PEOI
SAY NICE

"Pastor Chris Marley has written a very edifying work. Combining pastoral wisdom, insight into biblical texts, and a robust Reformed theology, Marley takes readers through Scripture using the lens of Christ as Husband and His people as Bride. Along the way, he constantly holds up the glory of Christ, our redeemer, and also calls us winsomely to live lives worthy of those wedded to Christ, whether we're husbands, wives, children, or unmarried. Readers will be challenged and blessed."

> Dr. David VanDrunen, author or editor of twelve books, most recently
> *Politics after Christendom: Political Theology in a Fractured World*
> and *Aquinas Among the Protestants*.
> His scholarly articles have appeared in many journals, including
> the Journal of Church and State,
> the Journal of Law and Religion, and
> the Journal of the Society of Christian Ethics.

"Pastor Chris Marley's book, *Scarlet and White*, delves into the mystery of Christ's relationship with His church. The author is deeply steeped in a strong theological background, and because of his unwavering fidelity to Scripture, he has a clear understanding of both the subject at hand as well as other related biblical texts. This topic has been avoided by most theologians who fear merely romanticizing it. However, one might see the prime importance of this relationship by its pervasiveness both in the Old and New Testaments, oftentimes under the cover of metaphors, similes, and allegories. Therefore, a firm understanding of this relationship proves invaluable for one's Christian walk, as well as one's marriage. Once you have started reading this book, you won't want to put it down."

> Dr. Raymond Perron, missionary in the Province of Quebec;
> apologetics and systematic theology professor at
> Faculté de théologie in Montreal;
> professor of missiology at the Institute for Reformed Baptist Studies;
> author of *Plaidoyer pur la foi chrétienne, l'apologétique de Cornelius Van Til*.

"I want this book! Chris is a really good writer who grips your attention, fascinates your mind, warms your heart, and challenges your soul. I hadn't realized that my Bible was so teeming with breathtaking romance. There are mountains of pastoral material here for wedding ceremonies, marriage counseling, romance enriching, church polity, membership motivation, ministerial inspiration, etc. Best of all, it will make you fall in love with the Savior. I see myself getting it, underlining all over it, and constantly referring to it."

Mark Chanski, pastor of Harbor Church in Holland, MI,
professor of hermeneutics at Reformed Baptist Seminary;
coordinator elect of the Reformed Baptist Network;
author of *Encouragement: Adrenaline for the Soul*,
Manly Dominion, *Womanly Dominion*.

"Want to better understand and savor Christ and His relationship with His church? Chris Marley here gives us a fresh and enjoyable look at this topic in his unique writing style. He combines exegetical faithfulness, salvation history, and biblical metaphors to give us an exquisite depiction of 'the Bridegroom and His Bride.' As one who has known Chris for many years, I can assure prospective readers that his life radiates Christian joy and the truth of the gospel, which echoes a strong 'amen!' to his message."

Dr. James Adams, pastor of Cornerstone Bible Fellowship of Mesa, AZ;
author of *War Psalms of the Prince of Peace*.

"I'm a big name . . . I'd be willing to endorse you!"

Dustin Battles

SCARLET AND WHITE

SCARLET AND WHITE

CHRIS J. MARLEY

Dedicated to my lovely br

Thank you for always supporting me an *me
as I learn what it is to honor God thr* *.age.*

Special thanks to my parents, who taught me about godly marriage through example, to the saints of Miller Valley Baptist Church for their patience and help while I wrote, and to Luke Walker for his contributions in bringing this book to life.

SCARLET AND WHITE

A Practical Examination of Biblical Theology Focusing on Christ and His Church Through the Metaphor of the Ideal Husband and His Princess Bride

Copyright © 2022 Chris J. Marley

All rights reserved

Published by Founders Press
P.O. Box 150931 • Cape Coral, FL • 33915
Phone: (888) 525-1689
Electronic Mail: officeadmin@founders.org
Website: www.founders.org

Printed in the United States of America

ISBN: 978-1-943539-37-6

Library of Congress Control Number: 2022952348

All rights reserved. No part of this publication may be reproduced, stored in a retrieval system, or transmitted in any form by any means, electronic, mechanical, photocopy, recording or otherwise, without prior permission of the publisher, except as provided by USA copyright law.

Contents

I. Recovering the Bride 1
II. Beginning in the Beginning 7
III. Cycles of History 39
IV. Be Ye Not Ruthless 59
V. Bridal Songs 71
VI. Marrying into Shame 103
VII. Emperor Seeks SWF 135
VIII. Husband in the Flesh 145
IX. Paul and the Bride I 169
X. Paul and The Bride II: The Quickening 197
XI. Paul Outside Ephesians 231
XII. Revelation of the Bride 237
Bibliography 249
Appendix 255
Scripture Index 257

Foreword

I remember the first time I heard about the content of Pastor Chris Marley's book, *Scarlet and White* in late 2021. One day, while speaking with Wrath and Grace Publishing, I was asked to look over a manuscript in consideration of editing it. "It is doctrinally rich," I was told, "And I think you'll enjoy it." Both of those statements could not have been truer. *Scarlet and White* is thoroughly biblical and incredibly enjoyable to read.

Reading through it for this first time, I discovered within Marley's book a kindred spirit, a brother in Christ, an able theologian, and gracious pastor who aimed at nothing less than drawing Christians into sweeter joy and comfort in contemplation of what God had accomplished in the storyline of the Bible. From Old Testament to New Testament, and through to the present day, Chris illuminates the ways in which the gospel story is the story of God redeeming sinners to create a Bride for Himself. It regularly brought a smile to my face and warmed my heart as Chris led me along the *scarlet* tapestry woven throughout Scripture, continually pointing me to Christ's plan to secure His Bride through His own blood.

By focusing primarily on one biblical metaphor—that of the Bride of Christ—Chris is able to help readers understand the biblical, historical, and practical implications of this doctrine. Here, Chris has written a powerful work on an oft-neglected doctrine, doing the Church a great service in writing it.

After reading it the first time, there was, of course, no doubt in my mind that I wanted to help edit this work. I knew it was something special. I also wanted to see it receive the widest reading audience possible. Thus began the talks between Wrath and Grace Publishing and Founders Press to co-publish this work. I am thankful we were able to work together on *Scarlet and White* and think all that have worked on it can agree that it is a phenomenal piece of writing that deserves your attention. We pray it will be a blessing to those who read it.

One further note on the author: This is a theologian who can be trusted. As I had the opportunity to get to know Chris better, I quickly realized that there was no disconnect between the author and his work. His authorial voice is who Chris truly is. He loves the Lord Jesus, His Word, and His people.

One cannot ask for a better set of criteria than this in a Christian pastor or writer. In fact, his personality shines through the pages. Between his love for Christ and His Bride, a fascination with old—sometimes obscure—Christian writings, and his general penchant for humor, it was clear that we had much in common. I am glad to now call him a friend.

So, as you read through this book, make sure to savor the words and theological teachings, because Chris is both a great writer and teacher. Pray over what you read. Keep a Bible open nearby and go to it frequently. Allow Chris to guide you from Old to New Testament as he explains the beauty behind the Church as the Bride of Christ, and remember the glorious truth that, if you have repented of sin and trusted in Jesus, *you*, dear reader, are part of this Bride!

Pastor Chris Marley writes with pastoral warmth, theological clarity, and a distinct wit that few can replicate. This is a theological work that can equally produce smiles and tears as it points Christians to the most beautiful union that exists between us and Christ. The Bride of Christ must remember who she is, and this is the book that the Lord has prepared for such a time as this.

Scarlet and White is a phenomenal piece of biblical, historical, and practical theology which explores the doctrine of the Bride of Christ with the utmost care and devotion. I commend this work to you, dear reader, with the utmost confidence that, if read faithfully, it will pour out a manifold stream of blessings upon you.

—Jacob Tanner

> Pastor, Christ Keystone Church; author, *Union with Christ: The Joy of the Christian's Assurance in the Doctrines of Grace*; editor, Wrath and Grace Publishing.

I
RECOVERING THE BRIDE

An Introduction

Most people are familiar with William Shakespeare. You probably had to read him for high school, or you at least watched the DiCaprio movie. I love Shakespeare's work, and not just because of the flowery language or iambic pentameter. I have always admired the breadth of his audience. The aristocracy and the poor all came to see Shakespeare's plays because there was something for each of them.[1] In the Globe Theater of London, poor people had the best view of the play. They paid a penny to stand in a dirt pit in front of the stage, so they were called "penny stinkards" or "groundlings." Sometimes, God's groundlings have the best view of grace in the Theatre of Redemption.

This book is written for groundlings, the common saints of Christ's church. There are astounding theology books out there. Systematic theologies by men like Berkhoff and Bavinck, Turretin and Calvin have influenced my work (as my footnotes bear out). There are innumerable others who have influenced my thinking; some are even still alive and writing. I love their works despite how long it took me to understand them. I am not the *Next Great Theologian*, but I want to write a book that everyone in my congregation (and other congregations) can read and enjoy. I want to help people fall in love with Jesus all over again. I want to help you see more of a God who loves beyond measure, gives grace to his people beyond comprehension, and saves groundlings like me.

Why I Wrote This Book

Years ago, I had a conversation with a friend from seminary about modern Christian music. He commented that, when working with young people, he encouraged them to avoid music with lyrics in the "Jesus is my boyfriend" genre. Nicolas Alford makes a similar statement regarding worship: "Worship songs shouldn't be able to be sung to a boyfriend or girlfriend with minor

---

[1] Shakespeare had a knack for humor, which was mostly for the common people. I have the same sort of humor, but I will keep most of that in the footnotes.

edits to the personal pronouns."[2] You have probably heard songs like this, where the sovereign, holy, omnipotent creator of the heavens and the earth is reduced to a teenage love interest. This is a major reason why Protestant theologians are hesitant to write about the church and its relationship to Christ in terms of the Bride. They have done what Christians do best: overreact to error. Overly sentimental pseudo-churches water down theology (the study of God) to prevent any kind of offense to the hearer. In a nutshell, it is immanence (God-with-us-ness) for them over transcendence (God-above-us-ness). It is the God-man without the God. They want to say, "Jesus is my homeboy."

The other primary group that has twisted this metaphor is none other than Rome.[3] In her claims to be both visible and invisible church, all in one bejeweled package, they have infected the beautiful Bride with all manner of unwholesome characters. Theologians talk about this idea regarding the visible/invisible church distinction, which is to say that becoming part of the visible church (walking an aisle, saying a prayer, and even being baptized and becoming a church member) does not make someone a Christian. Salvation makes Christians out of sinners by grace through faith. This is what makes someone a part of the Bride.

Rome also makes the Bride "brides" in the plural. These are the nuns, known to most of us for art history documentaries, an array of strange white hats, and the vigorous application of rulers. "After all," says the papist, "if Jesus is our husband, we should save ourselves for Him and never marry."

This way of thinking is so infamous for theologians that many, especially the Reformers and their intellectual offspring, are hesitant to do much work on this line. Personally, I was unaware of how bad this was until I started researching the subject during seminary. I was surprised to find only scant references in the books on my shelf. I only found a few books of extensive use even in the campus library. I have since been able to find more material, but in the Reformed community, references are still scarce.

You may be thinking, "Why is this subject so important?" I'm glad I made you ask. The Bride of Christ is the most extensively used metaphor in Scripture, providing a through line for the covenants and uniting God's people.[4] As Dietrich Bonhoeffer said, "Something of the divine splendour

---

[2] Nicolas Alford, *Doxology: How Worship Works* (Conway: Free Grace, 2017), 91–92.

On the other side of things, a lot of secular love songs have a disturbingly idolatrous tone to them, evidencing that subconscious need to fill a void left by our alienation from our creator with other people that fail to fulfill.

[3] An inference drawn from the work of Claude Chavasse, *The Bride of Christ: An Enquiry into the Nuptial Element in Early Christianity* (London: Faber and Faber, 1911).

[4] It is through these masculine and feminine counterparts that we come to understand the masculine self-revelation of God. God is pure spirit, and obviously does not contain a Y chromosome, reproductive organs, or any other biological metric for male sex. So why does God

is here reflected in our earthly relationships, and this reflection is something we should recognise and honour."[5] It is the source metaphor for two other highly used metaphors: the Children of God and the Body of Christ. The Bride of Christ also sheds a great deal of light on our ecclesiology (the study of the church), the nature of Christ's immanence to His people, and union with Christ. Understanding this metaphor affects how we live our Christian lives, evangelism, and even eschatology (the study of Christ's return and the end times). If Scripture spends so much time on it, we should too. In his book *God's Unfaithful Wife*, Ray Ortlund Jr. writes about one aspect of this metaphor:

> The biblical theme of spiritual harlotry is not the whole of theology. It is only one strand woven into the fabric of Scripture, along with others, all of which are needed for the whole tapestry to shine forth in its complexity and fullness. But this strand of God's marital love and of his people's presently harlotrous but ultimately faithful response is too much neglected. And it is the overlooked themes of Scripture to which any given age of the church must pay special attention, for it is precisely there that we most urgently need to hear the Word of God again.[6]

God values the marriage covenant as *His* institution. He teaches doctrine and His attributes through that metaphor. Together these form the meta-narrative of human history.

On the Limits of Metaphors

In literature, we have allegories, metaphors, and similes, and we try to keep them quarantined from each other. The challenge is that the Bride of Christ is used as all three at different points in the Bible. Paul's usage covers metaphors and similes, but Hosea cannot be anything but an allegory because of its sheer

---

identify Himself as male? Because it is in the divinely created male roles that God has revealed Himself; i.e., God created the role and gender of "male" in order to reveal Himself. So God does not conform to gender, gender conforms to God's purposes. We are as much born of a father as a mother, but it is from the church's womb that we proceed. The Son is the Bridegroom who counts Himself as incomplete without His Bride the church, protecting, leading, and loving her. The Son is also the exact imprint of the Father, as Hebrews tells us, so with the Son revealed as masculine, it befits the Father to reveal Himself as the same. As for the Holy Spirit, we see the noun in Hebrew, Ruach, is feminine, but its form in Greek, Pneuma, is neuter, neither masculine nor feminine. We might add that another title for the Holy Spirit, Parakleytos, is masculine. So clearly, the "gender" in the text is dictated only by the noun in the given language.
5 Dietrich Bonhoeffer, *Letters and Papers from Prison* (Glasgow: Fontana Books: 1962), 152.
6 Raymond C. Ortlund Jr., *God's Unfaithful Wife: A Biblical Theology of Spiritual Adultery* (Downers Grove: Intervarsity Press. 1996), 176.

volume.[7] In scriptural matters, we talk about this as *sign and thing signified*, or *type and antitype*. Historical narratives, poetry, and all the rest can have a literal meaning while pointing forward to Christ and His church.[8]

But first, we need to talk about limitations in metaphors. Any time we use metaphors, similes, and allegories, we must acknowledge that these figures of speech eventually break down. Some metaphors extend further than others, but it is important to find that termination point to avoid error.

For example, when Christ says that He is the Shepherd and that we are His sheep, we learn about His sovereignty, the constant care He gives to us, and how foolish we can be as creatures. There is more to it, but there are boundaries.

While this may seem like common sense, it is important to always keep in mind that a metaphor has its limits. When dealing with the church as the Bride, we need to be careful not to make the church into something it is not. Perhaps the most significant error we wish to avoid in this vein is perceiving the church as *equal* to Christ. A wife is no less valuable as a human being than her husband, but the church is not intrinsically equal in significance or importance as her Savior.

I may come close at times to violating the principle of singular meaning.[9] There are layers of meaning that exist within certain texts, though not all. Many of the psalms were simultaneously recording the author's experience and prophesying about Christ. Certainly, we want to avoid the use of the Quadriga[10] interpretation principles, but we do not want to over-simplify the text. The Reformation ESV Study Bible points out that "although today's Western world often regards using words that carry a double sense as confusing and ambiguous, in NT times such wording was commonly used to add weight and enrichment."[11] Arthur W. Pink, writing on Hebrews 12, says, "We feel it safest to regard the clause thus, for God's commandment is 'exceeding broad' (Ps. 119:96), and very often a single word has a twofold or threefold

---

7 Admittedly, this conflicts with Louis Berkhoff's definition of allegory because the elements are historical and not fictitious. Louis Berkhoff, *Principles of Biblical Interpretation* (Grand Rapids: Baker, 1950), 89.

8 John Owen provides a great summary of this: *An Exposition of the Epistle to the Hebrews Vol. 2* (Evansville: Sovereign Grace Publishers, 1960), 133.

9 WCF I.9, 2nd LBC I.9— "... the true and full sense of any Scripture (which is not manifold but one) ..."

10 Named after the Roman chariot pulled by four horses, this system of interpretation extracted literal, anagogical/ eschatological, typological/Christological, and tropological/moral interpretations from a text whether they were there or not. It was pioneered by Origen, though his was a three-fold interpretation. See Phillip Schaff, *History of the Christian Church Vol 2* (Grand Rapids: Eerdmans, 1970), 521.

11 Reformation ESV Study Bible, ed. RC Sproul, Notes on Romans 1:17 (Lake Mary: Ligonier, 2005), 1613.

reference, and therefore we need to be constantly on our guard against limiting the meaning or restricting the application of any utterance of Holy Writ."[12] So also Thomas Goodwin, "It being a rule I have always measured the interpretation of Scripture by, as I have oft professed, to take Scripture phrases and words in the most comprehensive sense; yea, and in two senses, or more, that will stand together with the context and analogy of faith."[13] And finally, regarding Paul's use of Psalm 68 in Ephesians 4, Lloyd-Jones writes:

> The difficulty reminds us of something which we must always bear in mind when we read the Bible. If we fail to do so our reading will often be unintelligent and confused. It is that we will often find a double meaning in statements in the Old Testament. This is so in many of the Psalms; it is equally true of many of the prophets and their writings.[14]

In preaching and in writing, I have repeatedly found these layers of meaning to a text, but there is always a danger in seeing what is not there. My test throughout has been whether the deduced doctrine or idea can be proven from clearer texts in Scripture. That way, even if I have erred in seeing a doctrine in a passage, the doctrine itself stands as true.

The Conflicting Views

While the theological ideas and principles I am presenting in this book are extensively well-documented and supported by orthodox theologians throughout history, there are many who view the use of the metaphors differently. Like Claude Chavasse and Benjamin Keach, some see the metaphors as connected and treat the church as the wedded bride.[15] Many have treated each occurrence of the bridal metaphor as unique to the context, so the bride in Hosea is not meant to be connected to the bride in Ephesians. They would not regard the children metaphor as connected to the bridal metaphor.

Perhaps the greatest contrast is with those who hold the church to be in a state of betrothal but not marriage to Christ. In the ancient Near East, betrothal was covenantal and not easily broken, as we see in the case of Joseph seeking to put Mary away quietly even though they were only engaged. Michael Horton puts it this way:

> Once more, the eschatological aspect must be recognized: the visible church is the bride of Christ; the invisible church is his wife, the

---

12 Arthur W. Pink, *An Exposition of Hebrews* (Grand Rapids: Baker, 2006), 1006.
13 Thomas Goodwin, *An Exposition of the Epistle to the Ephesians* (Evansville: Sovereign Grace Book Club, 1958), 90.
14 D. Martyn Lloyd-Jones, *Christian Unity: An Exposition of Ephesians 4:1-16* (Grand Rapids: Baker, 2003), 150.
15 Benjamin Keach, *Preaching from the Types and Metaphors of the Bible* (Grand Rapids: Kregel, 1972), 327.

church as it exists on the other side of the marriage supper of the Lamb. The "already" of union with Christ must always confess the "not yet" of the nuptial wonders that yet await Christ's bride, arrayed in the precious garments and jewels he gives her.[16]

What Dr. Horton describes in the above quote is not theologically in conflict with the unfolding of the metaphor in this book. Rather than placing the current earthly church as somewhere between betrothal and marriage, I am placing her as between marriage and consummation, which is the language Scripture uses to describe her. As for the betrothal covenant, it is the covenant of redemption outside of time, not the covenant of grace.

So with all that said, let us take a walk through Scripture, trailing behind Christ the Bridegroom and His Bride, the church. We will follow them from her birth in Genesis to the suspense-filled "to be continued" of Revelation. We will trace her through the cycles of history, her reflections in Ruth and Esther, while hearing her songs in the Psalms, Proverbs, and Song of Solomon. We will stand in the crowd at the bridal feast and wedding before hearing Paul's instructions to the Bride from Ephesians.

---

[16] Michael Horton, *The Christian Faith* (Grand Rapids: Zondervan, 2011), 726–727.

II
BEGINNING IN THE BEGINNING: GENESIS
Before the Beginning—Arranged Marriage

IT MIGHT SEEM ODD to start before the beginning but, in this case, it is necessary. The beginning would be Genesis 1:1, but our narrative begins even before Scripture, in a doctrine only alluded to by various passages (Eph. 1; Ps. 110). This is known as the *Pactum Salutis*, or covenant of redemption. As we see in the doctrine of election (of which Paul and Christ so often spoke), the real narrative begins outside of time within the council of the triune God. God determined the what, the how, and the why—what would be created, how it would be created, and for what purposes. To be specific, before the beginning of the world, God chose who would be His. He chose to love.

So what bearing does this have on the Bride of Christ? It means we are looking at an arranged marriage. Those whom the Father chose, the Son redeemed (Rom. 8:28–30). The Father in glory, before the beginning of the world, chose who would be the Bride for whom the Son would give his life.

Now, I am not arguing for a return to arranged marriages in our culture. But in this case, it is a most beautiful thing. Even within Scripture, we see clues that arranged marriages were atypical. The danger in earthly arranged marriage is the fallibility of the parents and inherent disunion with the children, but in our case, the Father is *perfection* itself. He is in *perfect* harmony with His *perfect* Son, and He changes the heart of the *imperfect* Bride.

This means that the intimate love of the betrothed husband originated before the world began. "The Son," says John Owen, "rejoices from eternity in the thought of undertaking this work [of redemption]."[1] God's love for His people and Christ's dedication to His elect began in the perfect unity of the Trinity before the earth was created. John Stott writes, "God put us and Christ together in his mind. He determined to make us (who did not yet exist) his own children through the redeeming work of Christ (which had not yet taken place)."[2] Christ's love for every Christian began before He spoke

---
1 John Owen, *Communion with God* (Carlisle: Banner of Truth, 2013), 134.
2 John Stott, *The Message of Ephesians* (Downers Grove: Intervarsity Press, 1979), 35.

the heavens and the earth into existence. There is intrinsic value in longevity. People are fascinated by pyramids, Stonehenge, Newgrange, and other ancient structures because they have withstood the test of time. How much more peace and confidence does the Christian have in knowing that the love and dedication of God for and to them is older than the universe itself? As A.W. Pink says, "What assurance would be ours if, when we approached the throne of grace, we realized that the Father's heart had been set upon us from the beginning of all things!"[3]

One of the major issues seen in arranged marriages throughout history, especially in the ruling class, is that they were often marriages of convenience. Typically, they were mutually beneficial (politically or financially) for the parents. In 1478, the inbred prince Hufflepuff in England was married to the inbred princess Cossette of France to build alliances and fortify their parents' respective empires. The Puritan Daniel Rogers dedicated an entire chapter in his book on marriage to the value of parents' involvement in arranging a marriage. However, it did more to show how he was a product of his time rather than provide a theological rationale for arranged marriages. There is value in the parental approval and blessing, but that value is in direct correlation to the wisdom of the parents, their selflessness, and their desire for what is best for the children.

However, with the Bride of Christ, we find a marriage of vast inconvenience for the one who does the arranging. God *gains nothing* from us by orchestrating our salvation. God had no need of us, in and of himself, but desired to display His grace and love through a marriage of His perfect Son to an imperfect and sinful bride. God does not need us, but He does love us.

People marry for many reasons: money, security, physical attraction, status, or even just companionship.[4] Edward Pearse asks his readers if they "are for" such things, only to go on and declare how Christ fulfills all the things that people seek in a spouse to a far greater degree than any human could.[5] Pearce says the marriage is not one of mutual benefit, but of extraordinary and exclusive benefit to the believer in his segment on riches. "You are poor, miserable and naked; and will you not embrace this Christ offering Himself with all these riches toward you?"[6]

---

3 A.W. Pink, *Exposition of the Gospel of John*, (Grand Rapids: Baker, 2006), 925–926.
4 My grandmother used to say, "People get married because they're lonely when they should really just get a dog."
5 Edward Pearse, *The Best Match or The Soul's Espousals to Christ* (Morgan: Soli Deo Gloria Publications, 1994), 56–70.
6 Pearse, *The Best Match*, 60.

Though we cannot know the mind of God and the nature of the Trinity in fullness because we are limited as created beings, perhaps an imagined dialogue is helpful . . .[7]

Peace, Father.

Peace, Son.

Peace, Spirit.

Peace to all in one.

Son, You know whom I have chosen; on whom I have set my heart. Does the covenant please You?

Yes, Father, I love her.

You know what will happen, what she will do, and what You must do to have her?

Yes, Father, but I love those whom You have given Me, the Bride whom you have given Me.

Spirit, You know what You must do to apply the Son's work, dwell within, and endure their grieving of You?

Yes, Father, but she will be loved in spite of herself.

Then when the LORD has sworn by Himself, He shall not repent of it. When it is spoken, then shall it be.

Benjamin Keach, in his book *Preaching from the Types and Metaphors of the Bible*, says:

> A man that intends or is disposed to marry is not contented . . . how happy soever he is otherwise, in the enjoyment of all outward good things in his father's house. Jesus Christ, notwithstanding all the glory he had with the Father, being the joy and excellencies and perfections, dwelling in the fruition of eternal bliss, yet thought upon a spouse, and judged it meet to enter into a marriage relation, Prov. 8:31.

> An obedient and wise son takes advice, and consults with his father, being fully resolved to change his condition, and enter into a contract of love, and marriage union; and then fixes upon a particular object. Jesus Christ took counsel with the Father about that glorious design of love and good-will he bore to mankind; and hence he is said to be "delivered by the determinate counsel and foreknowledge of God," Acts 2:23. It was no less than the great result of the blessed Trinity,

---

[7] I should note at this point that this brief poetic tangent is purely pedagogical. I am convinced that these works of the three persons of the Godhead are unable to be recorded because they exist outside of time on an archetypal scale.

that the Lord Jesus the second Person, should espouse sinners to himself: "I proceeded," saith he, "and came from God; neither came I of myself, but he sent me," John 8:42. He fixed not his choice on the fallen angels, but on the offspring of fallen man, who were given unto him by the Father.[8]

Genesis Creation

God's Word begins with the creation of the heavens and the earth. The word *Genesis* comes from the Greek word for beginning. This is where it all started. God speaks, and whatever He says *is*. It is not that it soon will be, or the angels will rush out and accomplish it right away, but it actually *is*. He created everything that you and I have ever known out of nothing, *ex nihilo*. The most important elements are very clear in the first chapter of Genesis: that God is the source of all creation, and He is omnipotent. God is sovereign, all-powerful, and beyond our comprehension.

The starting point of theology must *always* be God in His transcendent glory. You do not get starstruck meeting an employee at the local fast-food restaurant, but meeting the Queen of England would be an unforgettable event. We cannot appreciate God's immanence (His closeness through Christ) without understanding His transcendence (how far beyond comprehension He is as enthroned creator). To appreciate God becoming man in Christ, we first must see Him as God in eternity; otherwise, His becoming man does not matter.

So God creates man on the sixth day, after pigs and earthworms. God makes him out of dirt and breathes life into him.[9] Now, Adam is alone as far as intelligent, image-bearing creatures go.[10] God declares in Genesis chapter 2 that it is not good for man to be alone.[11] So God takes Adam's rib and makes a wife for him, establishing the first marriage in creation through Adam and Eve. As A. W. Pink says:

> All other ordinances or institutions (except the Sabbath) were appointed of God by the Medium of men or Angels (Acts 7:35), but marriage was ordained immediately by the Lord Himself—no man or angel brought the first wife to her husband.[12]

---

[8] Benjamin Keach, *Preaching from the Types and Metaphors of the Bible* (Grand Rapids: Kregel, 1972), 323.

[9] Notice, the first chapter of Genesis declares the majesty and sovereignty of God, while describing us as walking dirt clods. Perspective is important. As Job 4:18–20 describes, we are made of lesser stuff than angels, houses of clay with foundations of dust.

[10] 2LBC, IV.2.

[11] He's right. You should have seen my first two apartments in college.

[12] Pink, *An Exposition of Hebrews*, 1126.

Before dealing directly with Eve's creation narrative, it is necessary to deal with the concept of man needing a helpmate. There are entire devotional books written for women on the subject of being a helpmate/helper/helpmeet. Specific aspects should be acknowledged here, though, given the metaphor of the Bride of Christ. Namely, there is something to be learned about earthly marriage by Christ's example. Geoffrey Bromiley says, "As God made man in His own image, so He made earthly marriage in the image of His own eternal marriage with His people."[13]

Christ accomplishes salvation, provides all means for salvation, and yet calls upon His church to labor in redemptive work for her sake. God could do it all, but it is a privilege for us to participate. He assumes the responsibility, and in what He calls the church to do, He equips her. She is the helpmeet of Christ in this sense.

So how does this apply to earthly marriage? Everything starts as the husband's work, obligation, and responsibility. The husband's job is not just to go to work and then come home to his wife, nor is it the wife's job to raise the children, tend the home, cook the meals, wash dishes, change the bio-hazard diapers, etc. It is the husband's job to care for the family in all aspects, but it is the wife's job to help/obey her husband in whatever capacity she is needed. This is why it is the husband's responsibility to tend and maintain the marriage, lead his household, and raise all family members up in prayer and the Word of God (i.e., loving her as Christ loved the church). He cannot do it all, so he must delegate and trust his wife. Practically, this may not change a great deal of how the home functions, but it should drastically affect the husband's attitude toward his wife and family.

On the flip side, the wife should own those endeavors of helpmeet-ness and treat them with sober-mindedness. If the husband-wife ratio of labor was 50/50, we would quickly become consumed with whether the other is really giving 50 percent. Each should be striving to fill the 100 percent.[14]

Likewise, the church must treat what God has called her to do with the utmost diligence. As the church, it looks like we do 100 percent of the labor. The people build the physical church building, members invite others to come, the preacher studies and prepares a sermon, and so forth. Yet we realize that it is truly 100 percent God, as He calls, equips, affects the heart, and saves sinners.

In Genesis, God declared that it was not good for man to be alone. This was not because Adam lacked the creativity to name all the animals on his own, nor was it because Adam was unable to cook or clean. This declaration of

---

13 Geoffrey Bromiley, *God and Marriage* (Grand Rapids, MI: Eerdmans, 1980), 43.
14 This mentality is crucial when crisis strikes the home, like chronic illness, physical disabilities, or dementia in old age.

God strikes at the fundamental principle of this book. Humanity could best understand the unfolding of redemptive history through this living metaphor. Eve would provide Adam a living means of comprehending the nature of God's love for humanity, and Adam would serve in the same capacity for Eve.

In Paul's first letter to the church at Corinth (chapter 11), we find one of the more controversial passages of Scripture. I am not about to unravel the idea of head coverings, but we need to get at the heart and underlying doctrine of the passage. In verse 7, Paul declares that man "is the image and glory of God, but woman is the glory of man." There is a very real sense in which man is meant to learn about his relationship with God by examining man's relationship with a woman. It is a two-way street of sorts because men and women learn about heavenly marriage from earthly marriage and about the earthly from the heavenly.

It is the same with Paul's writings in Ephesians 5:22–33, as we will see in chapter 8, but it is worth briefly addressing now. The wife is to submit to her husband, the head of the family, as the church is to submit to Christ, the head of the church. This troubles a lot of people, but it is not even the more demanding of the two charges. The husband is commanded to love his wife as Christ loved the Church and gave Himself for her. Jesus is the perfect example of love in sacrifice, care, and preservation. That is the standard for husbands. The closer a husband gets to loving his wife as Christ loved the Church, the easier (and more likely) it will be for the wife to submit to her husband.

Thus, the stage is set for the creation of Eve, the production of types and shadows, and the progressive revelation of the mystery of the gospel. As John Owen says, it is called a mystery because it requires God to reveal it to us, or we could never find it out.[15]

> And the rib, which the Lord God had taken from man, made he a woman, and brought her unto the man. And Adam said, This is now bone of my bones, and flesh of my flesh: she shall be called Woman, because she was taken out of Man. Therefore shall a man leave his father and his mother, and shall cleave unto his wife: and they shall be one flesh. And they were both naked, the man and his wife, and were not ashamed. (Gen. 2:22–25 KJV)

Genesis 2:20–25 recounts an act of what we call *Creatio Passiva* or *Creatio Secunda*, where God creates something out of something that already exists, as opposed to the first part of creation where He created something out of nothing. As a type of Christ, Adam is made flesh and blood from the dust of the earth.[16] Then, as a type of the church, Eve is formed from Adam's side. As

---
[15] Owen, *An Exposition of Hebrews*.
[16] There's also an interesting way in which Christ's incarnation fulfills the "bone of my bones

William Gurnall says, "The church is taken out of dying Jesus' side, as Eve out of sleeping Adam's."[17] We need to draw several major themes from this for the Bride of Christ.

The first is the rib of Adam becoming Eve. While tradition has translated this as "one of his ribs," the most literal rendering of *tsela* is simply that she is taken from his side. Some artistic traditions reflect this[18], but we will go with "rib" for simplicity's sake. There is no other ancient Near-Eastern creation narrative that parallels this. In and of itself, the rib-woman is a phenomenon that holds many facets of application as a metaphor of the church.

The concept of Eve's creation from Adam's rib teaches the principle of gain from loss. He loses a rib to gain a wife. As Adam's bride was gained from loss, so was Christ's bride. Christ descended from the glory of heaven, endured the wrath of God, and even surrendered His spirit in death to gain for Himself a people to call His Bride.

This applies to our own losses in life as well. Job lost more than most, but it was restored twice over. Charles Spurgeon once said:

> Adam was laid asleep, and God took a rib, and made it into a help-meet for him. If God shall take anything from you, yea, though it lies near your heart, do not mourn as one that has no hope; in patience possess your soul, rest on the Lord, for He will bring it to pass that out of all this shall come a spiritual life-power, which in after days shall gladden your heart, and make you the joyful parent of much good to others in this world of sin and woe.[19]

Eve being made from a rib showed much being made from little. This was a small matter for the God who spoke and created from nothing, but it is impossible for man to create a hundred-pound anything from something that is only a few ounces. Then God took Adam and Eve and produced the entire human race from them. From Abraham, He produced all of Israel. God produced a church that would span the globe from such unlikely sources as fishermen, a tax collector, and a murdering Pharisee.

The forming of Eve from a rib taught Adam that his completion was outside himself, and vice versa. In Ephesians, we learn from Paul that Jesus counts Himself incomplete without the church. As Daniel Rogers put it:

> It is not for nothing that the Lord brought Adam a meet helper for him; that is, not only one created in the same image as he; but made

---

and flesh of my flesh" aspect in the other direction. As Hebrews tells us, He was made like us in all ways except sin.
17 Cited in *Bible Illustrations: Consisting of Apothegms [&c.], Grouped under Scripture Passages, Vol.1.*, ed. James Lee (London: Alfred Gadsby), 11.
18 Buonarrotti's *Creation of Eve* (1509-1510), or Lucas the Elder's *The Paradise* (1530).
19 C.H. Spurgeon, *The Treasury of The Bible Vol 1* (Grand Rapids: Zondervan, 1968), 385.

of himself, flesh of his flesh, and bone of his bone; woman of man, equal to him in dignity; not of his head, nor his feet or lower parts, but of his sides and ribs, in token of one that was to side with him and agree with him in the married estate.[20]

The world is filled with people seeking happiness within themselves. They seek wisdom within themselves. They think that they can become complete in and of themselves through self-confidence and ego. Even "religious" people believe that they can save themselves. Yet the Scriptures teach that the salvation, joy, and peace that surpass understanding are found in God alone, who is completely *other* than us.

Eve-from-a-rib points to Eve's identity deriving from Adam. Calvin writes, "In this manner Adam was taught to recognize himself in his wife, as in a mirror,"[21] and in the same way, Eve saw herself in Adam. Likewise, the Church must derive her identity from Christ, just as her existence is derived from Him. In my state, we have biker and cowboy churches. Many "churches" derive identity primarily from one person's ideology (other than Jesus), philanthropic interests, human heritage, or even ethnicity. A true church should have an identity founded foremost upon her Savior and Husband, Christ. Or, as Michael Horton put it in *The Christian Faith*, "A local church (or wider body of churches) is not free to develop its identity in continuity simply with the givens of racial, ethnic, socio-economic, or consumer affinities. Each particular expression of the church must seek to exhibit the catholicity that is grounded in God's electing choice rather than in our own."[22] The church's understanding of Jesus in terms of who He is, how He saved her, and how He labors in and through her should shape her identity. The identity of the church is in the very gospel that created her.

When the Eve-rib was taken from Adam's side, he was under a sort of "divine general anesthesia" described as sleep. Adam felt nothing as God took the rib from his side. It was a painless creation of the bride in a sinless world. In the pre-fall cosmos, the creation of Adam's bride required no pain. This contrasts drastically with the identity of the Bride of Christ formed after the fall. For that Bride, the Bridegroom did not lose a rib during sleep but was bruised in the heel (body). Adam's account would serve as a more peaceful foreshadowing of Christ's passion with a surprising number of correlations. Claude Chavasse writes, "Christ's Death and Passion would thus be prefigured by

---

20 Daniel Rogers, *Matrimonial Honor* (Warrenton: Edification Press, 2010), 55. When he says she is "to side with him and agree with him," he does not mean she is to be a "yes woman" who agrees with everything he says, but that she is by his side and working with him, like we would say food agrees or does not agree with us.
21 John Calvin, *Calvin's Commentary Vol. I*, Trans. John King (Grand Rapids: Baker Books, 2005), 132.
22 Michael Horton, *The Christian Faith* (Grand Rapids: Zondervan, 2011), 852–853.

Adam's sleep, and the opening of his side to take out the rib; his Resurrection, by Adam's waking again. Round the Rib was built up the new Bride, who may thus be said to have slept and woken again with the new Adam."[23] So here there is a kind of death-resurrection motif as well. The first and second Adams both had to "sleep" for the bride to be created.

Finally, Eve was taken from life to perpetuate life. This woman would be the mother of all living men and women. Therefore, Adam would call her Eve (Gen. 3:20). Her life would produce life, which we will tie in shortly regarding the union of the husband and wife producing life. God chose not to create Eve in the same way as Adam. Life follows a consistent pattern in the world we know and through all of history excluding Adam and Christ. People come from parents before them. She was not formed from dust to have life breathed into her. Adam was formed in an event unique to only him, but Eve was created from the first Adam.

From Christ's life, His Bride's life would be produced. A Roman spear would open his side following His real death, paralleling Adam's figurative death. The church's life would then be the source of life of children beyond count or measure.

"A man shall leave his father . . . and shall cleave unto his wife." Man is meant to leave his father's home, his place of origin, wherein he lacks no need and has the comfort of familiarity, out of a desire for a bride. He must then cleave to his bride and undertake the responsibility of the head of the new household. He should become the provider of his family and leader in the new home. The now-husband assumes the debts and needs of his new bride.

Christ came from heaven, leaving the heavenly home and Father, where He held the glory and sovereignty he shared with the father (John 17:5), to redeem a bride. In John 16:28, Christ says that He came from the Father to come into the world. He left an earthly mother, Mary, to endure the hardships of life in a fallen world. He lived a perfect life of obedience to glorify His Father, all for the sake of the Bride. He would even be obedient unto the death of the cross, declaring vows that sealed the Bride to Himself.[24] In doing these things, Jesus assumed the debt of the Bride and paid it in full. He took the federal headship, leaving home, father, and mother, in order to cleave to His Bride. "Sin brought the Son of God from the heights of heaven to the depths of hell."[25] But it was not sin only; it was love for those sinners.

---

23 Claude Chavasse, *The Bride of Christ: An Enquiry into the Nuptial Element in Early Christianity* (London: Faber and Faber, 1911), 79.
24 This concept will be explained when we get to the crucifixion itself but is derived from Titus 2:14 and other passages.
25 Owen, *Communion with God*, 91.

This image is more common in Scripture than we might realize. David uses this same *cleave* word in Psalm 63:8, where he declares to God, "My soul clings to you." His soul was wed to Christ through faith.[26]

The second theme at hand is that a man and his wife shall be one flesh. Now, remember, this is God creating. He could have made us asexual creatures, but one of the major reasons He did not was to provide us with a metaphor of His relationship to us. On the pragmatic side of things, it is important to note that this is about a *wife*—not a girl in a committed relationship, not a girl man has very strong feelings about—but his *wife*. This is about covenant relationship.

Men and women should not seek the physicality of marriage without the covenant of marriage. On the other side of the metaphor, we should rejoice that Christ's love is within the confines of covenant. It is not seasonal, it will not fade, and it will not forget. It is the thing signified by marriage and is greater than earthly marriage. There is no "till death do we part" clause in the covenant of grace.

The bridegroom and bride will become one flesh. How mysterious and beautiful is the union with Christ! The doctrine of union with Christ is both delicate and volatile. Some would ignore it for fear of straying into error. Others may be too bold, even claiming that saints become God in some way, as if they merge into some ephemeral Christian version of nirvana. There is a balance, and it is most easily found through this metaphor.

When a husband and wife become one in marriage, there are imputed values that take place.[27] A wife is given all her husband's assets and/or debts. Likewise, a husband receives all that belongs to his wife. They share a last name, a home, finances, a bathroom sink, and possessions. There is a physical union in the marriage bed. They should speak with a united voice on decisions made for the household. Everything becomes shared.

Yet distinctions do exist. There are still two physical bodies, two minds, two souls, two sets of interests and opinions that will never fully merge. It is foolish to pretend otherwise. The wife of a surgeon may receive esteem and the financial stability of a doctor's salary, but she should never take up the scalpel and attempt a heart transplant just because of what has been imputed to her. My wife is trained as a florist, but that does not make me capable of building a bridal bouquet.

Even more so, the union of the believer with Christ is extraordinary. By imputation, the believer is counted as holding the righteousness of Christ's

---

[26] The same image is repeated in Deut. 11:22, 13:4, and 30:20. To be clear, this is the dedication of the heart, not the covenant itself.

[27] This is a balance-transfer concept. It declares assets of person A belong to person B. This is how God's people are clothed in Christ's righteousness and is a crucial part of justification. This is one of the major themes in Romans, especially chapter 5. See also Jeremiah 33:17.

earthly ministry. How beautiful! How mysterious! The more the believer grows in grace and knowledge of their Lord and Savior Jesus Christ, the more his mind is conformed to Him and the more his heart desires that which is good and holy. The saint has the security before God that the Son does! However much the saint is one with Christ, though, they are still separate and distinct. The believer will not achieve the archetypal, divine knowledge of God nor the power to speak and create *ex nihilo*. Certainly, the glory and honor owed to God will ever remain His own. Only Christ, being God, could claim before the Father, "All mine are yours, and yours are mine" (John 17:10). We can only declare to God, "What is mine is yours." Yet the believer's bond to Christ is more secure than a wedding license, more intimate than the wedding bed, and more magnificent than earthly marriage. This is union with Christ.

When the two become one in the earthly marriage, life is produced. This is not perfectly so, but nothing is in earthly marriage. It is a kind of bizarre mathematical concept that the one plus one equals one . . . plus one. God chose the intimacy of marriage as the means to produce new life. Bonhoeffer writes of earthly marriage, "God allows man to cooperate with him in the work of creation and preservation."[28] So it is also with the church cooperating with God in the work of creating and preserving believers. I will not belabor the earthly aspect, but the thing signified in Christ and the church bears exploring.

It is important to note that this does not deny the monergistic nature of salvation. This is a technical term stating that it is God alone who saves. Some would claim that man co-authors his salvation (synergistic), but that is wrong. The Father chooses, the Son redeems, and the Holy Spirit quickens (brings to life). I am not denying that God alone saves us, nor claiming that the church in some way co-authors that salvation, but God uses means and secondary causes.[29] God uses His Bride to accomplish salvation through the general call to salvation.

Paul states that faith comes by hearing and hearing by the preaching of the Word of God (Rom. 10:17). This is the ordinary means of salvation. God works through the "foolishness of preaching" (1 Cor. 1:21 KJV) to quicken the spirit, regenerating the heart to respond in faith to the message preached. It is not usual, ordinary, or expected that God should speak in an audible voice as He did with Noah, Abraham, and Paul. Rather, God uses His redeemed and already quickened children to share the gospel that quickened them. Not every faithful, clear, gospel-centered sermon results in sinners being saved. It requires the attending work of the Holy Spirit for redemption to happen.

---

28 Bonhoeffer, *Letters and Papers from Prison*, 153.
29 2nd LBC V.2, WCF V.2.

Here is where the metaphor applies. For children to be born, the husband and wife are to meet together in intimacy. For people to be born again as children of the kingdom of God, the Bride of Christ must meet with her Husband. When Christ chooses to visit His Bride through the Holy Spirit in that way, new life is produced. Not every sermon attended by the Holy Spirit results in salvation (though it will certainly sanctify), but a sermon cannot change the hearts of men without the Holy Spirit any more than a woman can make herself pregnant. Yet every sermon where God chooses to save sinners, those sinners will be saved, no matter how simple and stuttering the preacher. This is the nature of irresistible grace.

Scripture often uses the idiom of "know" to describe the intimacy between husband and wife. This is extremely helpful for us to understand the nature of intimacy between God and His people, Christ and His Bride. Knowledge and intimacy are intertwined. We would find it suspicious if a man said he loved his wife but knew nothing about her. But a lot of people say they love God while understanding very little of the Bible and theology. Part of growing intimate with our Savior is learning more about Him. We also see how Christ loves us and knows us perfectly. The two are inseparable.

There is a sense in which Christ's Bride is not born until after the fall. More specifically, the Bride is born when the gospel is applied to people after the fall.[30]

A Brief Tangent

It becomes immediately apparent that this relationship between intimacy and marriage is key to the beauty of the Bride of Christ. To interact with the earliest commentators on Genesis is confusing at best because many read Paul's comments on perpetual virginity and their own opinions of the nature of sex back into these passages of Genesis. Augustine writes that they were naked and unashamed because there was not capacity for physical intimacy.[31] He elsewhere claims that "it was by sinning that their bodies incurred mortality, and sexual union is possible only for mortal bodies."[32] Similar negativity regarding intercourse was espoused by Jerome, Ambrose, and Origen. The history of this perspective would take far more time than I can conscientiously allot here, but it is an important backdrop for why the Protestant church has dealt so little with the vein of nuptial metaphor in these passages. Suffice it to say, these men were mistaken, and the intimacy of the marriage is joyous foreshadowing of glory, not a shameful necessity of fallen man to be overcome.

---
30 We will consider this in more detail in chapter 3.
31 Augustine, *Concerning the City of God Against the Pagans*, trans. Henry Bettenson (London: Penguin Books, 2003), XIV, 17.
32 Augustine, "The Excellence of Marriage," *Marriage and Virginity*, trans. Ray Kearney (Hyde Park: New City Press: 1999), 22.

God created sex between a husband and wife as a wonderful part of His created order and as a metaphor for the gospel.

The Fall

Now comes the greatest devastation of Scripture, the fall. It is the flap of the butterfly wings that destroyed the world. It is the sin of the ancestor that bent nature and bound the will of all generations to come. Genesis 3 is where creation stops, and decay begins.

Eve is deceived by the serpent's lie and eats of the fruit, then gives it to Adam who eats as well. That lie echoes through history, wearing many masks, but hiding in every sin we commit. The heart of Satan's lie here is that God is withholding good, keeping back what is best for us, holding back what will bring peace, joy, and satisfaction. Whenever we sin, we break God's law in pursuit of what we think will make us happy, mirroring our ancestors. This is important for our metaphor, because God the Son always gives His Bride what is best for her—for us. And that is what husbands are called to reflect. God loves His people perfectly.

When examining the doctrine of the fall, it is important to take note of some of the pitfalls into which others have stumbled. There are men in history who set their blame on Eve and Eve alone. John Milton, in his epic poem *Paradise Lost*, blames Eve extensively for rebellion against her husband and disobedience to God.[33] As he fictionalizes the historical account, he strays extensively from the theme of the fall itself. Dante falls into a similar trap, blaming Eve for the fall in his *Purgatorio*.[34]

It is important that Eve is neither dismissed from guilt, nor given the full weight of the blame. The fact that Eve sinned first in the narrative does not increase her guilt. Some have tried to claim that the record of the fall is chauvinistic because it blames Eve more than Adam. In truth, it is men in subsequent history who poorly interpreted the text. Genesis itself actually addresses Adam and Eve both with equal harshness, indicating that they are equals before God. They may have different roles, different strengths, different weaknesses, and different sins, but they are held to the same standard as image-bearers who have violated the law of God.

If there is any prejudice in Scripture itself, it is against Adam. There is some sense of Eve's being a victim, though again, she is not considered innocent. Paul writes to Timothy, "Because Adam was formed first, then Eve, and Adam was not deceived and became a transgressor." (1 Tim. 2:13–14, author's

---

[33] John Milton, *Paradise Lost* (New York, NY: Barnes and Noble Classics, 2004), IX, 205–999.
[34] Dante Alighieri, *The Purgatorio*, trans. Henry Wadsworth Longfellow, (New York, NY: Barnes and Noble Classics, 2005), Canto XXIX, 19–30.

translation). She believed a half-truth from Satan as the serpent. The question is, how did this happen?

Adam had been informed that he was not to eat of the tree, or they would die. Eve says that they must not eat of the tree or even touch it, or they will die. How this came to be is not spelled out in the text, but perhaps Adam misinformed her. Satan promises that the fruit will make them like God, knowing both good and evil. Eve believes him and eats the fruit.

Nowhere in Scripture do we have any indication that Adam was likewise deceived, and given Paul's treatment of it in 1 Timothy, it is only logical to assume he knowingly and willingly sinned against God's command. This adds to the gravity of Adam's sin. Indeed, if either is treated as being the greater transgressor, it is Adam. He was to tend the garden and lead his wife. He was the head of his household. He would be blamed, not Eve, as the source of the fall in Romans (5:12ff.).

In all of these things, Christ is contrasted to Adam. Where Adam failed as the federal head of humanity, Christ succeeded as the second Adam and federal head of his church. Where Adam failed to lead his wife, Christ succeeded in guiding His Bride. Indeed, Adam permitted his wife to pass from life to death, while Christ brought His Wife from death to life. When Adam saw his bride in sin, he simply joined her. When Christ beheld His Bride in sin, He clothed her in His righteousness and took the curse meant for her upon Himself.

An exceptional thing takes place when Adam and Eve both eat of the fruit. Verse 9 tells us that after eating, they realized they were naked and tried to clothe themselves. It seems almost ludicrous to us as we read, as if the two of them had never before in their lives looked down. How can they have not known they were naked? The full understanding does not come until Adam speaks with God (v. 10). He admits that he hid because he was naked. He was ashamed of his nakedness, in contrast to when they were created naked and unashamed (2:25). The shame of nakedness was an outward manifestation of their shame and guilt for sinning against God. It was God's piercing eye that would no longer allow Adam to hide his guilt. Hebrews 4:13 says that no creature is hidden from the sight of God, but "naked and exposed" to His judgment.[35] We see passages of Scripture that deal with nakedness, and, with an exception for birth, they are always tied to concepts of poverty and shame.[36] Here, both are present. Adam once walked with God unashamed as the image-bearer. He had peace and glorified God with his life. Now, Adam was spiritually bankrupt, impoverished, and guilty.

---

35 For the account of day of judgment, see Revelation 3:17.
36 For poverty, see Job 24:5–10 and Ezekiel 18:16. For guilt, the dominant image, see Isaiah 20:4; 47:3; Ezekiel 16:37–39; Micah 1:11; and Nahum 3:5. For birth, which is essentially about poverty, see Job 1:21 and Ecclesiastes 5:15.

There is a secondary element that we do not want to miss, though. Even without God's unique presence, they felt that nakedness, that shame, in each other's presence. They had lost a unity and vulnerability before God, but also with each other. Humanity had lost trust and intimacy that would be reflected in the curses to come.

Adam's reaction to the nakedness is one that is all too common. Adam sought to cover himself. He and Eve made the first organic clothing line from fig leaves and sought to hide their shame, guilt, and spiritual poverty in an external way. When people are confronted with their sin, they do everything they can to cover it up. They will list the works of their hands in their lives that they believe are commendable. They want to prove their worth to hide their guilt. The problem is that man's works are always insufficient when it comes to God who requires absolute perfection, just as Adam's fig leaf loincloth was insufficient to hide his sin from God.

It was necessary for Adam to understand his guilt before he could be forgiven. He had to see himself as "wretched, pitiable, poor, blind, and naked" (Rev. 3:17) in order to understand his need for God's covering. The same thing is seen in Hosea chapter 2, where God says that He will take His Bride out into the wilderness and strip her naked. God had come in His omniscience to accomplish this.

For Adam's sin to be done away with, it would require the shed blood of Christ. This is included in a term often heard, but not fully understood: *atonement*. Atonement literally means "covering." It covers the nakedness, shame, and guilt of the sinner.[37] Blood had to be shed for Adam's sin, whether it was Christ's or his own. So God provides the image of Christ for Adam to trust. God clothed both Adam and Eve in the skins of animals (3:21). This is the first sacrifice recorded in Scripture, and it is provided and performed by God. As with all sacrifices, it points to Christ. The first and last sacrifices recorded in God's Word are both made by God.

The church's identity is found in Christ and in Christ alone. She is nothing without Christ and Him crucified. It is His shed blood that animates her. She cannot exist except through Him. There is no Bride without shed blood. The church is conceived in the first gospel, Genesis 3:15, the *protoevangelium*. It is in the twenty-first verse of the same chapter wherein they are clothed in the skins of animals by God. This is not just to show that God chose leather pants over organic fig leaves for clothing His people, but to show the need for atoning blood. From birth, the church is clothed through sacrifice, a promise by God who will not repent of His decision. She must be clothed in the "garments of salvation . . . as a bride adorns herself with jewels" (Isa. 61:10; see Rev. 3:18).

---

37 Atonement is used more broadly to cover various aspects of salvation, like imputation and redemption, but here we see its root.

The Bride exists only through the sacrifice of Christ on her behalf. This is orchestrated in God's perfect wisdom to show Christ's perfect love. By Christ loving a fallen Bride instead of a perfect one, a more beautiful love is shown. If my wife were perfect and without sin, never offending or making a mistake, my love for her would be untested and simple. I may love her just as much, but that love would not be *displayed* to the same degree. In the same way that a light is most evident in darkness, *love is most beautiful in a fallen world*. You might not even notice that a lamp is on in the middle of the day, but to turn that lamp on in a dark room while someone is trying to sleep might incite warfare. As Thomas Goodwin observes,

> Now, just thus hath God set up Christ and the Church, his spouse, to be married together in heaven for ever; that is his plot. But he first throws her into sin and misery, and then sends his Son Jesus Christ to rescue and relieve her, so to show his love unto her to the uttermost; and all this so to take our hearts the more when we shall come to see his person in heaven.[38]

God is love. God is unchanging. God did not start loving His creation at the fall. Yet because of the fall, we are really able to know God's love. The beauty, the depth, the magnificence of God's love is shown because He loves His church *after* the fall.[39]

If you are a husband or wife, you have a beautiful opportunity in tribulation and trial to show love for your spouse. Allow me to tell you a story.

In April of 2010, my wife and I found out that we were going to have our first child. It was three days before we were scheduled to leave for a three-week vacation, two weeks of which would be spent overseas in Ireland. We were absolutely overjoyed, and terrified, as most expectant parents are when they get the news.

When we had flown to Boston, there was a misunderstanding with the tickets, and we ran all the way to our terminal only to find out we had an hour yet to wait. I was trying to find food, but Leah was just starting to get morning sickness, and nothing sounded edible to her. When I finally came back with food to the gate, I found her finishing up a phone call to her mom with tears streaming down her face. She was exhausted, hormonal, and nauseous. She looked up at me and said, "You can just leave me here if you want." I laughed,

---

38 Goodwin, *Ephesians*, 121.
39 "This is the mercy, this is the top of the mercies of God; and the truth is, to show forth this, he shut up all under sin, that he might have mercy upon all. It was but to show mercy so much the further. There was his mercy in preventing this, but there is infinite depth of mercy in recovering out of this; when they were all scattered from him, to gather them together again." Goodwin, *Ephesians*, 183.

and hugged her, because I realized, by God's grace, that He had given me a wonderful opportunity to show Christ's love to my wife.

There are a myriad of other examples I could give, and I am sure that there are even more that my wife could give of me, but few that are as amusing. The point is that our trials, especially in marriage, are opportunities to live and reflect Christ to the world, and particularly our spouses.

Let us backtrack a little, though, and return to the curse. This proclamation is daunting but beautiful because it is as much a blessing as a curse. There is rich information for us here, as God does not just dole out punishment for sin but hints at far greater realities.

The temptation is to only focus on the second half of the curse on the serpent, which is the gospel in disguise. The first half is both important and prophetic, though. God declares that there will be enmity between the serpent and the woman. This is not just about women hating snakes, but about Satan (and his offspring) versus the church. There is an innate friction between the Bride and the prince of this world. Satan is ever at war with Christ's Bride, and his hatred for the Son becomes channeled into hatred for the church. For this reason, Peter warns us of Satan who seeks to devour the believer as a roaring lion (1 Peter 5:8). We see the same narrative played out in rich imagery in Revelation 12. Especially in the last paragraph of the chapter, we see Satan pursuing the woman to destroy her, though she is preserved by God. He then makes war on her children who follow after God's commands and Christ's testimony. This is Satan's war on the individual saints. It is important for us to ever be mindful of our battle, not against flesh and blood, but against powers of darkness (Eph. 6:12).

The second half of the curse is a blessing to us. There is an old proverb, "The enemy of my enemy is my friend." Well, a curse on our enemy is a blessing to us. As stated earlier, it is often referred to as the protoevangelium. This Latin term means "first gospel." God declares that there will be animosity between the serpent and the woman, and between the seed of the serpent and the seed of the woman. Just like in English, the Hebrew word here can represent one seed or many seeds (much seed). At first glance, it looks like not only will Eve hate snakes, but her kids will too. It will be an anti-reptile household, but, of course, this is not the significance of the passage.

The serpent would crush (or bruise) the heel of Eve's offspring. In turn, the offspring would crush (or bruise) the head of the serpent. Again, this is not proverbial-type warning about snakes. As any Arizona country boy will tell you, you either shoot a snake from a distance or use a shovel. Only an idiot would step on a rattlesnake's head with sandals. The heel here represents the body, and the head is the seat of power. This is about Christ, the ultimate descendent of Eve, and Satan. In His work on the cross, Christ would be crushed in body, dying for our sins. In doing so, He would crush Satan's power. Satan would be the enemy put under Christ's feet (1 Cor. 15:25).

This is magnificent! Notice, this is the first curse in the series dealing with the fall of man. No sooner does God begin the pronouncement of curse for sin than He offers the promise of salvation through Christ!

Now God pronounces the curse on the woman. There are four phrases here dealing with two concepts. The first two phrases are about children. Eve's punishment, and the punishment of female offspring, is increased pain in childbearing and bringing forth children. This repetition is common for Hebrew, and the emphasis is that childbirth will be a painful experience. It is important to note here that there is grace even in the curse. Eve is not declared barren and unable to bear children, only that she will endure great pain in childbirth.[40] Grace-in-curse is a beautiful theme of Scripture seen time and again. Chastisement of God's people will show the gravity of sin, but there is always grace amidst discipline. The author of Hebrews tells us that it is a sign of our being children of God (Heb. 12:5–11; Prov. 3:11–12). God loves us enough to reprove us as Father.

God would bring the greatest pain into her life in tandem with the greatest joy. Paul extends the metaphor beyond the church to all of Creation. In his letter to the Roman church, Paul speaks of all of creation in bondage to decay, groaning in pains of childbirth, and this applies especially to the saints waiting for redemption of their bodies (Rom. 8:18–23). Obviously, this is looking forward to Christ's return and the creation of new heavens and new earth. Let us return to the sign to understand the thing signified.

When my wife was pregnant, we were told that there is actually a chemical that the body releases after a child is born that causes the mother to forget much of the pain endured in the childbirth process.[41] I had the opportunity to watch this play out after my daughter was born as the memory of labor and subsequent emergency c-section became foggy for my wife. I believe this is a grace that God gives so that mothers do not begrudge their children (at least more than they already do) for the pain of pregnancy and childbirth, and it makes them more open to repeat the process of childbearing.

Returning to Romans 8:18–23, Paul describes the whole of creation, with God's people especially, groaning in pains of childbirth for redemption. It is the pain and grief of the fall as the new creation, the new heavens and earth, is anticipated. This parallel metaphor depicts the whole of fallen history (from

---

[40] Victor P. Hamilton, *New International Commentary on the Old Testament: Genesis Ch. 1–17* (Grand Rapids, Eerdmans: 1990), 200.
[41] Scientists think the hormone oxytocin accomplishes this kind of high and selective amnesia.

eviction from Eden to Christ's second coming) as one long season of labor. The Bride of Christ is being composed, constituted, and formed while the birthing pains ensue. Part of why Christ was born, lived, and died was to groan with us, to be our sympathetic mediator. Paul says in Romans 8:26 that the Holy Spirit groans with us too. Yet the labor is not in vain. When the child is born, the pain will be forgotten. Christ uses this same metaphor, explaining the joy of when He will see the disciples again as the joy of the mother after birth (John 16:21).

Certainly, Eve's sorrow in bringing forth children did not fully end after the labor pains stopped. Having known the garden, she would have to raise her children in a fallen world. Often, we forget the sorrow Eve must have faced in one of her sons murdering the other. The death of a child brings overwhelming grief to a mother, but to compound that with fratricide is unfathomable. While no record is given of Eve's tears, we see the grieving of Mary at the foot of the cross (John 19:25–27). As Christ was leaving His mother to cling to His Bride, fulfilling Genesis 2:24, He directed Mary's maternal instinct to the disciple John, so that she might see Christ's work as Savior. In this same narrative, later, there is a beautiful fulfillment of the rejoicing anticipated, when John, who was given charge of Mary, would have returned home to rejoice with her in the emptiness of the tomb, that Christ had risen (20:10).

The church today is often beset with collective grief as it strives to raise up saints in a fallen world. When a member of the church is excommunicated for sin that they will not abandon for Christ's sake, or they are removed from the rolls on account of death, the pain of childbearing reverberates throughout the church.

Returning to Eve, the second major section of the curse is about her relationship to her husband. The first phrase is that her desire shall be for her husband. At first blush, this does not seem like much of a curse, and might even be a blessing. Unless intimate desire is intrinsically fallen, like Augustine and others have claimed, God's declaration here should be a good thing. Right? This, however, is not about the wife having love and desire directed toward her husband; this is about insurrection.

The original Hebrew text is extremely concise. What the KJV takes eight words to say, Hebrew uses three. Given the statement which comes afterward about the husband's dominant role, and the placement of this statement in curse, the full meaning comes into view. Eve's desire/urge/craving will be against her husband or, to put it another way, for her husband's role as the head of the household. Up until the fall, subjection and authority were not points of contention. Now that Adam and Eve are sinners, authority and subjection become issues. Adam is no longer the perfect husband, and Eve is no longer the perfect wife. There will be struggles for power and abuses of power attained. This is not just the narrative of ungodly male domination and the rise of feminism in response, but the history of the church as well.[42]

Israel, the national incarnation of the church as covenant community for the OT, would always have desire for her husband. She would fall prey to the appeal of gods that can be ruled (or so she thought), subject to her authority by way of sacrifices to idols. The Roman church would claim absolute authority and the ability to absolve sin, things reserved for Christ alone. In the modern church, we find dictator-pastors claiming to have cornered the market on truth and knowledge. Individually, Christians struggle with idolatry of self, desiring to have authority that is not rightfully theirs. The desire of the bride, in the fallen world, is often for her husband in all the wrong ways.

The other side of this coin is that the husband will rule over Eve, the bride. Again, the weight of the curse is not immediately apparent, and the echoes of this reverberate throughout redemptive history. On the immediate level, this is descriptive of the struggle women will have with foolish and oppressive husbands. For the Bride of Christ, however, it means that because of her sin, she will be ruled over and chastised, especially in the Exodus-to-Christ era, but we will get there in a little bit.

Finally, we look at the images of Christ the Bridegroom in Adam's curse. God subtly addresses Adam's attempt to make an excuse for his sin, that it was the wife God made for him who caused him to eat the forbidden fruit. God tells him that part of this curse is "because you have listened to the voice of your wife" (Gen. 3:17). This does not mean that husbands will be punished for listening to their wives. After all, we are called to live with our wives with understanding (1 Peter 3:7). What God is addressing is that Adam did not lead his household; his wife did. In contrast, Christ leads His church out of sin and into the paths of righteousness.

Then God addresses the whole pomegranate/apple/fruit thing. What we can easily miss here is that this is as much, if not more so, about disobedience than the actual fruit. God does not tell Adam that he ate the fruit of intrinsic cosmic power to evil, but that he ate the fruit God told him not to eat.

The first section of the curse is about unsanctified ground. Adam, and humanity with him, is losing dominion over creation. This is the injection site from which the poison of entropy and decay expanded outward through history and creation. One of the classic plot lines in literature is man versus nature, and that has been part of our story since Genesis 3. As John Calvin said, "The Lord . . . determined that his anger should, like a deluge, overflow

---

[42] There is a kind of male dominion that is good, rooted in creation and taught by Christ's example. Here I am referencing those who abuse that authority and seek to gain more than what is due to them.

all parts of the earth, that wherever man might look, the atrocity of his sin should meet his eyes. Before the fall, the state of the world was a most fair and delightful mirror of the divine favour and paternal indulgence towards man. Now, in all the elements we perceive that we are cursed."[43]

So now there will be painful eating, not just when the roast is overcooked. The word for pain (*atsav*) here can also mean "trouble" or "fatigue," which would also apply to dry roasts, but the image is that as humans after the fall, we wear out. There are thorns and thistles of frustrated labor. Severian, one of the early church fathers, wrote, "On account of the sin of man the earth has been cursed, so that it produces thorns, not in order that the earth, which is without feeling, may feel the punishments but so that it could always put the fault of human sin before people's eyes, by which we are admonished to turn back from sin and to turn toward the commands of God."[44] When we are frustrated in our efforts to accomplish a task or when creation itself brings sorrows, we should see these things as an effect of sin, to which we have made our own contributions.

There have been some interesting theories about the plants of the field, but the main thrust here is that man will no longer eat the fruit of the garden. Adam lived off the unmitigated favor of God. God will still send rain and give life and strength, but it will never be like the garden. God planted Eden, but now Adam will have to plant his own. And, of course, Adam's garden will have foxes that spoil the vines, as we will see in Song of Solomon.

All this toil will only stop in death. Man will return to dust—ashes to ashes, dust to dust.

In all these aspects of the curse, there is still mercy. God does not render Eve barren, only brings sorrow in her childbirth. The earth is not barren, but there is sorrow in its existence. One of the great mercies in the curse is that it points sinners to their need for a Savior. If life remained as it was in the garden, free of sorrow, sweat, and sickness, we would not have need to seek God and learn why the world is broken. Even the proclamation of death and the later banishing from the tree of life are mercies themselves, because by death man would see his need for redemption, and by death our Savior redeemed us.

But the beauty here is in seeing Christ taking on that curse for His Bride. Galatians 4:4–5 tells us that the Son was born under the law to redeem us from under the law, from under its curse. Christ came to become what Adam

---

43 John Calvin, *Commentary on the First Book of Moses Called Genesis Vol. 1*, trans. John King (Bellingham: Logos Bible Software, 173).

44 Severian of Gabala and Bede the Venerable, *Commentaries on Genesis 1–3: Homilies on Creation and Fall and Commentary on Genesis: Book I*, Eds. M. Glerup, T. C. Oden, & G. L. Bray, Trans. R. C. Hill & C. S. Hardin (Downers Grove: IVP Academic, 2010), 156. Severian had his problems, and this is not an endorsement for his work as a whole. Even a stopped clock is right twice a day.

should have been, the federal head who fulfilled the law, but also to take Adam's curse on Himself. Adam was cursed to eat bread by the sweat of his brow, but Christ would sweat "like great drops of blood falling down to the ground" in the anxiety of Gethsemane (Luke 22:44). Adam was cursed with the thorns of the ground, so Christ was given a crown of thorns as our federal head (Matt. 27:28–29). And Christ entered into the cursed earth in death as that seed that brought eternal life for His people. So, as we look to Adam's curse, we see Christ's suffering by which the curse is lifted from us. We still taste some of it, but the evil of suffering, the sting of death is taken away. And in the new heavens and new earth, the whole of the curse will be gone.

More is Less: Polygamy and the Bible[45]

R.C. Sproul was once asked if the Bible condones polygamy, and his response was, "Polygamy existed by God's patience and long suffering, not by His permission. Does your wife know you're thinking about polygamy?"[46] Though we chortle at these things, it raises a question that has often been left unresolved in the minds of believers and comes up quickly as we seek out the images of Christ's bride in Genesis. Even historically, this has not been a simple question.

While the early church unquestionably opposed the practice of polygamy, the reasoning behind it was fairly convoluted. Methodius of Olympus said,

> The contracting of marriage with several wives had been done away with from the times of the prophets. For we read, "Do not go after your lusts, but refrain yourself from your appetites." And in another place, "Let your fountain be blessed and rejoice with the wife of your youth" [Proverbs 5:18]. This plainly forbids a plurality of wives.[47]

Notice the assumptions that are in the background. By saying polygamy was "done away with" after the Old Testament era, it assumes that it was approved until it was abolished. The works of Augustine in *The Excellence of Marriage* and others show how this mentality worked. Since the Messiah was to come through the descendants of Eve (and then Abraham, Isaac, Jacob, Judah, etc.) there was an urgency for childbearing. Once Christ was born, that urgency ceased.[48] Polygamy was then, according to some, permissible as a means to the end of the Messiah being born.

---

45 Special credit is due to Covenant Legacy's article "Adam and Eve and The Problem of Polygamy," parts 1 and 2. Eric Ayala, Covenant Legacy, November 17, 2013, https://covenantlegacy.com/adam-and-eve-and-the-problem-of-polygamy-part-2.
46 R.C. Sproul, Twitter, March 25, 2015, 3:15 p.m., https://twitter.com/rcsproul.
47 Quoted by David Bercot, "Divorce" in *A Dictionary of Early Christian Beliefs* (Peabody: Hendrickson, 2003), 527. Methodius was a church father, opponent of Origen, martyr, and bishop.
48 There is a lot of truth in that, but what comes next in the logic sequence is where the problem is.

> Even when one man was allowed to have several wives, they behaved toward them with greater chastity than is shown now toward one wife by any of those others, when we see what the apostle [Paul] allows them as something excusable. They had those wives because of their task of having children, not because of unhealthy passion like the people who do not know God (1 Thess. 4:5).[49]

For Augustine, now that the urgency was gone to have the Messiah born, we can all start moving toward perpetual virginity, the polemic opposite of polygamy. To condone polygamy for its use by God, however, is akin to condoning Joseph's brothers selling him into slavery (Gen. 50:19–21).

A survey of the instances of polygamy paints a distinctive picture. As we have seen, Adam and Eve were created by God and set as husband and wife in the garden. There is no second wife in the garden, no polygamy, no polyamory, and no polyandry. It is one woman and one man suited for one another. After the fall, the first murder occurs in Genesis 4:8 as Cain slays Abel, but before the chapter is out, we are introduced to one of Cain's descendants, Lamech.

Lamech was a proud and violent man who boasted of the blood he shed as greater than his ancestor Cain. He is clearly presented to us in the record as an outstanding example of the repercussions of the fall, not a role model. Lamech is also the first polygamist in history, as we are told in 4:19. Calvin writes,

> We have here the origin of polygamy in a perverse and degenerate race; and the first author of it, a cruel man, destitute of all humanity. Whether he had been impelled by an immoderate desire of augmenting his own family, as proud and ambitious men are wont to be, or by mere lust, it is of little consequence to determine; because, in either way he violated the sacred law of marriage, which had been delivered by God.[50]

In like fashion, Victor Hamilton states,

> To be sure, no rebuke from God is directed at Lamech for his violation of the marital arrangement... But that is the case with most OT illustrations of polygamy. . . . In fact, however, nearly every polygamous household in the OT suffers most unpleasant and shattering experiences precisely because of this ad hoc relationship. The domestic struggles that ensue are devastating."[51]

Polygamy is not only practiced by the godless, but by God's chosen people. Yet when God's people practice it, blessing is not the result.

---
49 St. Augustine, "The Excellence of Marriage," *Marriage and Virginity*, 45. See also paragraph one of "Holy Virginity" on page 68.
50 Calvin, *Commentaries . . . Vol I*, 217.
51 Victor P. Hamilton. *NICOT: Genesis: Ch. 1–17* (Grand Rapids: Eerdmans, 1990), 238.

This practice resurfaces in Abraham's life in an attempt to bear the seed that God has promised. He takes Hagar as his wife (sort of) in Genesis 16:3, which produces strife in the household both momentary and far reaching (vv. 11–12) instead of promise fulfillment. Once again, we are seeing something that poses more of a warning against polygamy than a mandate for it.

After Lot's wife becomes a table seasoning, his daughters get him drunk and bear children by him (19:36–38), which we can all agree is one of the more disturbing OT sections. Jacob's two wives and the servants that they "give" to him live in a constant tension and contest with one another. Notice also that the child of promise through whom Christ would come, Judah, is by the first wife.

The book of 1 Samuel opens with the tension between the wives of Elkanah, Hannah and Peninnah. The tensions and competition for the husband's affection is reminiscent of Jacob's wives.

The next major polygamist figure is David. Of his children through different wives, one raped another, and a third killed the first. This was only part of the fulfillment of the curse brought on by adultery with Bathsheba and murdering her husband so that David could add her to his wife list (2 Sam. 12:11). Interestingly, David does seem to move toward a kind of monogamy near the end of his life. In 2 Samuel 20:3, he puts away the concubines that Absalom had visited (16:22), and in 1 Kings 1:1–4, he essentially refuses to take on a new mistress even when others push it on him.

Perhaps the most famous polygamist of the Old Testament, though, is Solomon, if for no other reason than the sheer number of wives (700) and concubines (300). Solomon's polygamy was not praised by God, Instead, it brought about his downfall. Despite his wisdom, Solomon's many wives led him away from God and the worship thereof (1 Kings 11:1–8). Ironically, Proverbs 31:3 speaks against this very thing.[52] Solomon is the main one who put together that magnificent collection of wisdom, including the oracle of Lemuel, with the exhortation for a man to not give his strength to *women*. This is not about painting women as evil, but that a plurality of wives (and concubines) will "destroy kings."

Indeed, the Old Testament labors to show the nature of marriage as being monogamous. Malachi 2:14–16 addresses "the wife of thy youth . . . the wife of thy covenant. . . and let none deal treacherously against the wife of his youth" (KJV). Proverbs 5:18–20 tells us to "rejoice in the wife of your youth. . . . Let her breasts fill you at all times with delight; be intoxicated always in her love. Why should you be intoxicated, my son, with a forbidden woman and

---

[52] It would seem Solomon anticipated Oscar Wilde's character Lord Goring, who always passed along good advice since it was the only thing he knew to do with it.

embrace the bosom of an adulteress?" Notice that it says *wife*, not wives. David Dickson argues that Leviticus 18:18 expressly forbids polygamy, though that passage only explicitly forbids marrying two sisters.[53]

We can agree with John and Paul (the Feinbergs, not the Beatles or the apostles) that "both the OT and NT teach procreative, monogamous marriage as normative. God made human beings male and female in his own image."[54] It is certainly easy to prove the New Testament's opposition using Christ's words in Mark 10:2–9 and the moral standards set for elders in 1 Timothy 3:2–12.

Thankfully, this subject provides another category wherein we can agree with the Roman Catholics. As their catechism states, "Polygamy is incompatible with the unity of marriage."[55] The Westminster Confession echoes the same sentiment, "Marriage is to be between one man and one woman. It is not lawful for any man to have more than one wife, nor for any woman to have more than one husband, at one and the same time."[56] I appreciate Rome's language here, though, because "incompatible" is precisely correct. Marriage is about beautiful, ordered, monogamous union, and as such is the reflection of Christ and His church.

Ephesians 5:25–27 gives the command for husbands to love their wives as Christ loved the church. The polygamist husband cannot reflect Christ to his wives because his attention, affection, and time are as divided as he is. The Bride of Christ is singular, albeit composed of many members. God is not a polygamist, Christ is not a polygamist, and men must not be if they are to properly bear the image of God. A man is encouraged to single, celibate life by Paul (1 Cor. 7:6–8), but for those that do marry, they are to be "one-woman men"[57] in reflection of Christ.

Polygamy is essentially adultery masked by an unholy covenant. Like adultery, it is sin and a product of the fall, as we have seen evidenced by the Old Testament itself. Also, like adultery, it mirrors the idolatrous hearts of men. The polygamist does not resolve to find satisfaction in his one wife, but adds others. Perhaps as you have read this section, you have sat comfortably in criticism of those gross polygamists and their unfathomable sin. Yet do you not do the same to God? Do you not add in other gods, other idols, to try and satisfy your heart when you ought to be satisfied by Christ who sacrificed

---

53 David Dickson, *Truth's Victory Over Error* (Carlisle: Banner of Truth, 2007), 182.
54 John S. Feinberg and Paul D. Feinberg, *Ethics for a Brave New World* (Wheaton: Crossway Books, 2010), Kindle Edition Location 5460.
55 Catholic Church, *Catechism of the Catholic Church* (New York: Doubleday, 1995), 463.
56 WCF XXIV.1, 2nd LBC XXV.1.
57 More literal rendering of 1 Timothy 3:2; see also Titus 1:6. Though these are listed as qualifications for elders/overseers, they are standards for which all believers to strive.

Himself for your sin?

On the flip side, there is an important lesson here about the metanarrative of Scripture. There is only one Bride. God does not have a separate bride from Christ; Christ does not have one bride in the Old Testament and then a new one in the New Testament. The Bride of Christ is *ekklesia*, the called-out ones, the church, the true Israel.[58] The *ekklesia* may grow, shift, develop, and mature, but it is the same Bride. Rob Westerman writes, "Either the woman and the bride are the same and The Church is the true Israel of God, or God has two wives. The teaching that the Jews and Christians are two separate peoples actually makes God out to be a polygamist."[59] It may be a tiny clump of cells in the ancient Near East at one point, and then a worldwide entity at another, but it is the same Bride. The Gentiles may be grafted in, but it is still Christ's Bride, a people He has purchased for Himself. As the early church father Justin Martyr says, "For the true spiritual Israel, and descendants of Judah, Jacob, Isaac, and Abraham (who in uncircumcision was approved of and blessed by God on account of his faith, and called the father of many nations), are we who have been led to God through this crucified Christ."[60]

Noahic Punctuation

Noah's story, which was told by God and recorded under inspiration by Moses, is dripping with Christological imagery. Christ is the Ark, enclosing His people within Himself to carry them through this baptism of the storm of death, riding through the waves and absorbing the impact of the manifestation of God's righteous wrath, creaking and groaning but never breaking. By divinely instituted structure and form, it endures when all else perishes.

Noah himself serves as a type of Christ, "flawless in his generations" and uncorrupted (after a fashion). He spares his bride and his children through his works in obedience to the Father. He even emerges after the judgment has passed with wife and children intact to a new earth, like Christ will at the end of days.

There is another aspect of this event in history that deserves our attention, a kind of punctuated event, wherein God separates His Bride, tearing her out of the world. He woos her again and marks a new "Ebenezer"[61] of history. The age of Noah is one of these events, where God's people are distinguished dramatically from the rest of the world, in God's election. There were only two

---
[58] Most people think of "church" as exclusively NT, but this word "ekklesia" that we translate as "church" occurs many times in the OT for the assembly of Israel.
[59] Rob Westerman, *The Millennium Mystery and Revelation Code Examined* (Self-published, 2009), 14.
[60] Justin Martyr, *Dialogue*, 11.5.
[61] A marker of God's providence. See 1 Samuel 7:12.

kinds of people in the world when the rains fell ... those who were in the ark and those who were not. Abraham, Isaac, Jacob, and Moses each mark such punctuations in human history.

Noah is not part of the godless murdering nations drowned in holy justice. Abraham is no longer another pagan of Ur nor a Canaanite. Isaac is not Ishmael, and Jacob is not Esau. Moses and the Israelites are not Egypt.

Yet our ego-centric worldview impedes our ability to properly grasp the significance of such events because we think it is either directly about us or it is irrelevant. What does Noah have to do with me? These events speak of the Bridegroom, and they speak of the Bride. It is not immediately about us, but it is about us because it is about God's people.

These events are a kind of rebirth recorded as the Bride appears to be pared down. She is stripped of the rags of social acceptance and anonymity. What is left is the naked and beautiful Bride.

In reality, though, the Bride never shrinks. The Bride of Noah's day is not just Noah and his family. That is the whole of the church militant on earth for a moment in time, but it must be combined with the church triumphant to see the whole Bride.[62] It is a punctuated event of history that sparks new growth of the same Bride.

Another point of separation comes in Christ's earthly ministry. He comes and delineates the true Israel from the broader national Israel. The cry of the gospel drops to a whisper, as it has done so many times before, only to grow again in magnificent crescendo. Each time this kind of refrain has been played, it has been clearer, each time more beautiful, like instruments added to the orchestra and enhancing the beauty of the gospel wedding song. From time to time, God refines this cry and song by canceling out the white noise of false Christianity through the refining fire of persecution. Not only is the exclusivity of the Bride shown in each of these instances, but as redemptive history progresses, a new aspect of the covenant of grace is revealed or elucidated. But whatever stanza of God's orchestral masterpiece we find ourselves in, the song of the gospel rings out and calls sinners to be saved and joined to the glorious Bride.

What we see recorded in Holy Writ is for our edification. It shows us the grand narrative of the Bride who is loved, rebuked, refined, and adorned. What we see there in the broad strokes of history plays out in our individual lives. Embrace the punctuation God drafts into your life. The commas, periods, and ellipses are written in the calligraphy of perfect wisdom. God repeatedly chastises us to pare away the attachments of this world in a *semicolon* to

---

[62] The church militant is the conglomeration of saints saved by grace here on earth, while the church triumphant is a term for the collective saints in heaven.

present a new time and season not entirely divorced from that which came before. Whether you are a sentence, paragraph, or chapter in the manuscript of redemptive history, rejoice in it. Embrace the punctuation God has written for you.

Hagar versus Sarah

Since we have now come to Abraham and the birth of the nation, I want to pull back and see the correlation of his brides through the inspired commentary of Paul. This will help us keep things in perspective. Here is my personal translation of Galatians 4:22–26:

> For it is written that Abraham had two sons, one of the slave-woman and one of the free, but he of the slave has been born of the flesh and he of the free through promise. Now (this) is allegorical: for these two are covenants, one from Mount Sinai birthing into slavery, which is Hagar. Hagar is Mount Sinai in Arabia but corresponds to present Jerusalem, for she is enslaved with her children. But above, Jerusalem is free; she is our mother.

Paul's interpretation of Abraham's wife and mistress of redemptive history in Galatians has caused no small degree of controversy. When Galatians is read in its entirety, and with Paul's letter to the Romans, Paul's declaration is self-evident. He is intentionally comparing the bulk of national Israel to Hagar *because* it is offensive. He wants to throw the audience off guard, especially the proud Judaizers who were trying to make Jewish culture obligatory for Gentile Christians. Being the people of God was always about faith. The bloodline was about Christ. So after Christ came, the bloodline was no longer relevant. The Jews who rejected Christ were not actually God's people; they were not children of Abraham and Sarah in the sense that really matters. Technically, they were sons of Abraham, so Paul labels them sons of Hagar.

Sarah Laughed (Genesis 18:12)

"So Sarah laughed to herself, saying, 'After I am worn out, and my lord is old, shall I have pleasure?'" (Gen. 18:12).

The context of this verse is the reiteration of the promise of Abraham's seed. God made the promise first in Genesis 12, then 15, and again in 17. When the angels tell Abraham again about the birth to come, Sarah's response is to laugh at the impossibility of it all. Abraham is 99 years old, and Sarah is not far off. By all earthly comprehension, it was impossible that after all those years of trying she would actually bear a son to her husband.

Sarah would later be granted faith in the promise of God. Hebrews 11:11

records, "By Faith, even barren Sarah herself, received ability to conceive of seed, and beside the season of life, because she considered Him who promised faithful" (author's translation). God granted faith to Sarah and she bore Isaac, who would be the ancestor of Christ Himself. It was "by faith" that she bore the impossible child. It was "by faith" in the God who promised, as being able to fulfill the promise, that Christ's earthly ancestor Isaac was born.

When we view Sarah as a type of the Bride, though, something else comes to light. Each believer is born again, as Christ said to Nicodemus (John 3:3). In commonly ordained means, the believer's birth is both through Christ (by the regenerating work of the Holy Spirit) and by the testimony and preaching of His Bride, the church. The regeneration catalyzes the response in faith to the preaching of the gospel that justifies sinners.

Often the individual, local church falters in her faith. Like Sarah, she laughs at the possibility of a birth or, more accurately, a rebirth. She looks at the Muslim or the drug addict, the atheist or the politician, then at how long her baptistery has remained dry and thinks, "After I am worn out, and my lord is old, will I have pleasure?"

There is a rebuke to Christ's church in these words. We may look at the labors of evangelism that have so long been unfruitful, at prayers repeatedly answered with a "no" (or a "not yet" that we thought was a "no") and assumed that all hope is lost. We forget that God is mighty to save and willing to forgive. We might even attempt means that God has not ordained to try and bring about salvation. Churches resort to gimmicks and bribery of the lost, thinking that a "Hagar" of prosperity preaching or pop psychology might bring about the promised birth.

We must return to the promises of the gospel. God promised to save sinners by the foolishness of preaching. Jesus promised that hell will not prevail against heaven. God promises that He will grant the "impossible" children in His perfect timing, not ours. Cry out again like the father of the child in Mark 9:24, "I believe; help my unbelief!"

Courting Rebekah (Genesis 24)

Genesis 24 deserves a thorough exposition unto itself in its redemptive-historical context, but we do not really have time for that. Our focus will again be restricted to the bridal narrative therein. First, we will briefly look at the narrative as a whole.

Abraham called, instructed, and equipped his servant for a specific task. He established an oath with the servant to seek out a bride fit for his son. The covenant was established with the placing of the hand under the thigh, a common practice of the era, tied to fertility and offspring, fitting for Abraham with the covenant of the seed.[63] The servant was not to take a bride from the Canaanites God had condemned, but from the land of Abraham's origin. The servant asked what should occur if the woman is unwilling to come; should Isaac go and get her? Abraham answered that Isaac was to remain in the promised land.

Abraham's servant prayed that God would grant success (vv. 12–4), worshipped at the first signs of providence (vv. 26–27), and worshipped with prayer when further success was granted (v. 52). Having brought with him a portion of Abraham's treasures (v. 10), and having found Rebekah, he offered her a foretaste of the wealth she would know in the promised land (v. 22). Her adornments were witnessed by those around her (v. 30), and the servant proclaimed the wealth of his master's house and of the son (vv. 34–36). He gave more to the bride and paid the bridal price from his master's store (v. 53).

In all these events, there was a sense of urgency to the servant. He hastened from Abraham's side after preparation and was unwilling to serve himself until he proclaimed his good news and fulfilled his calling (v. 33). After he secured Rebekah's hand, he was urgent to return to Canaan (vv. 54–56), and Rebekah herself shared this urgency (vv. 57–58). The servant rushed home with her (v. 61), and she met the bridegroom in the promised land (vv. 63–67).

Each piece of the narrative laid out above carries a point of correspondence to evangelism when viewed through our bridal lens.[64] Every believer who shares the gospel—from the faithful family member to the professional theologian—engages in this sequence to some degree. For the sake of simplicity, let us examine it in its primary form: the minister. He is called by the heavenly Father, instructed, and equipped for the task that lies ahead of him, having been saved by covenant and ordained in covenant with the church. Though he cannot perceive who is a reprobate (symbolized by Canaanites) and who is elect, he knows that he will not gather the Bride of Christ from among those not ordained. In all this work, the salvation occurs by faith and not by sight. Excepting a thirty-some year span, in all of human history the salvation of sinners has occurred with the Bride unable to see the Bridegroom. God's people on earth were only able to see Jesus in person during that brief window of time.

The task of the servant is to be saturated by prayer, understanding that it is God alone who grants success. He worships when God gives first signs of success, such as a willingness to listen to the gospel. He praises God and prays even more when a work of grace appears to be taking place.

---

63 Calvin, *Commentary . . . Vol. 2*, 12.
64 Benjamin Keach makes such a reference in *Preaching from the Types*, 327.

The minister, like Abraham's servant, presents a portion of his master's treasures. He proclaims the beauty and precious nature of the gospel. This is intrinsic to his part in the wooing of the bride. He continues in the proclamation of the wealth, far surpassing what is seen and tasted of in the earth, that awaits the bride in glory. The new convert (bride) is adorned with grace, new life, and a testimony to those who are around her. Just as with the servant and Rebekah, there is a progression of "gift giving," but ours is a growing in grace, development of spiritual gifts, and conforming to Christ. It is our sanctification.

In the Genesis narrative, we see the reluctance of Rebekah's family to release her. They try to detain her and delay the departure. While this is innocent and understandable in the context, its antitype in the Bride of Christ is more nefarious. Evangelism has many opponents in this world. The unholy trinity of this world (Satan, the world, and the flesh) do all they can to stave off the listener. "Not now. There will be time for that later. Enjoy your youth and worry about the afterlife another day." The world, Satan, and flesh all press lethargy and delay.

This is why there ought always to be a sense of urgency to evangelism, though not hasty recklessness. As the servant was unwilling to serve himself until he had proclaimed the good news, the minister ought to be cautious of tending to his own rest until he has fulfilled the task God has called him to do. There ought also to be an urgency to journey to the promised land. In all this, there is a balance between the urgency and waiting upon the Lord. The messenger does not hog-tie Rebekah and run off, but he is not content to leave her where she is. This is admittedly a difficult balance for believers to strike in evangelism, but we must work while it is yet day.

There is a bridal price for the church that we shall see again and again, but here we see a kind of dowry given to the bride herself and her family.[65] It is a taste of the treasures that await her in the bridegroom's home. All the blessings, all the fruit of the Spirit we taste of here and now—the joy, peace, and love we currently enjoy—are nothing compared to what is to come. As Isaac Watts wrote in his hymn "We're Marching to Zion":

> The men of grace have found glory begun below
> Celestial fruit on earthly ground from faith and hope may grow.
> The hill of Zion yields a thousand sacred sweets,
> Before we reach the heavenly fields or walk the golden streets.
> There shall we see His face and never, never sin;
> There from the rivers of His grace drink endless pleasures in.

---

[65] As Rebekah's family received a small portion of those riches, so are those who surround the new convert made aware of the miraculous change wrought in them.

Then let our songs abound, and every tear be dry;
We're marching through Immanuel's ground to fairer worlds on high.

Finally, in all these things, Abraham's servant never exalts or extols himself. He is feet for delivery, a voice for the message, and hands for the service. So ought every pastor to be. I have mixed emotions whenever people are excited about a doctrinally sound preacher. It is a joy to hear that people are excited about being taught, but it is precarious when the focus becomes too much on the messenger. It is a joy to listen to great orators boldly proclaim the gospel, and pastors should always strive to be better in these things. But let us never forget who gives the talents, who animates their preaching, who put the treasures in their hands, and who has sent them in the first place.

III
CYCLES OF HISTORY
Survey of Historical Books and Prophets

The remainder of the Pentateuch (Exodus through Deuteronomy), the historical books, and the Prophets continue to give us living metaphors and direct references to the Bride of Christ. Much of this is scattered and repetitive, though, so we will do a brief flyover. Later, we will deal with specific books with denser references to our subject.

After finishing Genesis, Exodus 4:22 is the first indirect encounter we have with the bridal image. Israel is described as the son of God. The most straightforward sense of this verse is that Jacob (renamed Israel) was born again into the family of God, and therefore the nation embodies this sonship. Jacob was saved through Christ, even though the incarnation would not occur for several thousand years. In Romans 9:4, Paul tells us the "adoption" first belonged to the Israelites; they were the first substantial, identifiable group to whom salvation "belonged."[1]

As we delve deeper into the imagery and meaning, the family tree becomes a bit complicated. Jacob also serves as an image of Christ as father and a kind of federal head to a nation. Thus, when God says that Israel, which means "he who strives with God,"[2] is His first-born son, it also refers to Israel's son Christ, the greatest fulfillment of the Abrahamic promise and the "only begotten son" of God. Jacob was saved through the promise of Christ and the atoning work Christ accomplished. Jesus identified with Jacob and all of Israel to be the sympathetic mediator. So all this together makes Christ simultaneously Jacob's father, descendent, and brother. This kind of imagery becomes

---
1 This also introduces for us the convoluted nature of the Bride of Christ imagery in a way reminiscent of Ray Steven's redneck ballad "I Am My Own Grandpa."
2 While this represented Jacob's striving against God at the Jabbok, it also foreshadowed Christ striving with God to accomplish salvation and suffering under God on the cross. As "Israel" denotes the sacred assembly, the church, it carries dual meaning. We strive "with God" but often strive against Him as we saw in Eve's curse of her desire being "for" her husband. There are some interesting plays on words with "Israel" throughout the OT.

increasingly convoluted when we look at Paul, who describes himself as a mother representing the church (Gal. 4:19), a father as representing Christ (1 Cor. 4:14–15), yet their brother as one likewise born again through Christ's work (1 Cor 1:10; Gal 1:11; and many more).

The Fifth Commandment—Exodus 20:12

The Decalogue, or Ten Commandments, is one of the best-known elements of Scripture. People raised in the church have mental images of artist renditions or the flannel-graph Moses carrying the two tablets. Some envision Charlton Heston or Mel Brooks in a robe on the mountain wielding the stones before the Israelites. Even non-Christians can name a few of the ten.

When theologians approach the Decalogue, they often refer to the first and second tables. The first table consists of commands regarding God in the first four, and the second table is commands regarding men in five through ten. I think most who have dealt with these categories have intellectually winced at the imbalance of four to six, and wished for a moment that it was five and five. However, I plead the fifth commandment has two aspects: one vertical and one horizontal.

Commandment number five, first found in Exodus 20:12, states, "Honor your father and your mother, that your days may be long in the land that the Lord your God is giving you." The horizontal, man-ward meaning of the command is easy enough to understand. It also provides parents with biblical grounds to say that disobedience shortens a child's lifespan.[3] In its original context, the Israelites were called to obey in their youth and provide for their parents at the end of life as part of the contract for residence in Canaan. Today, the moral exhortation carries over with an understanding that we look toward an eternal residence in the new heavens and new earth. Along with the other nine, these commands summarize what we call the moral law, which applies to all people in all places at all times.

But how can this have a vertical or God-ward element? Because we are likewise called to honor our spiritual Father and mother as children of God. Our spiritual mother is the church, as Cyprian, Calvin, and others suggest, and it is through her that we receive our regular exhortations and encouragements. This also provides a natural flow from the fourth commandment about honoring the Sabbath. So by honoring Christ and the church, by obeying the exhortations they give us for repentance and faith, we cling to the promise of eternal life.

---

3 That is a joke, just to be clear . . .

The Bored-Out Ear

Exodus 21:2–6 presents us with a prescription about slaves. This bondservant concept has been frequently referenced in terms of the Christian life alongside passages like Ephesians 6:6. If a slave was satisfied with life under his master, he could choose to remain in master's service. If he had a wife and kids in slavery, that too would motivate him to stay. His ear would be bored through with an awl, and he would remain a servant for life.

There is an important shadow of Christ here, but to see it, we have to first turn to Psalm 40:6, where David literally says that God has bored through his ear. This is normally translated as God giving him an open ear, indicating his obedience, which is understandable given the kind of imagery we find in Isaiah 32:3. But if we take this as a reference to the slave ritual of Exodus 21, it has a fuller meaning of making the psalmist a servant for life out of love for his master.

The climax comes when we see its citation in Hebrews 10:5, where the author of Hebrews clearly states that it is Christ's voice in David's words. It is Christ who said, "You have bored through my ear." When we take all of this together, it means that Christ's incarnation, taking on the body which God prepared for Him, was like the marking of a servant who has humbled himself and surrendered freedom for the course of an earthly life. Part of this was out of love for His master, and Christ repeatedly speaks of delighting in doing the will of His Father. The element often missed, however, is that this willful indenturing of Himself was also out of love for His Wife and children. The Son took on flesh to glorify His father, but also because He loved His Bride (the church), and their offspring (the individual believers).

Adulterous Israel

The first time we encounter *explicit* marital imagery in the Pentateuch is in Exodus 34:11-16, where the concept of Israel as the Bride of Yahweh is surprisingly assumed.[4] It introduces the harlot concept that will constitute the majority of the Bride of Christ references in the historical books and prophets. Leviticus 17:7 speaks of the people (corporately) offering sacrifices to goat-demons as harlotry or adultery; then 20:4–6 shows idolatry to Molech in terms of an individual committing adultery against God. So this sin can be either corporate or individual because Israelites are the Bride corporately and individually.

While not referenced in bridal language, there is a section in the Pentateuch that played out through Israel's history that we might refer to as "Bored Housewife Syndrome." Israel will be gifted a land of plenty by the same God

---
4 Ortlund, *God's Unfaithful Wife*, 25.

who spoke it into existence. She will have great seasons of bounty, and that is dangerous. As Jeremiah Burroughs puts it, most Christians will pass the trial of persecution, but most will fail the trial of prosperity.[5] To that end, God warns the children of Israel before they ever set foot in the promised land that they will be prone to forget the God they love in those seasons of prosperity. God speaks to this in Deuteronomy 31:20. It is the same tendency Robert Robinson strives against in his hymn "Come, Thou Fount of Every Blessing" when he says, "Prone to wander, Lord, I feel it, prone to leave the God I love. Here's my heart, oh, take and seal it, seal it for thy courts above." This is a temptation we all must wage war against in our own hearts.

The Cycle

When surveying the body of the historical books, a dominant pattern of behavior characterizes the Bride of Christ image. For example, the book of Judges has often been explained in terms of a repeating cycle that goes something like this:

Israel sins.

God brings chastisement in the form of an oppressing nation.

Israel repents.

God raises up a judge to free them.

Israel follows God for a season.[6]

To put it more simply: ***Sin, Chastisement, Repentance, Mercy.***

If we are paying attention, though, we see this pattern throughout the historical books. It starts in the wilderness and continues until the exile. Israel grumbles in the wilderness, casts idols for profane worship, rebels, doubts, and falters. God chastises her, she repents, God "relents," and they journey on.[7] The history of Israel from Egypt to exile gives a recurring sense of idolatry déjà vu.

Part of the challenge is in understanding the overlapping themes of the individual lives, the generational gaps, and the Mosaic scale model. Each true Israelite lives this cycle in his personal life, while his generation does the

---

[5] Jeremiah Burroughs, *The Rare Jewel of Christian Contentment* (Carlisle: Banner of Truth, 1964), 104ff.

[6] I thought about trying to put this in an actual circle, but my graphic design skills roughly equate to a toddler with a crayon.

[7] This language of God's relenting, His sorrow and anger from betrayal, and the like are what we call anthropopathisms. God does not have passions like us, and He is not reactive in His emotions, but God reveals Himself in terms that we can understand. This is called the doctrine of impassibility.

same. God shows glimpses of what Israel deserves in His "outbursts of wrath"[8] revealed at key points after their breaking of the covenant. Yet God continually displays mercy through a mediator so that He can foreshadow Christ and preach the gospel in signs and symbols. We say "glimpses" of judgment because the real cost of sin is eternal damnation. When these are applied corporately to the nation, there is chastisement for the elect within the nation as well as "fair warning" to the reprobate, leaving him without excuse. We also have to realize that almost every generation had to go through this for themselves, just as we each have our own journey to the cross.

Mosaic Economy

Life for God's people between Sinai and Jesus is often referred to as the Mosaic economy, referring to Moses as the first mediator figure, and has nothing to do with the tiny tile pictures. The whole Mosaic economy is a kind of scale model, shrinking down the elements of redemptive history into distinct tangibles. The tabernacle with its furniture, the sacrifices and priests, even Moses himself, are all types and shadows that find their fulfillment in Christ. The judges, the kings, and the prophets point to aspects of the great Redeemer and Ruler, while each man shows his own inadequacy necessitating the real fulfillment.

Another way to think of this Mosaic structure of diet, clothing, feasts, and sacrifices is in terms of scaffolding. In the construction of a building, scaffolding is built up on the perimeter to assist the construction of the actual building. You can even see the basic outline of the building by the scaffolding. Yet once the building is constructed, the scaffolding is taken down, just as the ceremonial and judicial laws of Israel are abrogated and taken away (this is a major theme of Hebrews). Likewise, the Mosaic law (with the exception of the moral law that transcends it) has no place after the church is revealed in its new form after Christ's resurrection and ascension.

God's law shows Israel their sin, and a cornucopia of images shows them God's provision of a Savior. God shows them their infidelity as well as the Bridegroom who woos them and saves them.

One of the more fascinating and obscure references to this is in Numbers 5:11–31, where we find a prescription for discerning unwitnessed adultery. If a husband suspected his wife had been unfaithful but did not catch her in the act, he could call for a unique kind of trial by the priesthood. The priest would take dirt from the tabernacle floor (holy dust representing God's presence in the trial) and put it into sacred water. She would hold a grain

---

[8] These are not actually outbursts, but perfectly contained within the immutability of the divine character.

offering without oil or frankincense, take an oath to receive judgment, and drink muddy waters.[9] If she was innocent, nothing would happen, but if she was guilty, her womb would swell, her thigh would fall away, and she would be rendered barren.

Because the grain is not anointed with oil or frankincense, the sacrifice does not represent Christ. Without Christ's sacrifice to intercede, she is judged by God's presence in the muddy waters and rendered barren. I believe what God is showing us here is not just that He hates adultery, though that is true, but what happens to the Christ-less church who is adulterous/idolatrous. Her womb may swell with the appearance of many converts, but she is ultimately barren and unable to produce living children, true saints, and she is unable to stand on the day of judgment (Ps. 1:5) because her thigh is wasted away.

David and Abigail

In many ways, we can think of the unfolding of redemptive history in the form of an opera. There is certainly a lot of singing in the Bible. In an opera, there is a theme that is repeated over and over in variations. A recognizable sequence of notes recurs in various pieces of music, but it is not identical in each recurrence. They are noticeably similar, but it is not the exact same song over and over. In a sense, that is what I am pointing out in this book—a recurring theme in variations that builds to a climax in Christ's work of redemption.

We find a familiar bridal theme in 1 Samuel 25 with the story of David, Abigail, and Nabal. David and his men are in the wilderness of Paran and petition Nabal for food for a feast because they have protected Nabal's sheep-shearers, but Nabal rudely refuses.[10] David is preparing to come wipe out Nabal's house when his wife Abigail hears what has happened. She goes with servants bearing food and wine to assuage David's wrath. Upon hearing her plea, David ceases and Nabal's household is spared. God kills Nabal, and David takes Abigail for his wife.

As always, we have to remember that this is both real history and the "script" of God's cosmic theatrical production, which we will revisit in Ephesians. As such, God presents a familiar theme, foreshadowing Christ in real time with flesh and blood figures of history. We find a bride who is wed to a doomed husband. It is interesting to note that Abigail is recorded as discerning and beautiful. While we are not intrinsically so, by the work of the Holy Spirit and Christ, we are granted discernment and made beautiful. Nabal resembles the foolish and rebellious world that rejects God's anointed, mirroring the opening of John's gospel. It could even be argued that he represents the unregenerate mass of national Israel.

---

9 Muddy Waters will always give you the blues. Oh yeah, I went there.
10 This is not a mafia "protection" scheme, just to be clear.

David is obviously and repeatedly an image of Christ. The world rejected the Messiah, and were it not for the sake of both the Bride yet within and the intercession of the church, the wrath of God would have come. Scripture often speaks of God's longsuffering with the world because He delays the day of judgment until the last of His elect are gathered in. While it would have been unjust for David to take matters into his own hands, Christ would certainly be just to judge the world. In time, judgment does come upon Nabal as it will on the world, and the bride is taken into the arms of a better bridegroom.

When David sends for her, Abigail's humility is a model for us as the church. She proclaims herself unfit and willing to only be a servant who washes the feet of his servants. May this be our hearts, eager to serve our Savior and His people. In earthly marriage, it serves each of us well to see our sin and God's love for our spouse, that we might have a servant's heart toward them.[11]

Isaiah, Jeremiah, and Ezekiel

With each progression, Scripture records the cycle: The Bride commits adultery, she is indicted and convicted of her adultery, and the Bridegroom woos her again. There was adultery in the wilderness and in the promised land. In the judges, we see the Bridegroom conquering enemies and the heart of the Bride. In the kings, we witness the husband/king governing his household, though these human types *often* do it poorly and *never* perfectly. It is in the prophets, however, that we see the hard work of the marriage. We see the rebuking of sin, the dealing with adultery, and the labor of reconciliation in the marriage. Especially in Isaiah, Jeremiah, and Ezekiel we see these themes revisited again and again because the Bride whores herself out to false gods again and again.

These prophets give us some of the most disturbing texts of Scripture. Pastors do not like to preach these passages because they are uncomfortable and the language shocks us. As Ray Ortlund Jr. says regarding one of these passages in Jeremiah, "The disgusting image of the covenant people driven with an animal craving to be sexually satisfied by someone, anyone, shocks and offends. It was meant to."[12] Here are some of those texts:

> "How the faithful city has become a whore, she who was full of justice! Righteousness lodged in her, but now murderers." (Isa. 1:21)

> "If a man divorces his wife and she goes from him and becomes another man's wife, will he return to her? Would not that land be greatly polluted? You have played the whore with many lovers; and would you return to me? declares the LORD. Lift up your eyes to the bare

---
11 Daniel Rogers, *Matrimonial Honor* (Edification Press: Warrenton, 2010), 20.
12 Ortlund, *God's Unfaithful Wife*, 88.

> heights, and see! Where have you not been ravished? By the waysides you have sat awaiting lovers like an Arab in the wilderness. You have polluted the land with your vile whoredom." (Jer. 3:1–2)

> "How can I pardon you? Your children have forsaken me and have sworn by those who are no gods. When I fed them to the full, they committed adultery and trooped to the houses of whores." (Jer. 5:7)

> "For long ago I broke your yoke and burst your bonds; but you said, 'I will not serve.' Yes, on every high hill and under every green tree you bowed down like a whore." (Jer. 2:20)

This last passage of Jeremiah is especially memorable given its connection between those actions of idolatry and sexual acts. Jeremiah goes on to record God's description of her like a donkey in heat.

We need the passages of the prophets to shock us. We need to be appalled by the words of Isaiah, Jeremiah, and Ezekiel. We need to see how God sees our sin. When Ezekiel gets to chapter 23, he escalates the language to drive home the horror of Israel's sins, first with the northern kingdom, and then the southern.

> Yet she increased her whoring, remembering the days of her youth, when she played the whore in the land of Egypt and lusted after her lovers there, whose members were like those of donkeys, and whose issue was like that of horses. Thus you longed for the lewdness of your youth, when the Egyptians handled your bosom and pressed your young breasts. (Ezek. 23:19–21)

I would guess that was not a memory verse you learned in Sunday School, but it is part of the inspired Word of God. It is profitable for reproof, for correction, and for instruction in righteousness (2 Tim. 3:16). It is necessary for us to see sin how God sees it, as adultery to a faithful husband.

Yet in the cycle of indictment and condemnation, there is the promise of God, the gospel with all its shadows of Christ and Him crucified. One beautiful example of this is a bridal reference that recurs in Jeremiah. In 7:34, God tells Jeremiah that He will silence the voices of the bridegroom and the bride as the land becomes a waste. The same concept repeats in 16:9 and 25:10. So immediately, this is about the impending exile of the nation. There will be no wedding celebrations in Judah. But there is another layer. The Bride of Christ will be taken out of the land, and the wooing voice of God as the Bridegroom will seem to be gone for a time.

Yet in 33:11, God promises that the voices of bridegroom and bride will be restored. The people will be brought back from exile, but more importantly, the church will be formed and the Bridegroom will come, God in flesh, to wed His Bride.

The Faithless Bride and Grace—Ezekiel 16

In Ezekiel 16, we have a strange chapter in an even stranger book, but before we begin, we need to remember the nature of Old Testament prophecy. These prophets are like prosecuting lawyers for God, sent to proclaim how God's people have broken the law. These condemnation passages set the stage for the brief declarations of gospel shrouded in prophecy. Commonly in cycles, the prophet will move from indictment to curse to promise. Time and again, the New Testament takes these segments of promise and declares them fulfilled in Christ, teaching us an interpretive paradigm and method.

God tells a heartbreaking story of an abandoned child of pagan parents, covered in blood as a metaphor for Jerusalem which is a metaphor for Israel which is also (partly) a metaphor for God's elect. This is what we call prophetic idiom, but we will come back to that. She is covered in the blood of her birth, umbilical cord uncut, unwashed and untended. The rubbing of salt referenced here is a practice thought to harden the skin so that a child can endure the environment outside the womb. If left to fend for herself, she will die of exposure, but God twice commands her to live. This strikes us as strange, unmerciful, and futile unless we take into account the authority of divine decree. God spoke light, heaven, earth, water, even life into existence. He spoke each of these once, but He commands life for this infant Jerusalem twice, showing particular care for her. He *causes* her to grow and flourish. Her body matures, her hair grows, and she becomes a woman. She is adorned with beauty, but she is naked and bare.

We cut to a scene when she is at the age of love, or marriage. God passes by and wraps her in the corner of His garment. He establishes covenant with her and adorns her. She becomes royalty! For Israel, this is her journey through the wilderness and being brought into Canaan. If we take this as the city, it would be when David makes Jerusalem the ruling capital.

It is after this that she whores herself out, spending her husband's gifts on adulterous lovers. God's response is to give her over to them so that she can see what they really are and what really matters to them. They rob her and leave her destitute.

Verses 15 to 41 provide an extended discourse on Israel's adultery, the atrocities those generations of the Bride committed. God comes to Jerusalem as a grieved husband consumed with sorrow and anger over his wife's betrayal.[13] He lists her "lovers" and her sins with each of them. Not only is she a whore, she even does that poorly. A prostitute gets paid, but Israel pays her

---
13 This is what we call anthropopathy. We cannot really understand how the perfect God emotes, and it is conveyed to us in human language. God is not actually overwhelmed by His circumstances and emotions, though He does hate sin.

customers, these false gods and earthly powers. She has taken her clothing and jewelry, the gifts of her husband, and worn them for her lovers. She has taken her food, gifts of her husband, and fed her lovers with it. She takes from the only one who actually loves her and gives to those who use and abuse her.

All of this, of course, is an image of idolatry in the lives of God's people. They sacrifice to idols with what God has given them, ignoring the true source of all they are and have. They sacrifice to gods of wealth and sex, thinking they will be the richer. As Israel did, so do we. As Christians we know this is sin, but often diminish its significance.

One specific element of Ezekiel worth noting is the shift away from direct reference to idols. God is not speaking of the gods of Egypt and Assyria, but the nations themselves. Part of this is Ezekiel's focus on rebuking Israel for their trust in alliances with pagan peoples. She sought to shore up her defenses against invading nations by forging alliances with others. From a geo-political standpoint, this makes perfect sense and seems to be justifiable. Why is God pronouncing condemnation for that, especially in terms of harlotry? Because Israel was not like other nations. She was a theocracy whose defense and hope rested in the Almighty Yahweh. Israel sought strength and security in the arms of other nations like Egypt, proving her distrust of God's ability to save her.

This is important for us to see because it strikes closer to home than worship of idols of wood and stone. We are tempted to put our hope in princes and presidents, in our employment, bank accounts, and retirement plans. We should be wise with our finances and good stewards of what God has given us (and there are passages of God's Word that speak to that), but they are never meant to be our hope and security. Our hope for things eternal and temporal ought to be in God who provides for His people.

Picking back up in Ezekiel 16:21, we see the most horrifying image of Israel slaughtering God's children and offering them up as burnt sacrifices to her idols. This may be a reference to Molech worship practices that are referenced elsewhere.[14] There is another layer to it, however. The children of Israel were led blindly (albeit willingly) to eternal condemnation for idolatry by "mob mentality" and leaders of the nation accepting these pagan practices. The Reformers and Puritans spoke of heretical teachers being the worst of murderers because they murder the soul. This is a stark reminder of how our idolatries are never isolated, but affect and influence all those around us.

At the very end of this oracle, God promises to accomplish redemption for her.

---

14 First referenced in Leviticus 18:21, but a recurring idol in Israel's history.

> For thus says the Lord GOD: I will deal with you as you have done, you who have despised the oath in breaking the covenant, yet I will remember my covenant with you in the days of your youth, and I will establish for you an everlasting covenant. Then you will remember your ways and be ashamed when you take your sisters, both your elder and your younger, and I give them to you as daughters, but not on account of the covenant with you. I will establish my covenant with you, and you shall know that I am the LORD, that you may remember and be confounded, and never open your mouth again because of your shame, when I atone for you for all that you have done, declares the Lord GOD. (Ezek. 16:59–63)

There are key elements here for us to understand the nature and narrative of redemptive history. In traditional prophetic idiom, God speaks alternately of a physical city (Jerusalem), then the nation whose capital it was, and then of the true Israel within her. Let us then examine how the narrative bears on each of these subjects.

Calvin basically ignores the literal city and claims it is purely representing Israel and the church. He begins the narrative with Abraham as the child of pagans and carries it through the Egyptian captivity, return to Canaan, marriage life under Mosaic law, exile, and the promised return. Calvin rightly sees the closing section as a promise of the new covenant in Christ, but because he ignores the literal city, he interprets the shame-silence as only an absence of reproach against God, akin to Job placing his hand over his mouth. It is not, therefore, according to Calvin, an absolute silence but aspectual. A similar claim is made by Patrick Fairbairn:

> So ought it to be also in our experience. The humbling and salutary lessons, so strikingly brought out in this wonderful history, should take such deep and abiding hold of our hearts that we shall ever be careful to avoid the evils against which it warns us. And especially since God has now laid open to us the marvelous riches of his grace and called us to the inheritance of his kingdom, we should strive to remember how unworthy we naturally are of such singular goodness, and how often, by our light and sinful behavior, we have provoked him to withdraw it again; so that we may give to him all the glory, and may set our hearts more upon that better country, where imperfection shall be for ever done away, and the strivings between nature and grace shall be wholly unknown.[15]

Daniel Block presents this shaming in a distinctly positive light. "This passage offers helpful insight into the biblical perspective on guilt and shame.

---
15 Patrick Fairbairn, *An Exposition of Ezkiel* (National Foundation for Christian Education: 1969), 179.

Against the grain of popular thinking today, this oracle is unrestrained in its shaming of unfaithful Israel."[16]

Shame is a precarious doctrine, as volatile as it is useful and perhaps more so. Many a believer has been stunted in his spiritual growth by an excessive and improper use of shame by well-intentioned ministers and fellow believers. Any and all approaches to the concept of shame for Christians must come in context of a robust doctrine of justification. We are saved by grace alone through faith alone in Christ alone. When our sins were paid for on the cross by Christ, they were paid in full. Not part, not most, but all. There is no more guilt in that sense. Yet internally, God may use a memory of past sins to draw us away from future sin. And the church should treat sin with gravity, as that which slew our beloved Savior. Our knowledge of our past produces humility and love. As Daniel Block said, "Accordingly, to experience divine grace is never a cause for pride and should not dull one's consciousness of sin. On the contrary, the gift of grace quickens the memory to past infidelity and present unworthiness, and heightens one's amazement at God's love."[17]

Another important factor here is that the public shaming is only prior to Israel's repentance. She is not meant to wear the scarlet letter for the rest of her history, so to speak, perpetually stripped and shamed after repenting. This ties into the church's use of excommunication. Where there is repentance, there is reconciliation, and the shame is removed.

The last factor we have to understand before moving on is that God is speaking to corporate sin. Corporately, Jerusalem has sinned and therefore corporately she will no longer speak. All that being said and acknowledged as true in principle, let us move on to a different aspect of this passage.

The chapter begins with the literal city that was built by pagan peoples. Jerusalem did not become Israel's capital until David took it in 2 Samuel 5, which is why it is called the city of David.[18] That may be the point at which God comes to Jerusalem and speaks life into her, or perhaps David's conquest is when God covers her and makes her the Bride. Then the city represents the nation for the bulk of the remaining narrative. Israel broke the covenant and despised her oath. Hosea speaks of God's divorce from the northern kingdom (Israel), but Ezekiel reveals the divorce of God from Judah. God showed love to her, covenanted with her, adorned her, clothed her, and blessed her above other nations. Yet she broke that covenant which depended on her obedience to the law. Her reproach is greater than Sodom, who only had Lot as a witness to God beyond natural revelation. Her reproach is even greater than Samaria, northern Israel, whose exile should have warned Jerusalem to follow God.

---
16 Daniel Block, *The Book of Ezekiel NICOT* (Grand Rapids: Eerdmans, 1997), 522.
17 Block, *The Book of Ezekiel*, 522.
18 Jerusalem was first taken in Joshua's time but was retaken by Canaanites later.

The most important element to identify is the greater covenant in the background. It was the promise to Abraham and the promise to David, the covenant that would be ratified in innocent blood. This covenant of grace will be established by God when He atones for her and all she has done. Contrasting like chiaroscuro,[19] the darkness of her adultery enhances the beauty of the light of the gospel presented here. Israel is not going to re-establish the covenant from Moses. After all, she would only continue to break it. God will make a *new* covenant. Israel will not atone for her sins; God Himself, born into flesh under the law, will atone for all that she has done. The true Jerusalem—the real, spiritual Israel—will be saved by grace through faith in Jesus Christ, and it is all right here in Ezekiel. The Bridegroom is God who atones for His people as the Messiah.

Let us look at the passage again with these clarifications. The italicized words are added.

> For thus says the Lord GOD: I will deal with you as you have done, you who have despised the oath in breaking the *Mosaic* covenant, yet I will remember my covenant *of grace* with you in the days of your youth *from Abraham and David*, and I will establish for you an everlasting covenant *in Christ's blood*. Then you will remember your ways and be ashamed when you take your sisters, both your elder and your younger, and I give them to you as daughters, but not on account of the *Mosaic* covenant with you. I will establish my covenant *of grace* with you, and you shall know that I am the LORD, that you may remember and be confounded, and never open your mouth again because of your shame, when I atone for you for all that you have done, declares the Lord GOD. (Ezek. 16:59–63)

My only significant deviation from the traditional interpretations is in regards to the silent shame. The silence of Jerusalem is a prophecy of the city after the apostolic era. Samaria and Sodom are given to her as daughters, meaning the gospel would go out from Jerusalem to these regions, to Gentiles, and to the ends of the earth. We can say that the Jerusalem church really is the birthplace of Christianity, but she is now silent. In history, we find different Christian epicenters: Geneva and Wittenberg during the Reformation, London during the Puritan Age, and perhaps places like Escondido, Grand Rapids, or Philadelphia in the U.S. today. But Jerusalem from whence we come is silent. The city "remembers" her glories and her sorrows as the one of whom Christ said He wished to gather her children under His wings but is now desolate (Matt. 23:37–39) and silent.

---

[19] A painting technique made famous by Rembrandt where contrasting light and dark colors are used to produce a dramatic effect.

In near parallel, we see our own individual stories. We are born into this cold, cruel world as naked and bloody. We are sinners from the womb, yet God preserves us. He gives us life, grows us, clothes us, and gives us all that we have in this world. What do we do with that? We chase after idols. We whore ourselves out to this world until God brings us to an end of ourselves, reveals our sin in His holy law, and establishes covenant with us. He covers our sins in the blood of Christ. We are wed to the Bridegroom despite our sin and because of His inestimable love. However, we will not be silent. We will spend our forever praising God.

Most of these subjects will be explored in greater detail in Hosea, but before leaving this section, we do well to look carefully at Micah's treatment of the unfaithful Bride (Israel). In 1:7, God speaks through Micah about the wages of Israel's whoredom: "And all her graven images will be crushed, and all her wages will be burned up in fire, and all her idols I will set as desolation, because from wages of a harlot she has gathered, and as wages of a harlot they will return" (author's translation).

God accuses Israel of using the income of her adultery to purchase idols, and part of the condemnation will be that these idols will be "returned to" harlot's wages. That sounds awkward, but there is a point to it. There are three ways to view this text, and perhaps the Holy Spirit intended all three.

Interpretation 1: Israelites paid a fee to have sex with temple prostitutes. Those funds were used to create idols for worship. When Israel is conquered and exiled, those idols will be taken by conquerors and used in the same cycle of pagan worship. The metal images will be melted down and recast as Babylonian gods, and the wooden ones will be used as fuel for sacrifices.

Interpretation 2: The wages of Israel's idolatry/harlotry are sorrow, given to her with interest. They will receive the wages/repercussions of sin in abundance as they are exiled to a pagan nation where they will be forced to worship pagan gods. In other words, God will give Israel over to what she chose over Him (we will see a similar concept in Hosea).

Interpretation 3: Given Paul's statement that idols are actually representing demons in 1 Corinthians 10:20, the Israelites' wages might be short-term financial "blessings" that they received from consorting with demons. That money was used to further pagan worship in the land of Israel for a season but will now be confiscated by pagan conquerors in the sacking of the northern kingdom.

On Violence

Before we move on, I need to address something about the shocking language of the harlot image in the prophets. In the wide, wide world of what passes for theology, there are some feminist "theologians" who have taken great offense at the prophets' language. They claim it is a misogynistic narrative that despises and demonizes female sexuality while exalting male sexuality. They say it condones domination and violence toward women through these images. While I hope that is not the impression you have gotten from these passages, I will briefly address it here. A more scholarly, apologetic approach can be found in the appendix to Ortlund's book *God's Unfaithful Wife*.[20]

Violence and abuse toward women is a real and terrible thing. The exaltation of male sexuality combined with objectifying female sexuality is also a terrible reality. In the modern era of internet pornography, these horrors are rampant and enthroned to the point that non-Christians have even spoken out against the psychological damage it has on men. The church should reflect the Scriptures in not only identifying male and female roles in life, but also preventing the exaltation of one to the degradation of the other. Oddly enough, these passages should prevent such prejudices rather than perpetuate them, if we actually grasp what God is saying.

Scripture teaches that Christian men are part of the Bride of Christ. In some aspects, they *individually* participate in that identity. A man should behave toward God the same way a wife should behave toward her husband. Though wives may sin against husbands, the husbands have sinned more grievously toward God. They cannot pridefully assert their masculinity if they are striving to reflect Christ (who set the bar for humility) to their wives.

Men should see these harsher treatments of Israel as descriptive and not prescriptive. God has the ultimate moral high ground and perfect wisdom regarding what His people need. If a man has any real perception of who he is, he cannot claim such wisdom. He does not know *perfectly* what his bride needs and must treat her with grace. He does not have the moral high ground because husband and wife are both sinners in need of a Savior. Above all, the bridal metaphor is exactly that, a metaphor, extensive as it is. God is sovereign and has rights over His creation that husbands do not have over their wives. Women are as much bearers of the image of God as men and carry equal dignity before God, despite the different roles. They are not clay in men's hands as humanity is in God's.

---

20 "The harlot metaphor and feminist interpretation," 177-185.

Beloved Harlot[21]

Pen to paper
    Countless writers strive
To make a story
    Come alive
Bleeding in ink
    What they think
Readers will identify
    And make the link
Love stories
    In lace and pink
Gifts of affection
    Roses and mink
But the perfect story
    That captures true love
Doesn't start below
    But rather above
It has love, adventure,
    New life
An ideal husband
    And adulterous wife
That transition was harsh
    So let me explain
To understand mercy
    You must see the pain
The perfect love story
    Takes imperfect people
Under that steeple
    Proud made feeble
There's sin
    And there's ugliness
The idols
    Of the covetous
Deserving damnation
    A whoring nation
Trading God's love
    For a moment's sensation

But elation
    Is temporal

---

21 This is an original spoken-word poem.

And in the covenant
    Moral
In place from
    Creation . . .
Adultery ends
    In desolation
So Israel was given
    Moses' code
But couldn't escape
    Her sinful mode
She broke the covenant
    Again and again
From Sinai to exile
    Beginning to end
It couldn't be fixed
    Nothing could mend
The law only breaks
    Never bends
But that is the message
    It sends
That sinners
    All men
Are broken
    And bent
And when
    They are left to fend
For themselves
    They are lost
Lacking the means
    To pay the cost
For their own
    Unrighteousness
        Unholiness
            Lawlessness
The whole point
    Of Moses
Was always to
    Show us
The need for a sacrifice
    A Lamb to pay the price
But we're
    Jumping ahead

And there's much
>To be said
About why those
>Old Prophets
Offend us and
>Shock us
Calling Israel
>A whore and a harlot
But they called
>As they saw it
See, the nation was privileged
>With law straight from God
Chock-full of commands
>To inherit the sod
Of Canaan, of Palestine
>In ancient Near East
With vineyards pre-made
>Milk and honey to feast
But God said up front
>Clear and outright
They would play harlot
>Adulterous bride
And they'd be exiled
>To Arabian nights
In breaking the law
>They'd lose all their rights
And when they did
>God held to His Word
They lost that land
>Where Joseph's interred
But in the next breath
>Following curses
God gave those prophets
>Benevolent verses
About a new covenant
>A whole new wedding
That she couldn't fail
>One where she'd sing
Like she once did
>In the days of her youth
A marriage of mercy
>Steadfast love and truth

God promised that He
>   Would save them alone
No horsemen or chariots
>   Could ever atone
For their sins
>   And transgressions
See the whole law
>   Was a lesson
About men's
>   Iniquity
How Holy God
>   Can't let sin be
But humanity
>   Is a travesty
Of unending
>   Adultery
Until she was remade
>   In the image of Christ
No amount of works
>   Could ever suffice
It took a new marriage
>   Covenant of grace
For the perfect love story
>   To ever take place
And instead of a house
>   With white picket fence
Or earthly Jerusalem
>   Or living in tents
For the newly washed Bride
>   Reformed and recast
Whom he atoned for
>   Sins future and past
He'll give her a home
>   Befitting romance
In a city to come
>   That's not built with hands

So with this brief overview of Israel's history and prophets, we are prepared to see the Bride in a more positive light through the living allegory of Ruth.

IV
BE YE NOT RUTHLESS
Ruth

EVEN IF IT WERE NOT INCLUDED in the annals of Holy Writ, the book of Ruth would be a beautiful story. In fact, Ruth has been described as the *perfect* short story.[1] It has tragedy, intrigue, and romance, though no sword-fights or pirates. It follows that traditional format of rising action to a climax and resolution. Encapsulated, Ruth is fascinating, but in its context of redemptive history, it is beautiful and foreshadowing. Alongside Hosea, it is one of the clearest books of the Bible for examining the metaphor of the Bride of Christ.

Part of what is so fascinating about this book is that it seems so perfect, and yet it is also history. We balk at concepts of foreshadowing and metaphors in history, because those are the tools of fiction. Yet what is fiction but a story wherein one author is sovereign over all the events? God can include foreshadowing, types, metaphors, and so on in real history because He is sovereign.

With that in mind, Ruth becomes more than a historical record, even more than a case study of God's faithfulness and grace, but a real-life allegory for us as the church in relationship to Christ. In particular, Ruth reflects the salvation story of those saints whose journey to the cross was longer than others. Not every elect person shows up one Sunday, is regenerated, repents, and believes before the sermon is over. Many of our narratives are hazy, with little more definition than "I know that I was an unbeliever in year X, but I was saved by year Z." As Ruth's journey ran from pagan Moabitess to an Israelite wed to the kinsman redeemer, so, too, are the redemption stories of many of God's saints.

---

[1] Weiser cites Goethe's view that Ruth is "the loveliest complete work on a small scale," and that of Rud. Alexander Schröder: "No poet in the world has written a more beautiful short story" (*Introduction to the Old Testament*, Darton, Longman and Todd, 1961), 305.

In not-so-fair Moab, we set our scene. Naomi has followed her husband Elimelech with their sons out of the land of Israel because of famine.[2] We are not told which famine this is in Israel's history, but it is fair to conjecture this is God's chastisement of the people for their sin during the book of Judges. Rather than repenting and waiting on God, they leave God's people to seek their fortune elsewhere. This is all the more ironic when we see that Elimelech means "my God is King." True, it is essential to the story that Naomi gain Ruth as a daughter-in-law, but that is God working through and in spite of these men's sin to accomplish good. Clearly God does not reward Naomi's husband for his departure or their sons for marrying pagan women, as they all meet untimely deaths. How often have God's people abandoned the assembly of the saints because they felt unsatisfied or under trial with the presumption that God would bless them? How foolish we are when we expect God to bless our disobedience.

Back to Naomi, though, she is left in a pagan land with two pagan daughters-in-law. It is important to notice that Naomi commits herself to the living God and how she refers to Him (1:13–21). She speaks of Yahweh even though she is in Moab. She does not pray to the pagan gods of the land but places her trust in the God of Israel because she knows He is the God of all creation. She sees Yahweh as sovereign, the Almighty, even in Moab. This is not Naomi on a good day, but in mourning. Yahweh has dealt harshly with her, but she knows there is no other god worth trusting.

As a side note, Naomi is an important figure for us in understanding the nature of grieving in a godly way. She does not curse God, but she does not feign happiness either. The church is a place where saints can grieve the effects of a fallen world, even of our own sin, as Naomi speaks of her trials as chastisement. Naomi, when chastised, evidences the soundness of her faith by going back to be with God's people.

Naomi prepares to return to Israel and trust in His providence there. She bids her two daughters-in-law, Orpah and Ruth, to return to their own people and start a new life. They are young and could re-marry unto fruitful and happy lives, at least in earthly terms. Naomi says that she cannot provide husbands for them, which foreshadows how God will provide Ruth a husband (just as we cannot wed sinners to Christ and provide salvation, but God is able). At first, both girls wish to go with Naomi, but Orpah relents and returns to the Moabites. Ruth, however, remains resolute and continues with Naomi. As a result, there is no book of Orpah or Orpah book club. There is a vague parallel here to what we see in the rich young ruler of Luke 18:18–30 who comes to Christ (which is commendable) but, after seeing the fullness of

---

2 If you say Elimelech's name four times in a row with the proper inflection, you get "In the Jungle" stuck on a loop in your head.

the cost of following Christ, relents and turns away (of course there is more to that narrative in Luke). Ruth's reaction, on the other hand, reads more along the lines of the Gentile woman who seeks after Christ in Matthew 15:21–28. She pleads with Christ and He answers her harshly, but she persists. Ruth's persistence is likewise rewarded. Perseverance, though ultimately granted by God, is a mark of God's people we should emulate.

Ruth follows Naomi back to the land of Israel. She chooses to live in a land and with a people foreign to her as she follows the example of a woman who trusts in Yahweh. It is through this woman that Ruth comes to know the bridegroom for whom she is destined. An Israelite bride brings a pagan to be wed into the nation of Israel. As with Abraham's servant, we again see the image of evangelism.

There is also a lesson here for the women of Christ's church, especially widows. Women are not called to preach or serve in the eldership, but that in no way diminishes your significance or usefulness. Women are not second-class Christians because of their gender or status in life. Naomi was not an elder or priest in the nation, but those elders and priests do not have their names recorded in Scripture either. Naomi is honored where men are not, like Deborah and Jael are honored in Judges. God used Naomi as a catalyst in a series of events for the coming of the Messiah. Christian women, you are instruments of God and trophies of His grace.

On the symbolic side of the book, we are meant to see Ruth as a foreshadowing of the Gentile church that would be grafted on to Israel through marriage. In that case, Naomi represents national Israel, left seemingly without children, which will tie in to the language of Hosea. The vow that Ruth makes in 1:16–17 reads like wedding vows (and has often been appropriated as such). Ruth's vow brings her into a covenant relationship with God's people, but it does not actually make her part of that people. What is fascinating is that while Ruth made that vow, it would be God who would fulfill it for her.

It is fairly unprecedented for a Moabitess like Ruth to join themselves to Israel. In fact, God speaks explicitly against it in Deuteronomy 23:3. She and her children for several generations to come would be forbidden from the formal assembly of God's people, but what is true of national Israel is not always true of spiritual Israel. Ruth may not have been considered a fully accredited national Jew, but she would become a child of God by faith and serve an integral role in Judeo-Christian history. It is worth noting that her descendant David would eventually entrust his aging parents to the care of the king of Moab to protect them from Saul in 1 Samuel 22:3–4.

While Ruth was knit to Naomi by her vow, she would not actually be part of Israel until she was wed to the bridegroom and kinsman redeemer, Boaz.

She would dwell among God's people, eat the food, and live the life of an Israelite. But until the redeemer wed her to himself, she was a Moabite. So, too, someone can dwell amidst the church, take in spiritual food of the preaching of God's Word, conform outwardly to Christian life, even take membership vows—but that does not make him part of God's people. Christ has to draw sinners out of death into life, make them a new creation, and "marry" them through repentance and faith.

Ruth follows Naomi back to Canaan, where she becomes part of the widow class. In order to provide for herself and her mother-in-law, she takes up gleaning. This was a provision of God for the sojourners, the orphans, and the widows prescribed in Deuteronomy 24:19–21. All three of those groups, after a fashion, represent Ruth and us as God's children.

Ruth is now a Moabitess in the land of Israel. We are sojourners in a foreign land, like Abraham, who told the Hittites of Canaan, "I am a sojourner and foreigner among you" (Gen. 23:4; Heb. 11:13–16). Ruth has been cut off from her earthly parents (and lost her father-in-law), just as we are separated from God until salvation, where we are adopted by God and separated from this world.[3] Psalm 68:5 tells us that God is the Father of the fatherless as well as the protector of widows. Ruth is left destitute by a dead husband, and God's elect are, prior to salvation, spiritually impoverished by their union to a fallen, dying world. When we are raised to newness of life, we are dead to the world as is the world dead to us.

Ruth ends up gleaning in the field of Boaz, seemingly by chance, but of course this is God's sovereignty echoing His description by Naomi as "Almighty." She has set out to find a field owned by someone "in whose sight I shall find favor" (2:2). The way Ruth stumbles onto the field of Boaz parallels the way in which many elect, in the first movements of the Spirit, learn of God as they seek to find what is missing in their lives.

In chapter 1, we were told that Elimelech was an Ephrathite, meaning the part of Judah's tribe tied to Bethlehem. Here we find out that Boaz is of that same clan and was born in Bethlehem, but we do not find out why this is important until chapter 4.

When Boaz enters stage left, we see a hint at the sovereignty of God running in the background. Boaz greets his servants with "Yahweh be with you!" But their response is "Yahweh bless you!" And indeed, he would be blessed.

Boaz takes notice of Ruth before she takes notice of him, and he even sets out to provide for her before she knows him. This shows the other side of the salvation narrative. Christ accomplished salvation centuries before many of

---

3 We will see this again in Hosea 14:3.

His elect are born and sends out the Holy Spirit to work in their hearts while they are yet in rebellion against God.

Boaz directly instructs Ruth in 2:9 to follow after his maids for the better gleaning, an image of the need for our proximity to the assembly of the saints. He urges her not to glean in fields that are not his, symbolizing false churches and worldly philosophies. Naomi would later reiterate this urgency for Ruth's safety.

He feeds her directly (2:14) so that she might have the strength and encouragement to continue gleaning. This is an interesting image of how Christ gives direct grace by His Spirit at times to drive us onward in laboring through His Word and the preaching thereof. God does not *just* make us work for the bread of life, neither are we to *only* wait for direct and extraordinary grace without laboring.

Boaz even provides through his servants (an image of pastors and elders) at multiple stages. Boaz warns his servants not to drive her away (2:15), just as God's ministers are called to serve, love, and teach all kinds of persons regardless of ethnicity, gender, or class. Ruth is told to gain her refreshment of water from those servants, like ministers extending the water of life that comes from the Bridegroom. So according to the bridegroom's instruction, the bride is to follow closely after his servants, gain her sustenance thereby, and be refreshed by their efforts. These are all undeserved, gracious provisions of the bridegroom that we find in greater form through Christ and His church.

Ruth 2:12 even records a benediction/prayer of Boaz for Ruth. This foreshadows the kind of intercession Christ gives in His High Priestly Prayer of John 17 as well as His ongoing intercession in glory. Like Old Testament Israel, Ruth sought Yahweh for refuge without knowing how the Kinsman Redeemer would be the vehicle of salvation.

It is true that Boaz does a great deal of this on account of what he has heard regarding Ruth. She loved and provided for her mother-in-law. Her faith has brought her to a foreign land. This is, in part, God's provision to inspire Boaz to love Ruth. If Ruth was an anti-Semite inciting rebellion against the judge of that era, Boaz would not likely have openly welcomed her into the barley field. Yet Christ approaches us as we are gleaning from His Father's providence while we are still in rebellion, even dead in our trespasses and sins. Yet He sets His love upon us and draws us into relationship with Him by irresistible grace. Ruth is amazed that Boaz overlooks her race, but we are amazed that Christ overlooks everything we are.

After a hard day's gleaning, Ruth returns home to Naomi and recounts the day's events. Naomi's response is to rejoice because Ruth has unwittingly found the redeemer of Naomi's people. Ruth has been shown grace by the one who is able to provide for her. Naomi rejoices and praises God while proclaiming/petitioning blessing for Boaz. How much more ought God's people to rejoice and praise God for the first signs of His work in unbelievers? We can learn from Naomi's example to pray and praise God when a sinner agrees to attend a church service, listens to the gospel, and hear the means of grace that is faithful preaching. Naomi knew that God could bring about great things through these events, and so ought we to rejoice knowing that God is able to save sinners.

Chapter 3 opens with a fascinating hope declared by Naomi. After Ruth has been gleaning for some time in Boaz's field, Naomi presses Ruth on a course of action in hopes of obtaining rest for her. She could have said wealth, security, even love, but Naomi is concerned with Ruth finding rest. Ruth has journeyed to a foreign land by faith. Ruth has tirelessly cared for her mother-in-law and labored in the fields and the threshing floor to provide food. Even though Boaz made sure that she gained much from that labor, Naomi desires better things for her, just as believers desire more for unbelievers than learning facts about God and morality in church. There is a desire for that faith that produces rest in the arms of the kinsman redeemer. There is a desire for marriage.

Naomi's second express desire is for it to "be well with" Ruth. This is likely a reference to Deuteronomy 6:3 and, thereby, offspring. Naomi wants descendants for the family line, but God had even greater things in mind.

To this end, Naomi prepares Ruth to woo Boaz. Ruth is bathed, anointed, and clothed before she goes to the threshing floor to meet with her future husband. In one sense, this represents the futile efforts of unbelievers to prepare themselves for Christ. Many believe wrongly that they must be clean, perfumed, and adorned in order to come and meet with Christ. They think they have to be good and pure in order to be saved, for Christ to desire them like Boaz desired Ruth. Even well-intentioned believers can give this impression to the unregenerate, pressing the law as a to-do list rather than a tool that exposes their need for a Savior. We do not prepare ourselves for salvation, it is God who regenerates and effectually calls.

This brings us to the second sense. Naomi, in a way, does the work of the Holy Spirit. She prepares and urges, laying the groundwork for the marriage. In the preaching of the Word, two unbelievers may sit side by side as they hear the gospel, while only one believes and is saved, even though they heard the same sermon. The difference is not that one person is more ethical, more wise, or more intelligent than the other. The real difference is that God has worked by His Spirit in the heart of the one who believed *before* he believed. In fact, God decreed it before the world began.

Now we follow Ruth to the scene of the threshing floor. Naomi gave specific instructions for Ruth to come to Boaz after he has eaten, drunk, and lain down at the threshing floor. Seeing ourselves in Ruth and Christ in Boaz, we approach our Savior after His work is complete. He ate and drank with His disciples, completed the work necessary for our salvation, and was laid in the grave. Christ is no longer in the grave, but because His work is complete, we can come and find grace.

The threshing floor is largely foreign to us in the modern age, but it was an integral part of agriculture once upon a time. This is where the sheaves of wheat or barley were beaten to separate the grain from the husks. The mixture was then tossed into the air with winnowing forks so that the chaff (unnecessary and undesirable) was driven away by the wind while the grain itself fell to the ground where it could be collected. The threshing floor is a useful metaphor frequently used through history. One example is the term "tribulation." It actually comes from the Latin *tribulum*, which was a farming implement. A set of boards were fixed together with nails protruding through the bottom. The tribulum was then weighted down with stones and dragged, often by animals, over the wheat on the threshing floor to accomplish the aforementioned process.[4] Tribulation is a metaphor for trials in life that separate out the grain from the chaff. (See Ps. 1:4; 35:5; 83:13; Isa. 17:13; 41:15–16; and Matt. 3:12 for just a few of God's uses of this metaphor). Corporately, tribulations sift the unbelievers out from the true believers. Individually, tribulation purifies God's saints. In coming to the threshing floor, Ruth is separated out from the world to be the bride of Boaz.

Ruth approaches under the cover of darkness to where Boaz is sleeping on the threshing floor. Boaz had a few drinks that night, enough to make his heart merry and sleep well on what was undoubtedly an uncomfortable bed. When Ruth approaches, she follows her mother-in-law's instruction and "uncovers his feet."

Many of you have probably read this story before and wondered why she would do that. As a kid, I thought it was so that he would get cold and wake up. Many scholars believe that this is a euphemism for uncovering more of Boaz than just his feet. This may be linked to Exodus 4:25, where Moses' wife Zipporah symbolically touches Moses' "feet" with the foreskin of his son when she rebukes him for his disobedience. That would make a weird passage even more disturbing, if that is even possible.

If that is what our passage means, it is descriptive and not prescriptive. Courtship rituals should not involve telling a woman to go disrobe a man,

---

4 *Civilizations of the Ancient Near East Vol. 1*, ed. Jack M. Sasson (Hendrickson: Peabody, 1995), 195.

lay down with him, and wait for him to tell her what to do. Maybe God gave Naomi an extraordinary impulse, or she wanted grandchildren more than she should. We do see how honorable Boaz is in this, because he does not take advantage of her.

The best way to understand this, however, is Ruth uncovering Boaz so that she might cover herself in the corner of his cloak. They are not even married and she is stealing the covers. The covering of the widow is a symbol of protection.[5] In Ezekiel 16:8, God covers Jerusalem with the corner of His garment as a symbol of covenant security. Later we see Ruth ask Boaz to cover her with his wings, foreshadowing Christ's lament over Jerusalem in Matthew 23:37. After all, the term *atonement* literally means to cover.

Boaz rejects intimacy outside the marriage. He does not reject Ruth altogether, but he makes clear that the covenant has to be established first. He commends her for following the law and coming to him as the redeemer. She will be covered, but in the covenant. He gives her a gift of food, a foretaste of blessing, but it is nothing compared to what she will have in his household. It is the same for us coming to Christ.

He also tells her to remain with him until the morning (3:13). He gives no reason for this, but it is presumably for her protection. In Song of Solomon 5:7, we see the bride assaulted by the watchmen of the city, and perhaps there was an issue with such crimes in Israel. Here again, we see the bride is safest when she is close to the bridegroom. How often have we seen someone come near to Christ and the true gospel only to be drawn away to a different field of gleaning? Sometimes they are led astray only to be beaten down by a works-based "salvation." In Bunyan's *Pilgrim's Progress*, Faithful recounts his run-in with Adam and Moses that leaves him beaten and bruised, not to mention Christian's Mount Sinai detour earlier in the book.[6]

It is in the midst of this narrative that Ruth refers to Boaz as a redeemer, bringing to the forefront a major theme of the book. This category of a kinsman redeemer has a few echoes through the Old Testament. When Zimri destroys the household of Baasha in 1 Kings 16:11, we are told that he killed all his relatives, or redeemers. In Job 3:5, he laments the day of his birth, calling upon night and darkness to "claim it" or redeem it (a verb form of the word in Ruth). Most importantly, Leviticus 25 outlines the nature of the kinsman redeemer.

---

5 See Neufeld, Ephraim *Ancient Hebrew Marriage Laws* (Longmans, 1944), pp. 31ff. There is also the well-known statement of Ṭabari quoted by W. Robertson Smith, "In the Jahilya, when a man's father or brother or son died and left a widow, the dead man's heir, if he came at once and threw his garment over her, had the right to marry her under the dowry (mahr) of (i.e. already paid by) her (deceased) lord (sahib), or to give her in marriage and take her dowry. But if she anticipated him and went off to her own people, then the disposal of her hand belonged to herself" *Kinship and Marriage in Early Arabia* (Black, 1903), 105.

6 John Bunyan, *Pilgrim's Progress* (Uhrichsville: Barbour, 1988), 71, 22–27.

There are two kinsman redeemer concepts in Leviticus. The first is about buying back a relative's land for him after he sold it in poverty. This way he got it back before the Year of Jubilee. The second is about buying a relative out of self-imposed slavery, again so that they do not have to wait for Jubilee.

The book of Ruth, on the surface, is dealing with the first kinsman concept, in coordination with the Levirate marriage.[7] Were Ruth not in the picture, a redeemer could have bought Elimelech's land for Naomi and then inherited that land for his descendants after her death. But Boaz is redeeming the inheritance of Elimelech with marriage. Given the dialogue with the other kinsman in chapter 4, Boaz purchases the land for Naomi—providing her with a 401(k)—and marries Ruth, thus ensuring Ruth's financial security. It would be Ruth's children, carrying the Elimelech name, who would keep the land.

Because of the mixture of elements in the story, we can fail to see some of what is going on here. Ruth is bought out of "slavery" as a Gentile pagan before the real Year of Jubilee. She was part of a generation of Gentiles that were left to their own sins. It was not until the atoning work of Christ was accomplished that the true Jubilee occurred and the Gentiles were brought into the church en masse. The year of Christ's Jubilee was prophesied in Isaiah 61:1–2. When Jesus reads that passage in Luke 4, He says, "Today this Scripture has been fulfilled in your hearing" (4:21). He is the one who brings in the Year of Jubilee as the ultimate Redeemer who sets the captives free—not from Assyria, Babylon, or Rome, but from their sin.[8]

When Boaz buys the land of Naomi, he also buys a family line that would have been lost because of the deaths of Elimelech and his sons. Their name would have been "blotted out from under heaven." In Judges 21, the rest of Israel scrambles to find wives for the Benjamites so that the tribe survives. So Boaz ensures that Elimelech's line is not lost. This foreshadows Christ marrying His Bride to preserve the line of men. Not all men are saved, but all men would have been lost to condemnation if Christ did not accomplish redemption. In the elect, the line of Adam, and what Adam should have been, is preserved unto glory.

This all brings us into the narrative of Boaz and the "first redeemer." Boaz says there is a closer blood relative to Elimelech who has first rights (or obligation) to redeem the land. Boaz goes to find him in the gate, a common place for meeting and judgment. We see this in Deuteronomy 22:15 and 25:7,

---

7 If a husband died and didn't have any kids, a relative was supposed to take the widow as his wife and have kids in lieu of the dead guy. It's creepy to us, but in a world of family lineage and a promise of Messiah through the family line, this was important. It was the Levirate marriage of Judah to Tamar his daughter-in-law that led to this pair and ultimately to Christ.

8 There is an already/not-yet concept here, as the Year of Jubilee for the land does not come until the new heavens and new earth.

Proverbs 22:22, and Amos 5:10–15. It was where the elders sat in counsel for the guidance of the people. This is the setting for the next scene of this mini-redemptive history.[9] Boaz offers him the opportunity to redeem the land of Elimelech for Naomi, and at first the unnamed relative says he will do it. When John Doe finds out that the land comes with a wife, he declines because he wants to preserve his own lineage. This is ironic, because he chose to preserve his own inheritance and name, but his family line is now forgotten and the land inheritance lost.[10] Boaz is willing to give up preserving his own name because he loves Ruth, and it is his name that is remembered through the ages and around the world. So he who seeks to keep alive his line shall lose it . . .

The first redeemer symbolizes Adam with the covenant of works. Adam was created under the law, and all of his descendants (i.e., all of mankind) are born with the same obligation for perfect obedience. In Eden, Adam was able to fulfill the law to the perfect standard and satisfaction of God. After the fall, that obligation remains, but man is incapable of fulfilling it. Just as the first redeemer in Ruth counts the cost to be too great, our cost for failure under the law is too much for us to bear. Adam cannot redeem us. The law cannot redeem us. The condemnation under the law, hell, is unending because man cannot absorb its fullness. This informs the rest of the narrative at the gates of the city.

Boaz offers to redeem the land and line of Elimelech, so they make a bizarre transaction before the witnesses. Boaz takes his sandal. We are told that this cryptic gesture was common for the era, but there is little else in the text to explain it. This is not to make John Doe limp home in shame or for Boaz to walk a mile in his shoe. It has to do with inheritance. Other passages of the Old Testament give us a little glimpse into the reasoning behind it. According to Deuteronomy 25:5–10, the first redeemer had an obligation to Naomi as a widow through Levirate marriage. If he refused, Naomi could remove his sandal, spit in his face, and his household name would bear the title of "he who lost his shoe," which goes poorly on the family crest.[11]

But why the shoe? In Deuteronomy 1:36, God promises Caleb the land on which he has walked as reward for his faithfulness. In Deuteronomy 11:24, God promises the Israelites all the land on which their foot treads. In Joshua 1:3, God makes the same promise to Joshua, and in Joshua 14:9, Caleb reminds Joshua of the promise made to Moses. In Psalm 60:8, God expresses His sovereignty over the foreign nations by saying that Moab is

---

9 Judge Judy was not around yet, so you would go to the gates.
10 Paulus Cassel, *Joshua, Judges and Ruth Vol. IV of a Commentary on the Holy Scriptures*, Ed. J. P. Lange (T. & T. Clark, 1875).
11 This has no connection to Shoeless Joe Jackson.

His washing basin and He throws His shoe over Edom. God does not wear shoes, but He does own the land over which He has "walked." So the shoe represents the land walked on and thereby possessed. Likewise, to be without the shoe is a sign of distress (primarily financial) and humiliation; it is to be without the inheritance.[12]

When Boaz takes the first redeemer's shoe, it is symbolic of Boaz taking possession of the land with its cost. Christ took on flesh and walked in the earth. John 1:14 speaks of the Word that was with God and was God in the beginning taking on flesh and dwelling among us. He was born under the Law (Gal. 4:4) to become our federal head in Adam's place. Christ did this in order to "take the sandal" of the Law. He fulfilled its obligations on our behalf in His life and absorbed the wrath due to our failure in His death. The second person of the Trinity temporarily "ruined" His inheritance of the glory of heaven and the adoration He had there so that He could redeem His people. Yet, like Boaz, Jesus was not forgotten nor did He lose His lineage. Rather, Christ bought for Himself a people with the price of His own blood. Just as the first redeemer is now forgotten, so is our condemnation before God.[13]

This also has unique bearing on the declarations of John the Baptist. When John was asked if he was the prophesied Messiah, he said that he was unfit to carry Christ's sandals (Matt. 3:11) or untie the straps (Mark 1:7). This has often been interpreted as humility, but this doesn't get to the fullest sense of all that is in this story. John knew he did not deserve a place in the kingdom of God, none of us do. He was unfit to accomplish the redemption for which the Messiah came. But this greater context indicates that John knew it was by grace alone that he was given an inheritance in Christ's kingdom. He knew Christ had to take the shoe.

In verses 9 to 12, Boaz addresses the judgment seat of the gates as witnesses to the transaction. The people and the elders respond with a proclamation of blessing. This benediction references Rachel and Leah, through whom the whole of Israel is descended. It brings up Tamar and Judah, a famous instance of the Levirate marriage. Boaz's marriage to Ruth would sustain that lineage from Jacob to Christ. This was more than a blessing; it was a prophecy.

In verses 13 and 14, the glory is not ascribed to Naomi, Ruth, or Boaz, but to God and His work. The author speaks of the child of Boaz and Ruth as Naomi's kinsman, the redemption of the family line. The women of the town suggest a name and Ruth and Naomi accept. He is called Obed, meaning

---

12 James M. Freeman, *Manners and Customs of the Bible* (Plainfield: Logos, 1972), 115, 131.
13 See Luther's treatment on the law from Galatians 4:1-5. *Galatians* (Wheaton: Crossway, 1998), 195ff.

servant.[14] Of course this foreshadows his descendent, the suffering servant Christ, who would redeem the line.

The book closes with a genealogy that includes Rahab (see also 1 Chron. 2:12–15). She is not named, but her husband is. This is not just because it is a patriarchal society, but because in the instances of Tamar, Rahab, and Ruth, they were foreign women. Their own names did not warrant placement in the line of promise descending from Abraham (though Matthew 1:2–5 does include all three). It was only because of kinsmen redeemers that they are in that line, because of the name placed upon them. God uses brides of questionable and illegitimate background to bring about important children.

So, too, we are the Bride of Christ and inheritors of the promise because the Kinsman Redeemer put His name upon us. We have a defiled background as well. You may not be a prostitute like Rahab or a Moabitess like Ruth, but you are a sinner. In and of yourself, you are not fit for the royal lineage of Christ, but God chooses to glorify His name through the weak and simple things of this world. God uses sinners to proclaim His gospel and save other sinners. We get to bring in born-again, adopted children who were condemned under the first redeemer Adam, so that we can receive the inheritance together.

---

14 You see, there have been pushy people in the church since the beginning. Just kidding.

V
Bridal Songs

The Psalms, Proverbs 31, and Song of Solomon

So now we come to a series of songs because what is a wedding without music, right? I want to start out with the Psalms, and then we will move to a song in Proverbs, then close with the Song of Solomon, which is actually multiple poems put together. Reading Psalms is a bit like a scavenger hunt. Christ is there, but the challenge is in finding Him. Sometimes it's in the description of a sacrifice, or He is the voice behind David's own, but He is always there. This is especially true in the bridal psalms.

The Joyous Marriage—Psalm 16[1]

Psalm 16

A Miktam/Treasure of David. Preserve me, God, because I have taken refuge in you.

(My soul) has said to Yahweh, "My Lord you are; my good is not upon/over you."

To holy ones in the land/earth are they and noble ones, all my delights are in them.

Sorrows multiply for those who run after another (or many are the sorrows of another dowry). I will not pour out their libations from blood, and I will not lift up their names.

Yahweh is my allotted portion and my cup; you hold my lot

The boundaries/pledges have fallen to me in pleasant (ways) also a beautiful inheritance over me.

I bless Yahweh who is counsel to me, also nights instruct me, my heart

I have set Yahweh always before me, because (he is) at my right hand, I will not be shaken

---

1 This is the author's translation of Psalm 16.

Therefore my heart rejoices, and my glory rejoices; also my flesh dwells secure

Because you will not abandon/forsake my soul to Sheol; you will not give your covenant-faithful-one to see corruption/a pit.

You reveal to me the path of life, abundance of joy before you, pleasures in your right hand forever.

Alexander Pope said, "A little learning is a dangerous thing; drink deep, or taste not the Pierian spring: there shallow draughts intoxicate the brain, and drinking largely sobers us again."[2] Scripture teaches us, in this psalm and elsewhere, that when certain truths are fully understood, they bring joy and peace. The greatest of these is the love of God. It encourages us to ask the question, "What brings joy and peace?"[3]

In most English translations of this text, it says nothing of marriage, so it may seem a strange choice for our study. When we look closer at the original text, however, and its themes, we find a duet of bride and bridegroom about joy and contentment that grows in proportion with knowledge. They sing to the honor of the father of the groom. With that in mind, let us see the text in three refrains: David as part of the Bride, Christ as the Bridegroom, and us as the Bride.

David

David begins by praying for God to preserve him, while declaring that he has already trusted in God as a refuge, themes we see often in Psalms. David's soul then speaks to Yahweh, "You are my Lord," acknowledging Him as sovereign, as protector, but also as the Bridegroom (see Gen. 18:12 and 1 Peter 3:6, where Sarah called Abraham "lord"). The next phrase is translated in the ESV as "I have no good apart from you," but it is more literally, "My good is not over you." David is saying that he can praise God, but can never add to God. It is the same sentiment he prays in 1 Chronicles 29:14, "But who am I, and what is my people, that we should be able thus to offer willingly? For all things come from you, and of your own have we given you." As Paul said in Romans 11:35, "Who has given a gift to [God] that he might be repaid?" So

---

[2] Alexander Pope, *An Essay on Criticism* (London: W. Lewis, 1709), 14. In Greek mythology, the Pierian spring was used by the Muses, giving knowledge and inspiration to the one who drinks.

[3] One of my favorite analogies for this is to tell people, "Imagine I have a box. Inside this box (which I pantomime) is what you desire most in the world. Think about that for a moment. Now what's in the box?" Then I proceed to explain how the pile of money or keys to a sports car are actually just symbolic for us of the peace, joy, and contentment we think that will bring. But they don't actually give us those things. It's always hollow. Only when we pursue Christ do we find the actual peace/joy/contentment that we are looking for.

David turns his service, love, and protection to God's people, those holy and noble, and finds his delight.

In contrast, David shows the multiplying sorrow of the pagan with language nearly identical to Genesis 3:16: "To the woman he said, 'I will surely *make great your pain* in childbearing'" Literally, David says, "Great are the sorrows/pains of another bride-price"[4] where, like we saw in Ezekiel, they lusted after other gods in spiritual adultery. David is saying that when people chase after the promised blessings of other gods, they give birth to sorrow after sorrow. In other words, not only have they abandoned the faithful, gracious God, but they have sought lovers/gods who lie. That's what idols do; they lie. David refuses to offer up the pagan sacrifices of blood, possibly a reference to human sacrifices like those for Molech, and will not even raise up the names of those false gods.

Turning back to the positive, he says that Yahweh is his portion and cup, like the Levites who were not given a land inheritance. Numbers 18:20 records, "And the LORD said to Aaron, 'You shall have no inheritance in their land, neither shall you have any portion among them. I am your portion and your inheritance among the people of Israel.'"[5] This meant that there was a conscious dependence on God to provide, and David knows that his real inheritance was not Palestine, just like Abraham did. We see this again in the words of Asaph in Psalm 73:23–28. David is saying that God is all he needs, provides all he needs, and that God preserves what He has given to David. The bride's cup at the wedding feast runs over, as David says in Psalm 23. Psalm 34:10 adds, "The young lions suffer want and hunger; but those who seek the LORD lack no good thing." And Psalm 84:11 says, "For the LORD God is a sun and shield; the LORD bestows favor and honor. No good thing does he withhold from those who walk uprightly." David rejoices in God's sufficiency, saying the bounds of God's providence are pleasant and beautiful.

David next praises God for the counsel He has given. This would include the direct guidance of God speaking to David, as well as the written Word, which David calls a lamp to his feet and a light to his path (Ps. 119:105).[6] God directly gives David the counsel needed and indirectly reins him in at night by his conscience. Christ guides David as the wise husband guides his wife, even creating boundaries for her sake when necessary.

Now we come to a key element in David's optimism. He has set Yahweh always before himself. He seeks God, prefers God above himself, converses

---

4 The word here, *mhru*, is really only found in Ex. 22:16, where it is used to reference a bride-price. Longman and Garland explore this in a footnote (*Expositor's Bible Commentary*, 188), though reject it in favor of "run." This concept is referenced more positively by others like Perowne as well.
5 This is a theme we will come back to in Revelation.
6 Psalm 119 may not have been written by David, and no author is given in the title of the psalm, but I am assuming Spurgeon was right on this one.

with God, and, most importantly, continually sees God's hand in his life. There is communion in the marriage! This is why David is so joyous in exile. God is at his right hand, counseling and guiding, and he will not be shaken. Because of this, David rejoices in heart, in glory (meaning his whole being), and in the security of his body. If God is for him, who is against him?

David declares his confidence that God will not, at this time, abandon him to the grave and the pit, or corruption, since God's promises had not yet been fulfilled. The covenant-faithful one will not be forsaken. This is only partly true for David, as he would eventually die and undergo the decay of the grave, but that is because it is not really about David. It is a prophecy.

He closes with God's revelation of a lifelong journey full of wisdom, joy, and pleasure in God. David knew that the narrative God had written for him did not end in the grave. Psalm 49:15 says, "But God will ransom my soul from the power of Sheol, for he will receive me." So also Proverbs 14:32: "The wicked is overthrown through his evildoing, but the righteous finds refuge in his death."

Christ

Next, we must see Christ's voice in David. As Peter teaches in Acts 2:22–32, this psalm is truer of Christ than David. Paul reveals the same in Acts 13:35–38.

Even though Christ was omnipotent and omniscient as God, He sought solace and refuge in prayer to the Father throughout His ministry. In death, He committed His soul to the Father (Luke 23:46).

Psalm 16:2–3: Christ's good works were not over the Father. He does not add to God but serves the Father to satisfy the debt of the elect. His grace is sufficient. He delighted in serving the elect by His life and death. He delighted and continues to delight in the noble, holy ones whom He has made noble and holy as the bride (John 17:1–6, 19).

Verse 4: As the Bridegroom long-promised, Christ lamented the sorrows of the adulterous Israel. He rebuked and pleaded with them. "An evil and adulterous generation seeks for a sign, but no sign will be given to it except the sign of Jonah.' So he left them and departed" (Matt. 16:4).

Verses 5–6: Christ delighted in the Father and served His purposes, as we see in John 4:34: "Jesus said to them, 'My food is to do the will of him who sent me and to accomplish his work.'" He delighted in His Bride, the people set as Christ's inheritance. D.R. Davis gives the account of Andrew Bonar on the Sunday after his marriage to Isabella. He wryly called the congregation to sing from Psalm 16, "Unto me happily the lines in pleasant places fell; Yea, the inheritance I got in beauty doth excel." Davis then comments, "Obviously, a lovely and congenial wife is not the whole of the beautiful 'inheritance' the Lord may give. But she may be a part of it. . . . Sometimes the Lord satisfies us by giving us someone who herself satisfies us."[7] When the earthly marriage reflects the heavenly one, the lines have truly fallen in pleasant places.

Hebrews 12:2 tells us that "the author/founder and finisher/perfecter of (our) faith, Jesus, for the joy before him, endured a cross, despising shame, on the right (hand) of the throne of God has been seated."[8] So it was prophesied in Isaiah 53:10–11: "Yet it was the delight of the LORD to crush him; he has put him to grief; when his soul makes an offering for guilt, he will see his offspring; he will prolong his days; the will of the LORD will prosper in his hand. Out of the anguish of his soul he will see and be satisfied; by his knowledge will the righteous one, my servant, make many to be accounted righteous, and he will bear their iniquities" (author's translation). Jesus knew the bride-price in His blood and gave it willingly.

Verses 7–9: He glorified the triune God, the counsel of which He was part. And the Father instructed Him in the night of Gethsemane. He set the Father's glory always before Him, and His redemption will never be shaken. He rejoiced in that work accomplished. Christ's heart rejoiced, but His glory of the triune God and the angels of heaven rejoiced as well. His flesh that is His body, which is the church, now dwells secure.

Verses 10–11: God did not abandon Him to the tomb and corruption, but raised Him in victory, revealing the path of life in Christ, and raised Him to heaven where Jesus's joys and pleasures are complete in the consummation of the wedding.

Us

Verses 1–2: Let us pray on this side of the cross that God would preserve us. What a concept this is! We are like refugees who have left everything behind and come to plead for sanctuary. We must confess our sins against a holy God and cling to Christ as our salvation. We must acknowledge, as David did, that all our works cannot add to God nor make Him our debtor. But those who flee to Christ and trust in Him alone for salvation will by no means be cast out. Only then are we part of the Bride.

Verse 3: We then must set to serving God in love and gratitude, first toward God's people. As Galatians 6:10 says, "So then, as we have opportunity, let us do good to everyone, and especially to those who are of the household of faith." As John Calvin puts it, "The only way of serving God aright is to endeavor to do good to his holy servants. And the truth is, that God, as our good deeds cannot extend to him, substitutes the saints in his place, towards whom we are to exercise our charity. When men, therefore, mutually exert

---

7 Dale Ralph Davis, *Slogging Along in The Paths of Righteousness: Psalms 13–24* (Geanies House: Christian Focus, 2016), 61.
8 This is a personal translation. The words in parentheses do not occur in the original text.

themselves in doing good to one another, this is to yield to God right and acceptable service."[9] This is the bride loving the bridegroom by tending to her own body.

This is crucial to a right Christian perspective on relationships. The worldly perspective is that we "love" people for our own sake and what we like about them. But as Christians, we are to love people for Christ's sake. We love because God first loved us, and we glorify Him by loving others.

Verse 4: Having been wed to the Bridegroom of our souls by faith, we must flee from idolatries rather than seek a second bride-price. This is what we do when we try to gain the benefits of Christ without letting go of our idols. The libations of blood that are poured out when we make idols of money, lust, comfort, or any other, multiply our sorrows.

Verses 5–6: Let us proclaim with David that we are satisfied in God's providence, that we will be satisfied in glory with God as our inheritance and know that He preserves us in that. This language of inheritance always draws us back to the bride and her children. How could the lines of our inheritance have fallen more beautifully than in heaven with our Savior? As Paul says in 2 Corinthians 5:8, "Yes, we are of good courage, and we would rather be away from the body and at home with the Lord." Then we can say what Paul does in Philippians 3:8, "Indeed, I count everything as loss because of the surpassing worth of knowing Christ Jesus my Lord. For his sake I have suffered the loss of all things and count them as rubbish, in order that I may gain Christ." So also James 1:17: "Every good gift and every perfect gift is from above, coming down from the Father of lights with whom there is no variation or shadow due to change."

Verse 7: As to God's counsel of us, Calvin says, "The counsel of which David makes mention is the inward illumination of the Holy Spirit, by which we are prevented from rejecting the salvation to which he calls us, which we would otherwise certainly do, considering the blindness of our flesh."[10] God counsels us to receive the wooing of the Bridegroom and see the immeasurable value of that marriage.

Verses 8–9: Let us set Yahweh always before us, and at our right hand to guide us. As Spurgeon puts it, "The worldling forgets God, the sinner dishonours Him, the atheist denies Him, but the Christian lives in Him. . . . Perpetual communion with God is the highest state of joy which can be known on earth."[11] Never has there been so happy a marital union! So let us say with Paul in Philippians 4:4, "Rejoice in the Lord always; again I say, rejoice."

Verses 10–11: Our final reason to rejoice comes in the last lines of the psalm that God will not abandon us forever to the grave or corruption. Romans 8:11

---

9 John Calvin, *Commentary on the Book of Psalms Vol. 1*, trans. James Anderson (Bellingham: Logos Bible Software, 2010), 218.
10 Calvin, *Commentary on the Book of Psalms Vol. 1*, trans. Anderson, 227.
11 Charles Spurgeon, *The Treasury of David Vol. 1*, 398–399.

says, "If the Spirit of him who raised Jesus from the dead dwells in you, he who raised Christ Jesus from the dead will also give life to your mortal bodies through his Spirit who dwells in you." And 1 Corinthians 15:20 adds, "But in fact Christ has been raised from the dead, the firstfruits of those who have fallen asleep." And finally, Philippians 1:23 states, "My desire is to depart and be with Christ, for that is far better." How easily we see these words as those of the enamored bride! God has revealed the path of life to his people, with pleasures and joy forever.

Bridegroom Sun, Won't You Come? —Psalm 19:4–6

A great deal of ink has been spilled over Paul's use of this psalm in Romans 10:17–18, "So faith comes from hearing, and hearing through the word of Christ. But I ask, have they not heard? Truly, they have, for 'Their voice has gone out to all the earth, and their words to the ends of the world.'" This led Luther and others to say that the sky is the church and the sun is Christ. Spurgeon also took the sun as representing Christ. Many today now denounce these and say that there is nothing more in natural revelation than God's general attributes and existence.[12] They claim Paul simply spoke of how God's testimony in creation left men without excuse, as he said in Romans 1.

As is often the case, men have spoken past each other rather than to one another, and the best course actually lies between them. Natural revelation alone cannot reveal the gospel. Yet God has hidden references, types, and shadows of Christ in the creation. Paul alludes to God's use of metaphors that we cannot understand until after we have known Christ. Some we may not even understand this side of glory. As Spurgeon said, "We can never err if we allow the New Testament to interpret the Old . . . and I feel therefore, that we shall not be guilty of straining the text at all when we take the language of David in relation to the sun, and use it in reference to our Lord Jesus Christ."[13]

The sun is a common image of Christ in Scripture. In Luke 1:78–79, Zechariah calls Christ a sunrise that gives light to those in darkness, and in the shadow of death, to guide them in the way of peace. In Acts 26:13, Paul describes Christ as "a light from heaven, brighter than the sun, that shone around me and those who journeyed with me." And Revelation 1:16 says, "In his right hand he held seven stars, from his mouth came a sharp two-edged sword, and his face was like the sun shining in full strength."

So what are these hidden metaphors? We could say that man once thought that the celestial bodies revolved around the earth, but now we see how the earth revolves around the sun. So also, we once thought everything revolved around us, but as God's people, we see that all revolves around Christ. We can

---

12 Natural revelation is those things which creation reveals of God, as opposed to special or supernatural revelation where God reveals Himself directly.
13 Charles Spurgeon, *The Treasury of David Vol. 1*, 418.

also see Christ's incarnation in the sun, coming from the hidden recesses of glory, the tabernacle of heaven, to journey through this earth and bring the light of the gospel to mankind.

If we can say such a thing, the clearest shadow here is the end of days. When the last of God's elect are wed in soul to Christ, He will come out of the wedding tent, marching joyously and triumphant as both Bridegroom and mighty warrior to draw His Bride, the church, to their eternal home together. As it says in Revelation 22:5, "And night will be no more. They will need no light of lamp or sun, for the Lord God will be their light, and they will reign forever and ever." Yet when He comes, what is warmth and joy to God's people will be fire and wrath to those who hate Him. As Psalm 19:6 tells us, nothing is hidden from His heat. What perfects, glorifies, and delights His beloved is what consumes the chaff. As Christ says in Matthew 5:45, "[God] makes his sun rise on the evil and on the good."

The question of "Who is God?" evokes a wide range of responses. Some would say He is the imagination of man, others that He is a benevolent old man in the skies who thinks little of man's sins. Some would describe Him as a wrathful and angry god. The Christian, however, should say that He is just, holy, sovereign, and yet merciful, gracious, and loving. They would point to the stars and say they declare His power and wisdom, but they would point to Christ and say with David, "Yahweh, my rock and my redeemer."

The Wedding Psalm —Psalm 45[14]

To the director on Lilies, of the sons of Korah, Maskil, a song of love

> My heart has overflowed of a good word; I speak my work to the king; my tongue is the pen of a quick/ready scribe.

> You are the most beautiful of the sons of Adam, grace has been poured in/with your lips. Moreover, you are blessed by God forever.

> Gird your sword on your thigh; mighty is your splendor and your majesty.

> And your majesty is successful/prospers, it rides on a word of truth and humility of righteousness, and your right hand teaches you fear/fearful things.

> Your arrows are sharpened, peoples under you fall, in the heart of the enemy of the king.

> Your throne, God, is forever and ever. A plain/upright scepter is the scepter of your kingdom

---

14 This is an author's translation of Psalm 45.

You have loved righteousness and hated wickedness. Moreover anointed you God your God, the oil of joy beyond your companions

Myrrh and aloes, cassia (are) all your garments. From temples/palaces of ivory, instruments make you rejoice.

Daughters of kings (are) in/with your precious ones. The Queen of your right hand has stood in gold of Ophir

Hear, daughter, and see and incline your ear and forget your people and the house of your father.

And the king will desire your beauty. Because he is your lord, bow down to him.

And the daughter of Tyre with an offering before you, rich people entreat/are sick

All-abundant (is) the daughter of the king within gold-woven/filigree clothing

To embroidered. She is brought to the king, virgins after her, her companions brought to you.

They are brought in gladness and joy; they come in to the temple/palace of the king.

Beneath your fathers are your sons; you will set them for princes/chiefs in all the earth.

I will cause your name to be remembered in every generation and generation. Moreover, peoples will praise you forever and ever.

You know how sometimes you are at a dinner party and someone asks you which is your favorite painting by fifteenth-century Dutch artist Jan Van Eyck? Well, my answer is always the Arnolfini Portrait, partly because it looks like Dracula is marrying his cousin, but mostly because of the detail. In the back of the room is a fisheye mirror that reflects the back of the two subjects and even the artist himself. It is a painting within a painting. That is what Psalm 45 is, a wedding portrait within a wedding portrait.[15]

Solomon

Tradition tells us this psalm was written to commemorate Solomon's marriage to Pharaoh's daughter. As the author observes the regime change from David to Solomon and the marriage of the king, he expresses adoration and hope for the king's reign. He says his heart bubbles over with a good matter,

---

[15] The sons of Korah even hint at this in the title by telling us it is a *maskil*, a psalm of instruction.

so he addresses the king with the careful words of a ready scribe. This hints that there is more to the psalm than just a royal wedding.

Solomon is described as the most handsome of the sons of Adam, so he apparently took after his ruddy, handsome father (1 Sam. 16:12). He has grace in speech, especially in wisdom, according to his request of God at his inauguration in 1 Kings 3:10–14. He is blessed by God, partially fulfilling the promise of the Davidic covenant in 2 Samuel 7:10–17.

The psalmist calls Solomon to display his military strength, girding his sword on his thigh, reminiscent of Song of Solomon 3:6–11, Psalm 2, Psalm 110, and many more. Though Solomon was not a man of war like his father, he had to be ready to defend the kingdom and commanded a substantial army (1 Kings 4:26). His sharpened arrows strike the heart of his enemies, and the people fall before him.

Yet his majesty prospers on the basis of truth, humility, and righteousness. These three horses pull the chariot of his throne. There is military might, but it takes a backseat to diplomacy. His right hand teaches him the fear of God, which is the beginning of wisdom.

Verse 6 shifts to addressing God, whose throne is eternal. God wields the scepter of uprightness while loving righteousness and hating wickedness. Solomon is called to be steward over God's chosen people, so his regal conduct should reflect God's reign. He is to wield the scepter in fulfillment of Genesis 49:10, "The scepter shall not depart from Judah, nor the ruler's staff from between his feet, until tribute comes to him; and to him shall be the obedience of the peoples." Solomon is being challenged to follow God's example of sound judgment, sidestepping the error of Proverbs 17:15, "He who justifies the wicked and he who condemns the righteous are both alike an abomination to the LORD."

Solomon is anointed to a reign of joy above all the people of God, and they were pretty happy. The Queen of Sheba said in 1 Kings 10:8, "Happy are your men! Happy are your servants, who continually stand before you and hear your wisdom!" Solomon's reign was Israel's golden age with broadest borders and a thriving economy.

He smells good, because the perfumed anointing oil has soaked into his robes. As his bride sings in Song of Solomon 1:3, "Your anointing oils are fragrant." And in 5:13, she says that "his cheeks are like beds of spices, mounds of sweet-smelling herbs. His lips are lilies, dripping liquid myrrh."

He is adored and serenaded by his people and even surrounding nations. He has princesses among his precious ones. "Daughters of kings" may be an exaggeration about his servants (Ps. 45:9), but it is more likely a reference to wives and concubines taken from foreign nations.

Egyptian Queen

When we get to the second half of verse 9, the psalmist shifts focus to the queen who stands in the place of honor, his right hand. The gold of Ophir she wears is referenced several times in the Old Testament. Ophir was a mining city going back to the patriarchal days (Job 22:24; 28:16) and possibly depleted by Isaiah's time (Isa. 13:12). The fleet of Hiram brought Solomon gifts of gold from Ophir in 1 Kings 10:11.

The author pleads with the queen to "hear . . . consider . . . incline your ear" to forget her people and country. This is the wife's side of Genesis 2:24: "Therefore a man shall leave his father and his mother and hold fast to his wife, and they shall become one flesh." As queen, her allegiance was now to Solomon, Israel, and Yahweh. She needed to leave behind the false gods of her homeland.

The author says that if she does this, the king will desire her, though that obviously proved not to be a prerequisite (1 Kings 11:1–8). She is exhorted to bow to Solomon as both king and husband, as Sarah had called Abraham "lord" (Gen. 18:12; 1 Peter 3:6). This is added to the previous conditions for her exaltation by the nations alongside her king, as in 1 Kings 10 with the gifts of Sheba's queen. D.A. Carson records, "Tyre came to typify the world in its proud independence and self-sufficiency, its accumulation of wealth without scruple."[16] So if the princess of Tyre brings gifts, how much more will the other nations give?

Her adornments will not only be great for her wedding and processions, but even in private. She will have gold-threaded and multi-colored or embroidered robes, the finest of pajama pants. The psalmist hopes that her descendants will be greater than the ancestors, but it would be the child of another wife who would take the throne. She will be remembered and praised forever.[17]

Now that we have seen the psalm in its original context, I want to look closely at the fisheye mirror of our Bride of Christ metaphor.

The Christ

The psalmist was overwhelmed as the Holy Spirit moved him to write something more than just a best-man speech. It is a prophecy. At every point, the psalm is better fulfilled in Christ than Solomon; so some, like Spurgeon, deny

---

16 D.A. Carson, *New Bible Commentary: 21st Century Edition*, Ed. G. J. Wenham & D.A. Carson, (Leicester: Inter-Varsity, 1994).

17 That part, like some of the previous hopes of the psalmist, goes largely unfulfilled. It may be that this is the same bride as in Song of Solomon, but even then, we do not know her name or much about her.

it had any origin in old Shlomo.[18] Matthew Henry writes, "This psalm is an illustrious prophecy of Messiah the Prince: it is all over gospel, and points at him only, as a bridegroom espousing the church to himself and as a king ruling in it and ruling for it."[19]

Christ may or may not have been physically handsome, but He is beautiful to the sinner saved by grace.[20] As Augustine said, "He then is 'beautiful' in Heaven, beautiful on earth; beautiful in the womb; beautiful in His parents' hands: beautiful in His miracles; beautiful under the scourge: beautiful when inviting to life; beautiful also when not regarding death: beautiful in 'laying down His life;' beautiful in 'taking it again:' beautiful on the Cross; beautiful in the Sepulchre; beautiful in Heaven."[21] He is lovely to the saints by virtue of His incarnation, as Edward Hyde declares: "In one Christ we may contemplate and must confess all the beauty and loveliness both of heaven and earth; the beauty of heaven is God, the beauty of earth is man; the beauty of heaven and earth together is this God-man."[22]

There is some debate as to whether grace is poured into the lips or poured out upon the world from the lips. We find both to be true of Christ, who was filled with the fullness of God and wisdom but also spoke the gospel to the world and gave it grace. Who could be said to have more grace in speech than He who preached the gospel and declared grace accomplished from the cross? As John 1:17 says, "For the law was given through Moses; grace and truth came through Jesus Christ."

Jesus was blessed and beloved of God and was the true fulfillment of that Davidic Covenant. Paul borrows this language to describe Jesus in Romans 9:5: "the Christ, who is God over all, blessed forever. Amen."

His earthly ministry was not militant in the usual sense, but we see His binding of the strong man and plundering (Mark 3:27), as well as His might and authority over demons and even death. As Matthew Henry said, "He is to rescue his spouse by dint of sword out of her captivity, to conquer her, and to conquer for her, and then to marry her."[23] Of course, this is but a shadow of the Parousia, the return of Christ in judgment of Revelation 19:11–16.

---

18 Solomon in Hebrew is actually *Shlomo*, but that sounds more like an off-brand clown than a king.
19 Matthew Henry, *Matthew Henry's Commentary on the Whole Bible* (Carol Stream: Hendrickson, 1991), 330.
20 Isaiah 53:2 prophesies that the Christ will not have beauty that we should desire Him, but that may be a reference to Him on the cross, bloody and beaten.
21 Augustine of Hippo, *Expositions on the Book of Psalms: Psalms 1–150 Vol. 2* (Oxford; London: F. and J. Rivington; John Henry Parker), 230.
22 Cited in Spurgeon, C. H. Spurgeon, *The Treasury of David: Psalms 27–57 Vol. 2* (London; Edinburgh; New York: Marshall Brothers), 325.
23 Henry, *Commentary*, 331.

This is crucial to our comfort and security as saints, knowing that nothing can separate us from the love of God in Him, as Paul tells us in Romans 8:37–39. No one can snatch us from His hand, as Christ assured us in John 10:28. The Second London Baptist Confession states, "For our rescue and security from our spiritual adversaries, we need his kingly office to convince, subdue, draw, uphold, deliver, and preserve us to his heavenly kingdom."[24]

The strangest line in Psalm 45 is in verse 4: "and your right hand teaches you fear" or "fearful things." But what is at the right hand of the king? Verse 9 tells us it is the queen. For Christ's church to be His Bride, He must undergo the outpouring of God's holy wrath, the most fearful thing that ever was. In His humanity, He feared for her and the cost of redeeming her.

Christ's arrows pierce the heart in conviction of sin, from the least of His enemies to the greatest, not to slay, but to convert them to His people. The peoples fall before Him, not in death on the battlefield, but worship.

Yet He rides upon truth, humility, and righteousness. As Christ said in Matthew 11:29, "Take my yoke upon you, and learn from me, for I am gentle and lowly in heart, and you will find rest for your souls." Calvin said, "At first sight, indeed, it seems to be a strange and inelegant mode of expression, to speak of riding upon truth, meekness, and righteousness, but . . . he very suitably compares these virtues to chariots, in which the king is conspicuously borne aloft with great majesty."[25] We are to imitate Christ in this as Paul did. In 2 Corinthians 10:1, he says, "I, Paul, myself entreat you, by the meekness and gentleness of Christ . . ." In Christ alone, we see the fullness of Proverbs 20:28: "Covenant-love and faithfulness preserve the king, and by covenant-faithfulness, his throne is upheld" (author's translation). What makes Jesus the perfect Messiah, the only one who can take away our sins? He proclaimed the *truth* of the gospel. He is the *truth* of God's love for us as sinners. He embodied *humility* as He took on flesh and suffered the cross for our sins. He did what was *righteous*, fulfilling the law so that we could be clothed in that righteousness.

Only in Jesus do we see the fullness of the Elohim digression in verse 6. It is quoted in Hebrews 1:8–9 as proof for the deity of Christ and His supremacy over the angels. Christ is God and the eternal King, risen from the dead to die no more. Revelation 13:8 describes Him as the Lamb slain from the foundation of the world.

The scepter is a symbol of Christ's administration. It is righteous and secure because He is God and the grand fulfillment of the prophecies already mentioned. He is upright, loves righteousness, and hates wickedness. He will by no

---

24 2nd LBC VIII:10.
25 Calvin, *Commentaries . . . Vol V*, 176–177.

means acquit the guilty (Ex. 34:7). Christ proved this love for righteousness and hatred of wickedness in His earthly ministry.

While it makes the most sense with Solomon to translate verse 7 as "God, your God has anointed you," with Christ, we can say, "Your God (the Father) anointed You, God (the Son), with the oil of joy." The anointing of Jesus' incarnation was unto sadness and sorrow, as Isaiah 53 foretold, but it later became the anointing of gladness. As we see in Hebrews 12:2, "looking to Jesus, the founder and perfecter of our faith, who *for the joy that was set before Him* endured the cross, despising the shame, and is seated at the right hand of the throne of God" (emphasis added). It is also an anointing of peace prophesied about in Psalm 133, where sinners are united fully to their creator and redeemer. This is an anointing above prophets with better prophecy, above priests with a better sacrifice, above kings with an eternal throne, above David with a universal kingdom, and even above the angels who minister to Him.

His robes are fragrant with myrrh, aloes, and cassia, parallel to the incense offerings and ingredients of the holy anointing oil for the tabernacle (Ex. 30:23–24), which was never to be poured on the body of an "ordinary person" (v. 32). Myrrh and aloes were bound in Christ's burial clothes to anoint Him in death (John 19:39). The original text says that myrrh, aloes, and cassia *are* all His garments. They are Jesus's righteousness that is fragrant before God. Its aroma is released in His suffering. With these garments, Christ clothes His Bride who needs it.

The adoration in song from ivory palaces glimpses the angels and church triumphant surrounding the throne singing His praises. The word for "palaces" can also mean "temples," pointing to the sacred nature of heaven. Though the earthly houses of ivory will perish (Amos 3:15), the city of God will endure forever.

He has saved unto Himself a people, His precious ones, from the lowly beggar to "daughters of kings." Whatever the past of the church, it is made the Daughter of the King by adoption.

The Church

At Christ's right hand is the queen, adorned with His wealth, far beyond even the gold of Ophir. All the treasure of the earth belongs to the Bridegroom, and around her neck lies the imperishable beauty of a gentle, quiet spirit (1 Peter 3:4).

The church is exhorted to pay close attention. She must turn from her ancestry, from Satan her father and the world her mother. Our allegiance to them has been severed in salvation, and we owe all adoration to our Savior, the Bridegroom and King of our hearts. "Since He is your Lord, bow to Him" (Ps. 45:11).

In these things, we will find the delight of our Savior. As Augustine says, "She was loved, while yet loathsome, that she might not remain loathsome."[26] So, too, we will be blessed. True, in this world, we will be hated and turned out. Some will even consider it the work of God to persecute and kill us, as Christ warned. Yet this is only for a time and a season. Revelation 21:24–26 says, "By [the Lamb's] light will the nations walk, and the kings of the earth will bring their glory into it, and its gates will never be shut by day—and there will be no night there. They will bring into it the glory and honor of the nations." The glory and honor of the nations are the people as we see in Proverbs 14:28: "In the multitude of the people is the glory of the king."

All abundant and glorious is the bride in her chamber. The church's adornment in Christ's righteousness is not primarily for her to incite jealousy and adoration from those around her.[27] In Revelation 3:17–18, we see the church at Laodicea. She thinks she is rich, but she is actually poor, pitiable, blind, and naked. She is instructed to "buy" without money fine gold and beautiful garments, white in purity, to clothe herself.

The primary goal is to bring her into an intimate connection with her Bridegroom and Savior. Perhaps in the many-colored robes, we are meant to see the diversity of the church. This is how Augustine interprets it: "It is one both precious, and also of divers colours: it is the mysteries of doctrine in all the various tongues: one African, one Syrian, one Greek, one Hebrew, one this, and one that; it is these languages that produce the divers colours of this vesture. But just as all the divers colours of the vesture blend together in the one vesture, so do all the languages in one and the same faith."[28] But we can also see here the spectrum of Christ's fulfillment of the law on her behalf.

Here, the bride and her pure companions are one and the same. With joy and gladness, they are brought into the palace/temple of the king. Indeed, as they cross the threshold into glory, they are heard to say, "Grave, where is your victory? Death, where is your sting?"

If we place the "wedding" of the church at the incarnation and crucifixion, then the fathers would be the saints of the OT. As we see in Hebrews 11 and many other places, God raised them up as great men. Yet by the fullness of the gospel revealed and the outpouring of the Holy Spirit on the church, the best was yet to come. Men walking by faith and not by sight would be animated by the Holy Spirit to carry the gospel to the ends of the earth. Isaiah 53:10 states,

---

26 Augustine of Hippo, *Expositions on the Book of Psalms: Psalms 1–150 Vol. 2*, 229.
27 Though v. 13b can be translated "before you rich people are sick (with envy)."
28 Augustine of Hippo, *Expositions on the Book of Psalms: Psalms 1–150 Vol. 2*, 253.

"Yet it was the will of the LORD to crush him; he has put him to grief; when his soul makes an offering for guilt, he shall see his offspring; he shall prolong his days; the will of the LORD shall prosper in his hand."

We can truly say the name of the church is remembered in all generations. Though it is not yet fully so, the nations will praise her forever and ever as the Bride saved by grace.

Proverbs 31 Woman

While on the topic of Solomon and his bride, it is fitting to deal with the excellent woman described in the final segment of Proverbs. It follows the oracle of Lemuel but does not appear to be part of that. Wolters observes how refreshingly unique this is from the heroic poem literature of the ancient Near East, which focused on women only for eroticism. Here we see the praise of a woman for her excellence in the mundane. I call it a poem because it is an acrostic, where each line begins with a successive letter of the alphabet, As Best Can Describe Excellence For Genial Harmony In Just Kinship. Solomon's father, David, employed the same technique in Psalm 119 and others. The acrostic conveys a sense of completeness, which fits well with this description of the excellent wife.

Whenever looking at the Proverbs 31 woman, there is a temptation to fall into moralistic, legalistic teaching, claiming that this is what every woman ought to be and whoever falls short is an unfit wife. To make this an absolute standard of ambition, stewardship, and industry is misleading and disheartening for many. While women do well to see the value in these things as general principles and strive for them, Christianity is not about standards of morality to be achieved by sheer human effort. All Christians, women included, are sinners saved by grace, not works. It is noteworthy that several of these attributes are not achieved by raw human effort but granted by God: wisdom, kindness, mercy, charity, and fear of God.

Likewise, men do well to generally consider these attributes in a prospective spouse because a slothful, wasteful, foolish, unkind, hateful, godless woman will make for a sorrowful marriage where the husband takes up residence on the roof corner (Prov. 25:24). Yet a man cannot expect to find a perfect woman. He should be searching for a fellow sinner saved by grace with whom he can unfold the love parable of Christ and His church. As my colleague Rob Cosby once said in a sermon on this passage, when Solomon asks, "Who can find an excellent wife (such as this)?" the answer is "no one."

Husbands, consider the attributes of the excellent wife and praise your wife wherever she lives out these principles. After all, that is what the author is doing! Value the wife of your youth above all the jewels of the world's offerings. Pray that God would give your wife more of these things because she will need them to put up with you. You cannot demand all these of your wife, especially in her youth, because they are attributes that come with time and are gifted by God. In all this, remember that you are not the ideal husband, Christ is. All of these things are found in Christ, as Psalm 112 prophesies of him.

Now we come to our central focus, examining the Proverbs 31 woman as a type of the Bride of Christ.

Verse 10: As the author proclaims, the value of the excellent wife is far above jewels, so Christ has valued His church as worthy of His blood. She is appraised at a value above all else in the world.

Verses 12 and 23: The bride is the glory of her husband and brings him praise. As the church follows after Christ and fulfills her purpose of proclaiming the gospel, she glorifies God.

Verses 13 and 19: The wife labors to clothe her children. As the church faithfully teaches the Scriptures, she sews together clothes from the precious fabric of graces purchased in Christ's sufferings by which the children of God, her children, are clothed and protected from the elements of this fallen world.

Verse 14: She labors to feed her children, gathering from afar. A faithful eldership, called to the ministry of the Word, searches the length and breadth of the Scriptures to feed God's children, to feed Christ's sheep, and fulfill Christ's exhortation to Peter.

Verse 15: She not only is diligent in her own tasks but also equips the household to labor. So, too, a faithful church and eldership labor to equip the saints themselves in discipleship.

Verse 16: She applies the wealth of which she has been made steward, investing it to increase it. The church labors to sow the gospel and invest her time and the riches of Scripture in sinners by evangelism.

Verses 17 and 25: The excellent wife dresses herself with strength and dignity. The royal Bride puts on the whole armor of God and prays for strength.

Verse 18: She properly values her possession, the gospel, and keeps her lamp lit by the oil of the Holy Spirit, unlike the foolish virgins of Matthew 25.

Verse 20: She labors for the poor, as the church must care for the poor in benevolence (especially within the body). She is also concerned with the spiritually bankrupt out in the world in need of a savior.

Verse 21: She clothes her household in the scarlet cloth of Christ's righteousness purchased for her in blood.

Verse 22: She prepares the coverings of the bed to be intimate with her husband, as the church makes ready for the consummation of the marriage at the end of days. She herself is clothed in royal cloth as the true queen of heaven. As Richard Sibbes says, "He [Christ] is the greatest king that ever was, and she [the church] is the greatest queen; for Christ, he is Lord of heaven and earth, and of all things; and her estate is as large as his."

Verse 24: She seeks to clothe the naked citizens of the world in linen garments by proclaiming to them the Christ who makes them a nation of priests (Ex. 28:42).

Verse 26: She proclaims the wisdom of God's Word and the kindness that is the fruit of the Spirit.

Verse 28: She is loved not only by her husband, but also her children. God's people are marked not only by their love of Christ, but for one another. As John Brown once said, "Happy is that Christian Society when the minister loves his people, and the people love their minister for the truth's sake."[29]

Verse 29: She surpasses all others. By God's grace, and grace alone, the church is made more excellent than all the world.

Verse 30: She is not consumed with the external appearances of beauty or charming others falsely into loving her. Her concern is with God, who loved her while she was yet unlovable.

Verse 31: The poet closes by calling for this excellent bride to be given the fruit of her labors and praise in the place of judgment, the gates. Though the church may be often mocked and maligned in this world, she will be judged as righteous on account of Christ. She will be called blessed in her labors when she comes to the day of judgment and enters the gates of heaven glorified and triumphant.

This description of the church as the excellent wife of Proverbs 31 must be viewed in terms of the already/not-yet concept. She (by which I mean we) falls short of these things. The church is not always wise or a good steward. We fall into the trap of concerning ourselves with the external appearance of the church without regard to the matters of the heart. In her varied manifestations of local congregations, the church is not always a good steward of that with which she has been entrusted, nor does she always care for the poor, blind, and pitiable citizens of this fallen world as she ought. Let us, men and women, daughters and sons of the King, see these things as callings to strive for and labor in until the day when we enter the gates of the heavenly Jerusalem.

---

29 John Brown, *An Exposition of the Epistle of Paul the Apostle to the Galatians* (New York: Carter and Brothers, 1853), 218.

In truth, there are several passages we might deal with in Proverbs beyond what are referenced in this book, but a short note will suffice. There are repeated exhortations couched in terms of wisdom granted by father and mother to son. Depending on the household in which you were raised, you may have heard all, some, or none of these principles of wisdom from earthly parents. Regardless, they are presented to you by Christ and His Bride from whom Christians are born again to newness of life and made sons by adoption. Heed the wisdom of your Father and Mother, and seek more of it in attending the means of grace through the church as well as through prayer to your Father. As James 1:5 tells us, "If any of you lacks wisdom, ask God for it, who gives generously to all without reproach" (author's translation).

Song of Solomon

Prelude

When you bring up Solomon's Song in the church, prudish nature kicks in and people get uncomfortable. The first time I told my congregation that I would be teaching through this book, there was a mixed reaction. Some were excited because they had never been through a study on it. Some made jokes that they wanted to know what the metaphors meant. The rest just waited nervously to see what it would be like.

When we come to the *Song of Songs*, which is what it calls itself, we have to do a lot of prefacing. Once we know what the Song is, we know how to deal with it. If we misunderstand what it is, we can get into some weird areas, like naming breasts the Old and New Testaments, but we will get there in a bit.

The Song of Songs is love poetry, similar to Egyptian love poetry of the same time, with equally weird imagery.[30] After the awkwardness of Scripture addressing sexuality, the next thing we think of is the unflattering aspects of Solomon's description of his bride. She has eye-doves and hair like a flock of goats. He is particularly fascinated with her teeth like a full set of shorn lambs, which sounds like a redneck pickup line. The pomegranate cheeks make a little sense, but the towering neck with shields sounds like she might have shingles. The gazelle-breasts and towering nose do not sound like charitable descriptions either.

Outside of synchronous literature, we find an unlikely parallel in the surrealist poetry of Andre Breton. In *Freedom of Love*, there is a cornucopia of bizarre metaphors. Asbestos, prison water, and a platypus are not usually synonyms for romance. They seem unflattering because the context is personal, just like the images in the Song.

---
30 Tremper Longman III, *New International Commentary on the Old Testament: Song of Songs* (Grand Rapids: Eerdmans, 2001), 43, 50–51.

The bridal song is a compilation of poems on the subject of romantic love, dealing with its joys and its woes, like the last few decades of pop music. The primary focus is on the joys, but the negative side is there. It explores the beauty of physical and emotional intimacy. While most of its explicit nature is lost in the English translations, the Hebrew has a very "if you know what I mean" double-entendre overtone.

This is important for the broader context of God's Word. We need the Song of Solomon in the canon of Scripture. When the early church reached a modicum of peace, asceticism and a doctrine of perpetual virginity spread like wildfire, which became foundational for monastic and convent life. The passages of Paul about blessed singleness (mostly 1 Corinthians 7) were emphasized to the point that sex and marital intimacy were considered intrinsically evil. Part of this is understandable, given what Paul writes, but we forget that Paul has a number of "givens" insofar as biblical principles. He was well versed in the Old Testament and knew the *Kethuviim*, or writings, including the Song of Songs. His writing assumes (without contradiction) the blessedness of marital sexuality extolled in the Old Testament. As John Piper says, "It is no accident that centuries of Bible scholars construed the Song of Solomon as a story about Christ and the church. They may have been too squeamish about letting it have its natural meaning for Solomon and his bride, but they were not wrong in seeing that the ultimate meaning of marital sex is about the final delights between Christ and his church."[31]

It is important that we understand that the Song of Solomon is not *immediately* an analogy of Christ and His church or of God and Israel, even though most of Jewish and Christian tradition has claimed that.[32] Let me explain what that means. The immediate (not-mediated) meaning is what you read above, that this is erotically charged love poetry. It celebrates human sexuality within the confines of the marriage covenant. That is something worth celebrating. This *Superlative Song* (which is what *Song of Songs* means) reminds us that there is good and beauty in earthly love between a husband and a wife. This is what God intended for His creation. I love the way D. Martyn Lloyd-Jones put it: "God ordained sex."[33] Song of Solomon is descriptive, not directly prescriptive, of a beautiful aspect of creation. We should not consider ourselves more prudish than God, who included these things in His Word.[34] I am not trying to offend unnecessarily, but we have to see the book for what it is.

---

31 John Piper, *This Momentary Marriage: A Parable of Permanence* (Wheaton: Crossway, 2009), 127.
32 We will get to the Christian history of interpretation in a moment, but for the Jewish side, see Longman, *Song of Songs NICOT* (2001), 24.
33 D. Martyn Lloyd-Jones, *God's Way of Reconciliation: An Exposition of Ephesians 2* (Grand Rapids: Baker, 2003), 42.
34 This is a paraphrase of Dr. Bryan Estelle.

However, the bulk of this book's pedagogical or teaching function in the canon of Scripture is about Christ and the church. What I will focus on here is how the immediate meaning relates analogically to the Great Eternal Marriage, which is what all good in earthly marriage points to anyway.

I have to emphasize that this is about analogy, not allegory. There is a long history of bad allegorical interpretation of the Song. Hippolytus was the first to claim the two breasts of the bride were actually the Old and New Testaments.[35] Origen was one of the most famous commentators on the book.[36] He did to the Song of Songs what he did to himself; he de-sexed the song. Jerome did much of the same.[37] Their interpretations are unanimous in denying the human sexuality and romance of the book because that is just too offensive to consider, apparently. Medieval theologians, while denying literal interpretation, were fascinated with the book. The *Patrologia Latina* (a collection of early and medieval writings) contains thirty-two commentaries on the Song, more than twice as many as Romans and Galatians combined.[38] Beyond that, however, they never agree. Keel claimed that if any two allegorizers agreed, it was only because one was copying the other.[39] We cannot even write this off as a medieval or Roman Catholic problem because Martin Luther did the same thing. He claimed Solomon was writing an allegory of the political state of Israel in relation to God, and John Owen seems to have largely followed suit, though he focuses on the church and Christ.[40]

I do not want to dwell too long on all of this, but we have to understand the history to distance ourselves from its errors while learning from its mistakes. My hope here and in the rest of this book is to draw analogies of the Bride of Christ in faithful form, following the example of those inspired New Testament authors interpreting the Old Testament. I pray that I have not demolished the text to draw out ideas that are not there. All this being said, the preface is ended, and the content begins.

Garden Lost and Found

There are particular passages in the Song that speak of what we will heretofore refer to as "outdoor recreations" of the Song of Solomon couple. One of the clearest is 7:12, "Let us rise early to the vineyards. Let us see if it has budded,

---

35 Marvin H. Pope, *Anchor Yale Bible Commentaries: Song of Songs* (New York: Doubleday, 1977), 114.
36 Pope, 115.
37 Longman, *Song of Songs NICOT*, 31
38 E. Kalas, "Martin Luther as Expositor of the Song of Songs," *Lutheran Quarterly 2* (1998), 323.
39 Othmar Keel, *The Song of Songs*, (Minneapolis: Fortress Press, 1994), 8.
40 Longman, 33. As to the John Owen reference, see his uses of the Song in *Communion with God*.

the vine has opened, the blossom has bloomed, the pomegranates. There I will give my loves to you" (author's translation).

Odd as it may sound, some have used this in a somewhat prescriptive manner to say this is what healthy, young, married couples should be doing. Remember what I said before, this is *immediately* a *descriptive*, not prescriptive, collection of love poetry. We are looking at a rather explicit record of the poet's adventures in marriage. In Christian marriage, intimacy (both emotional and physical) is important. But we need to be cautious of saying "this is what marriage should be" because healthy intimacy will look different for different couples. Some couples will stay indoors for their recreational activities.

On the redemptive-historical scale, the importance of these passages is to point back in Scripture to Genesis 1–3. Here we find a time in history when nakedness in that garden was about unashamed intimacy. It was unbroken and uninterrupted love between a husband and a wife as well as between Creator and creature.

All of this sheds light on a major theme of the book, what Bryan Estelle refers to as "redeemed eroticism." The state of Eden was lost in the fall. Humanity was kicked out of the garden and lost the communion it offered. Sin did this; sin continues to do this. Now, by grace-through-faith salvation, intimacy is recovered in an already-not-yet sense. This side of glory, love will never be what it was in Eden, but, at points, it becomes tangible. The outdoor recreation is unashamed, sinless, God-honoring sexuality of Eden for husbands and wives regained in part, just as joy and peace in God through Christ are regained in part with a yearning for the fulfillment. Christian marriage is meant to be the purest and greatest human intimacy that, this side of glory, can be found.

Plainness

As soon as the bride appears, she describes herself as plain (though she acknowledges that she does have some beauty). This is in verse 5 of the first chapter. She describes herself as dark but lovely. In the modern world of tanning beds, we associate dark skin with beauty and wealth, but like anorexic models, this is strictly modern. In the time of the Song of Songs, the wealthy did not spend time outside with the laborers, and pale skin was associated with wealth, decadence, and beauty. We still have remnants of this concept in an unusual term. "Redneck" is a derogatory term for Caucasian manual laborers, where the neck is red or tan, but the rest of the body is pale because of outside hard labor while clothed. A "farmer's tan" falls into the same category.

The bride furthers this concept by saying that she is ungroomed. This reference is easily missed in the following verse. Her brothers have forced her to work their fields, and as a result, she has not kept her own vineyard, meaning she has not tended to her own body and beauty.[41] This evokes an image of the bride with dirt under the nails and tangled hair. Basically, she is unpresentable, especially to a king. She even asks the chorus not to look at her. We are meant to see this as the pre-marriage bride who then is wooed by the shepherd-king.

This reflects Christ's Bride on multiple points. Before Christ, she has spent her time tending vineyards from which she does not reap. This is comparable to Ecclesiastes 2:18–23, where one sows and another reaps. We have been exhausted and unkept as we have poured our lives, time, energy, and heart into the world which has little to no regard for us. We are ugly with sin, and we only realize this as Christ draws us by an effectual call of grace into love with Him. The Bride is unpresentable, but Christ makes her presentable. As Thomas Goodwin says, "If thou sayest, thou wantest beauty, be not discouraged, he will take thee with all thy deformities, and put beauty on thee; for so the Apostle there goes on—he washeth and cleanseth his Church, to present her to himself in the end, glorious, and without spot or wrinkle."[42] John Owen describes this as the sanctification Christ purchased for the Bride. "He not only purchases love for his saints, He makes them lovely."[43]

Modesty and Chastity

With the abundance of evocative, sensual imagery, some people miss the theme of modesty and chastity in the book. Part of this is because in a book of "redeemed eroticism," we do not expect an emphasis on chastity, and partly because the first reference is a bit obscure.

In the first chapter, the bride asks where the shepherd will be keeping his flocks so that she can come to him directly. She further explains that she does not want to be wandering among the fields like a veiled woman. We might assume that a veil would be for the sake of modesty, but in the ancient Near East, this was not the case. The veil was a cultural marker of a prostitute.[44] In Genesis 38:12–15, Tamar veils herself so that Judah would think that she was a prostitute and not recognize her as his daughter-in-law, so he would sleep with her and give her a kid.

---

41 It is possible that we are looking at the abuse of the true Bride, the remnant within Israel, at the hand of the illegitimate children, the unbelievers in the nation. This would explain the language of "my mother's sons." Yet, as we have already observed, we need to be cautious of allegorization.
42 Goodwin, *Ephesians*, 40.
43 Owen, *Communion with God*, 129.
44 This is not absolute, as there also appears to have been a veil for marriage, which is referenced in 4:1. Presumably the prostitute's veil was for anonymity. There may be a reference to the prostitute veil in Isaiah 3:23.

The bride in the Song is concerned with modesty, not willing to be seen wandering about in the fields like a soliciting prostitute. She is single-minded in her pursuit of the shepherd. As Paul describes the qualification for deacon or elder as a one-woman man, the bride here is a one-person woman.[45]

The bridegroom describes the bride as a locked garden and sealed fountain or spring in chapter four. She is chaste, reserved only for her husband. This is connected to the value of the abundance of the restricted garden. It is locked, and the bounty of the garden has not been pillaged by passers-by. The garden is a repeated image in the book for the woman's body, especially her more intimate physicality. She has not given herself to other men but is reserved only for her covenant husband. Only he will have access to her "garden." Likewise, the owner of a "delicate spring of waters" may place a great stone upon it as in Genesis 29:3 so that others would not partake of it.[46]

At the end of the book, a parallel set of images is present in 8:8–10. The brothers of the bride, here a positive image, are concerned with guarding the chastity of their sister until her marriage. They bar the door and build a battlement of silver on the wall, silver being an image of purity. She even describes herself as a wall, guarded and impenetrable.

On the immediate level, all of this emphasizes the importance of chastity outside of marriage. Proponents claim that this is not an end unto itself, unlike the perpetual chastity. It is for the purpose of protecting intimacy in marriage. The garden is not guarded to remain untouched forever but so that the bounty thereof would be for the bridegroom alone.

This same principle applies to the church. The church should acknowledge the value of purity before marriage, even if the world does not. She should declare the destructiveness of adultery. However, we can fail to make the application to spiritual life. In some cases, God uses the same language very explicitly (as we have seen) to describe the negative side. He refers to our idolatries as adulteries. Our sin is to Christ what a wife's adultery is to her husband.

Here, we examine the positive side. Like Solomon's bride, we ought to reserve our best things for God. Our best singing, dedication, love, and adoration should be reserved for Christ. By doing this, by not giving ourselves over to adulterous idolatries, we are set free. We are at liberty to love our Bridegroom, Christ, with abandon.

---

45 1 Timothy 3:12 describes this qualification for a deacon. If it is required for a deacon, then it is certainly required for those called to the ministry of the Word, and every qualification therein should be a goal for every Christian.
46 Goodwin, *Ephesians*, 230.

Timing

The Song bears a trio of identical statements (2:7; 3:5; and 8:4) about patience. The bride exhorts the young women, the daughters of Israel, to not force love or fabricate it in immaturity. Rather, she calls them to wait on God's timing. The immediate lesson here is plain enough to see and timely for young women. Women are called to wait for God to bring a godly man into their lives who is suitable for marriage, not to force love or try to convert a worldly man by evangelistic dating. Being equally yoked is of great importance for a God-honoring marriage.

For the church, this exhortation is about how we do evangelism. God saves sinners when, where, and how He chooses. We should plead with sinners for God and with God for sinners, but we cannot force conversion. You can make someone read the sinner's prayer at gunpoint (that is not a recommendation), but God has to regenerate the heart.

Chapter 5 of the Song is challenging. The bride is awakened to the sound of her love calling to her, at which point she hesitates. She is bathed and dressed for sleep. To heed this call would mean dressing and soiling her feet. At last, her heart is stirred to love, and she goes to the door. When she opens it, he is gone, and she goes out into the street to find him.

This is a cautionary tale for us. Like the bride, comfort and aversion to inconvenience often deter us from intimacy with Christ. First, this is about dealing with sin. We have to soil our feet and gird ourselves for war in dealing with the sins we have harbored in our hearts. It is inconvenient and uncomfortable to mortify the flesh. Often the destruction of one sin reveals others that have been hiding in the shadows. Yet these sins alienate us from our Beloved. They do not divorce us from Christ, but they do create distance and do violence to intimacy with Him.

Secondly, we are tempted to neglect worship, prayer life, and personal study because of worldly distractions. Jude 21 exhorts us, "In the love of God, keep yourselves, waiting for the mercy of our Lord Jesus Christ into eternal life" (author's translation). When we fail to do that, it often reaps what the old Puritans called "winters of the heart." We desire and seek Christ when our heart stirs, but He seems unreachable, and our prayers seem to stop at the ceiling. In times like these, we have to be willing to persevere and endure hardship to find our love, Christ.

Thirdly, there is a caution to the unbeliever. In coldness of heart, they do not seek Christ while He may be found. The day is coming, either in death or in Christ's return, when it will be too late to seek salvation and its rewards.

> "When persons are generally uncompliant with such outward means
> as they cannot but acknowledge do contain warning from this and

invitation unto another frame. So the spouse acknowledgeth that it was the voice of her Beloved that knocked, saying, "Open to me, my spouse, my love, my dove, my undefiled; for my head is filled with dew and my locks with the drops of the night," Cant. V.2. Both the voice and the love, and the long waiting of Christ, were manifest unto her; and yet she complies not with him, but makes her excuses, verses 2,3. And the sloth of persons will be reckoned in proportion unto the means of diligence which they do enjoy. Some may not be sleepy, worldly, careless, slothful, at as cheap a rate of guilt as others, though it be great in all.... When persons are as it were glad of such occasions as may justify them and satisfy their minds in the omission of duties or opportunities for them. This casts off the duty prescribed unto us, Heb 12:1; which yet is indispensably necessary unto the attaining of the end of our faith. When men will not only readily embrace occasions offered unto them to divert them from duty, but will be apt to seek out and invent shifts whereby they may, as they suppose, be excused from it,—which corrupt nature is exceedingly prone unto,— they are under the power of this vicious habit. Especially is this so when men are apt to approve of such reasons to this end, as, being examined by the rules of duty, with the tenders of the love of Christ, are lighter than vanity. So it is added of the slothful person, who hides his hand in his bosom, that he is wiser in his own conceit than seven men that can render a reason," Prov. 26:15–16. He pleaseth himself with his foolish pretenses for his sloth above all the reasons that can be given him to the contrary. And such is the reason pleaded by the spouse when overtaken with this frame for a season, Cant. 5:3.... When there is a great neglect of our own prayers, when at any time we have been enabled to make them. So the spouse, in whom we have an instance of a surprisal into this evil, prays earnestly for the coming and approach of Christ unto her in the holy dispensations of his Spirit, Cant. IV. 16; but when he tenders himself unto her desire, she puts off the entertainment of him. So do men pray for grace and mercy sometimes; but when the seasons of the communication of them do come, they are wholly regardless in looking after them. They put off things unto another season and meet ofttimes with the success mentioned, Cant v.6."[47]

Because this section opens with the bride asleep (verse 2), the easiest way to read verses 7–8 is the bride's nightmare. When she goes out to find her beloved, the watchmen assault her. The original text uses forceful language that may even indicate sexual assault. Yet she presses on in her search, which

---

[47] John Owen, *Hebrews Vol 5*, 205-206. Cant. is an abbreviation for Canticles, the old-timey title for Song of Solomon.

is fairly unrealistic. An assault victim would not go on as if nothing had happened. This is likely a dream, and certainly not a prescription for young women who are victims of real assault.[48]

On the Bride of Christ level, the watchmen are the trials of this life and the powers, principalities, and authorities of darkness in this world. Revelation 12 shows the same narrative in a different image. The dragon, which is Satan, is in pursuit of the woman and her offspring. The woman is the church, with parallels to Eve and Mary. In Ephesians 6:12, Paul emphasizes that our battle and contention is not against flesh and blood, but spiritual forces of evil. This ties in to our next passage on a unique level.

The Garden Pests

In 2:15, the third antagonist surfaces. There are angry brothers, watchmen, and foxes—oh my. They impose themselves on a narrative where they do not seem to belong. While everything else is idealized, which we would expect from love poetry, these antagonists seem to break through the rose-colored glasses. The world is an ugly place, a fallen place, and love does not change that. Love does, however, make it endurable and worth enduring.

This is the mixed bag of the world's fallenness for the church, covering the whole range from mosquitos to martyrdom. They are metaphors for all the nuisances and dangers of life that wreak havoc on our Christian walk. Some sorrows are inevitable in a fallen world because of Adam's first sin and the abundance we have heaped on it. We should expect foxes, cruel brothers, and even watchmen over the course of our lives. The bride in 2:15 alludes to these sorrows and asks the bridegroom to deal with them, but they do not remain the focus of her attention. She does not spend the rest of the book bemoaning the foxes.

Spurgeon, in a devotional, narrows the scope of the foxes to only sin. "Little foxes spoil the vines; and little sins do mischief to the tender heart. These little sins burrow in the soul, and make it full of that which is hateful to Christ, so that He will hold no comfortable fellowship and communion with us."[49] This certainly fits the scheme of pests in this life that spoil the tender vine of spiritual fruit. Sin is often at the heart of trial, and we ought to use it as opportunity for self-examination and repentance. Not every trial is a

---

48 If you have ever been victim of sexual assault, please report it. It is not your fault. I should probably have this someplace more prominent than in a footnote, but it is terrifying that sexual predators are able to continue preying on others because their victims are silenced by shame. If you are a child of God, the stains of this world will be taken away, all the grief and sorrow, but for the sake of yourself and others, please do not keep silent.

49 Charles Spurgeon, *Morning and Evening*: May 30 (New Kensington: Whitaker House, 2002), 314.

chastisement for sin, but there is never a bad time to seek out sin in our lives, repent, and return to the cross.

We cannot ignore the problems of life. We should not pretend that our world is perfect, even under the guise of adorning the gospel. It violates the ninth commandment for Christians to lie by claiming that they have found their best life now, because we have not. Christians get their best life next, and we have to be honest with the people we know in this world. Christ did not promise a problem-free life, but rather sufficient problems for each day (Matt. 6:34).

There is also a crucial distinction between trusting God as a Christian and being oblivious. We are called to fulfill our responsibilities and trust that God will accomplish His will. It is irresponsible to do nothing and claim faith. For a husband to work hard at his job and provide for his family is not a lack of faith; it is stewardship. Moms should seek to provide general safety for their children. Letting toddlers play on the freeway is not "letting go and letting God."

But when we have problems, we should bring our cares to the Shepherd-King-Bridegroom. We should make our requests known unto God (Phil. 4:6). There are a lot of foxes we cannot catch, but God is able to provide far more than all that we ask or think (Eph. 3:20).

Finally, there is a temptation to only see the foxes, especially for those predisposed to melancholy. We can fixate on the issues of this life and forget about the grace God has shown us. Many Christians have been so consumed by concerns for important things that they lose sight of the eternal things. For some, politics become an all-consuming drive as they grieve and mourn for a loss in an election. For others, scarce finances are the fox that makes them forget the Bridegroom. We must always remember that our primary concern, our chief end, is to glorify God and enjoy Him forever.[50]

Solomon's Procession (3:6–11)

This passage has inspired a wide array of interpretations, including Solomon coming and stealing away the bride for himself. Of course, this reaches far beyond what is present in the text. Commentators assume this because the bridegroom has been presented so far as a shepherd, and now we see the bridegroom as Solomon in splendor. However, if we take the Song as an anthology of love poems, there is no problem shifting from shepherd to king. After all, Solomon's father David went from being a shepherd boy to king of Israel.

We see an extensive connection from the Davidic covenant between the immediate seed as King Solomon and the great seed as King Jesus (2 Sam.

---
50 Westminster Shorter Catechism, Q1 A1.

7:1–17). This link permeates the Song, but especially here where Solomon is named. The first glimpse of Solomon's company is the "columns of smoke," perfumed with frankincense and myrrh. The frankincense and myrrh, of course, tie in directly to Christ with the gifts of the wise men and the embalming of His body in burial. This also goes back to the Exodus narrative, where the children of Israel were led by God (Christ) in the theophany of a pillar of smoke by day. All of these are textual hints that this is more than just Solomon, but a shadow and type of Christ. It may be strange to go back and forth between Solomon as shepherd and as king, but it is nothing foreign for us to do that with Christ. He is the immanent Shepherd and the transcendent King; He is the Paschal Lamb and the Lion of Judah.

Solomon approaches in splendor and entourage. Perhaps the most striking feature in this is the lengthy description of accompanying warriors. There are sixty *gibborim*, or mighty men of Israel. They are experts in war and armed for battle against the terrors of the night. It would not be an unusual practice for guards to accompany the king, but why is there a focus on them in a collection of love poetry?

The answer comes from unlikely passages in John's Apocalypse. In Revelation 14:14–20, Christ comes with warrior-farmer angels to reap the harvest of the earth. The "fruit" of the earth is gathered in by sickle and treaded out in the winepress of the wrath of God. Blood flows in the streets up to the bridles of horses. In 19:11–21, Christ Himself comes with heralding angels to judge in wrath the men of the earth. The sword proceeds from His mouth and lays waste to armies of men. These two passages show Christ in terrifying judgment repaying the evil and rebellion of men. This should cause us to tremble and work out our salvation in fear. It is a call of alarm that Christ comes as a thief in the night to bring judgment we cannot withstand unless we are covered by the blood of Christ.

The depiction in the Song is the same event from a drastically different perspective. This is the arrival of king and warriors seen from the bride's point of view. This is what the saints wait for with great anticipation (Rev. 6:10–11). For God's people, Christ's entourage of warrior angels is our comfort and peace. If we are truly called and saved by grace through faith, we know that God has sent His angels to watch over us, and we look forward to the day when Christ comes with them to consummate His kingdom and bring us into glory.

Called to Give Account (5:8–16)

In verse 8, the bride petitions the daughters of Jerusalem to help her find the bridegroom. She says she is "sick with love." The daughters of Jerusalem ask why the bridegroom is worthy of attention in verse 9. What makes him worth seeking? From here, the bride launches into a lengthy description of the beauty of the bridegroom.

The immediate application is for husbands and wives. We ought to have the praises of our spouse at the forefront of our minds. We should be ready to give account for the love we have in our marriage. We might find it easy to give a list of our spouse's shortcomings and failures, but do we dwell on the good that God has given and developed in them? First, this guards against infidelity. If we are quick to remember what we love about our spouse, we are better defended from temptations to adultery. Secondly, it gives a good witness to godly marriage. Even children should be able to see from their parents' example that the best intimacy, sex, and love are within covenant marriage, despite what the world teaches. Finally, and most simply, this helps us to love our spouses more readily.

At the Bride of Christ level, these same things apply in terms of faithfulness and zealous love. We are the least tempted when we are most in love with our Savior. This is primarily about evangelism, though. It goes beyond an account of the hope in us, to which Peter exhorts us in 1 Peter 3:15. It is a description of love for a Savior who first loved us. The world should hear more than just intellectual apologetics from us, valuable as that is. It does not take a seminary degree for you to describe why you love Christ. The people to whom we bear witness should hear of the superlatives of Christ in a way that makes them want what we have. This is precisely the vein that Edward Pearce follows when he asks, "Are you for dignity and greatness? Are you for riches and treasures? Are you for bounty, for a noble and generous spirit? Are you for wisdom and knowledge? Are you for beauty? Are you for love as well as loveliness?" Each of these are found in perfect fullness in Christ.[51] Thomas Goodwin says, "The church there had withal in her eye all those gracious perfections his person was adorned with; which thus won her heart to him, and drew this from her."[52]

The bride of the Song speaks of love and beauty over benefit, security, and obligation. This is something we often neglect in our description of our God. When you speak of Christ, is it only in terms of benefit, regarding blessings of family, job, finances, and home? When you tell of your love for God, is it primarily about the security of knowing you are not going to hell? Do you only speak of loving your Savior because it is what is required of you? Or do you speak of how Christ loved you, saved you, and showed you what love truly is in giving His life for your sake? Is Christ beautiful to you? The praises of your Savior should flow from your lips as freely as from Solomon's bride.

---

51 Pearce, *The Best Match*. These are headings throughout chapter 7.
52 Goodwin, *Ephesians*, 27.

In all this, we should be affirming what the bride said of her beloved back in 5:10, that he is preferred above all others. Our adoration of Christ should be so fulfilling that there is no place for adultery with idols.

ON SEALS AND LOVE (8:6–7)

As the bride and groom come up from the consummation of their love, the bride petitions her husband. She asks him to set her as a seal on his arm and heart. Her reasoning is the jealousy of love, denoting the exclusivity of their marriage.

On the immediate level, this shows the nature of the love of marriage. Commentators have noted that this is the most substantial description of love in the book, contrasting the descriptions of superficial attraction. This teaches us that the love of marriage is invaluable and permanent. It is strong, it is jealous, and it is for life. The concept of jealousy here is positive. It is a desire for faithfulness in marriage, not consuming distrust. In 8:10, another aspect of this is added: "I am a wall and my breasts are like towers. Then I was, in his eyes, like she who finds peace [*shalom*]" (author's translation). The marriage bed is to be the place of safety and security for the bride, where love can be expressed without fear or hesitation. This beautiful peace is what adultery destroys.

One final note on the immediate application is that this is the wife speaking of seals. She wants her seal on the husband. The husband's seal is assumed. Here, the wife claims ownership of the husband. This points forward to the language of Paul in 1 Corinthians 7, describing the needs of intimacy for both spouses, acknowledging that the wife has needs to be met by the husband. He is no more the owner of his body than the wife is of hers. It is a two-way dedication. A husband must be as devoted and faithful as the bride; if he sins through infidelity of heart or action, it is as grievous, if not more so.

On the Bride of Christ level, the relationship is bi-directional as well. We should own Christ as ours. Not only has Christ purchased us for a possession, He has given Himself for us. In 7:10, the bride declares, "I am for my beloved, and over/upon me is his desire" (author's translation). For Christ and the church, this has been true from eternity. We were elected for Him, and His love and desire was set upon us before the world was made. The seal is set upon our hearts by the Holy Spirit after believing (Eph. 1:13), but it may be said that our seal is upon God's heart by His own work in predestination.[53]

For the next application, we begin in broader context. First, Exodus 28:11–12 and 28:21 describe God's requirements for the outfitting of the priest. He bears the names of the tribes over his heart and on his shoulders. He was to

---

53 Goodwin, *Ephesians*, 241.

carry the names of God's people in *heart* and *action* as he made intercession on their behalf. In a more perfect way, Christ accomplished redemption for His sheep known by name, carrying their names on His heart and atoning by His actions.

Christ bore our names on His heart on the cross and continues to do so in glory as He makes intercession for us. His hands and side were pierced for our sake. His arm, the symbol of strength, is mighty to save us, while His heart is set upon us. His love is stronger than death, and His jealousy is fiercer than the grave. It flashes with the fire of God.

The close of verse 7 speaks of a man being despised for giving the wealth of his house for love. Immediately, it speaks of the fact that a man would be despised if he tried to purchase love because it is invaluable. In terms of Christ, we see that He gave the wealth of Heaven itself, humbling Himself, taking on the form of a man, and redeeming His Bride. For this, Jesus was despised by men. He was crucified on a tree and received the curse of God for our sin. By the wealth of His house, Christ redeemed for Himself a Bride.

THE ABSENT FATHER

It may seem strange to fixate on what is absent, but it is striking that the whole book lacks reference to the father of the bride. There are allusions to the mother's existence, and the brothers even speak. The father never appears, though. If the father passed early in her life, that might explain some. Yet we would assume that a bride of Solomon would be of some royal lineage, which would emphasize the father's role.

This is not the only occurrence of it either. We never hear about the parents of Sarah, Tamar, Rahab, Ruth, or Mary, not because the Bible is chauvinistic, but because what matters is that they married into the line of Christ. Their identity begins anew with marriage.

When we look at this for the church, we see how we are born again into the marriage to Christ. Our new Father is united to Christ in the Trinity. Our former spiritual father, the devil, is no longer relevant. He no longer has a claim on us, nor does he have a role in our lives after that perfect betrothal. We are dead to him and his accusations, as he is dead to us.

VI

Marrying into Shame

Hosea

WE WILL NOW BEGIN TO unweave some of the most poetic, terrifying, and beautiful passages of Scripture: Hosea's prophecies to the nation of Israel. The final verse of the book, 14:9, calls the reader, in a Proverbs-esque fashion, to a wise, discerning consideration of the prophecy. We must perceive the mysterious ways of God, the righteousness of God, to keep from stumbling. Indeed, we need much wisdom and discerning consideration to draw the sweeter waters from the depths. Hosea is beautiful in its complexity, from mixed metaphors to Hebrew wordplay, as it unfolds the history and future of God's relationship to His people as the Bride.

One of the greatest challenges in expositing Hosea's prophecy is the fluid use of what is called the *prophetic idiom*. Dr. Bryan Estelle describes it as the way in which the prophets spoke of new covenant reality in old covenant language.[1] Hosea switches audiences seamlessly, from national Israel to the true Israel within the nation (the believing elect) to the church that will come out of Israel. I will try to mark these transitions as we progress through each chapter to avoid confusion.

Hosea's name was an abbreviation of "Yahweh Saves," and that theme shines in contrast to the black of the condemnation passages. Hosea was called during a time when Israel's exile was imminent (somewhere between 786 and 720 BC). The kings of Judah were still largely following God, and God was still largely pleased with them,[2] but Israel had one sinful king after another.[3] While the primary focus is on the Assyrian exile for the northern kingdom of Israel, the future Babylonian exile of Judah runs in the background.

The major theme permeating the book is infidelity/idolatry. Hosea was addressing a culture of idolatry and religious syncretism. The Israelites not

---

[1] This is based off my personal lecture notes from his courses, but it was also referenced in a blog post from *A Pilgrim's Theology*, "Calvin and 'Prophetic Idiom,'" June 17, 2010. https://theologiainvia.wordpress.com/2010/06/17/calvin-and-prophetic-idiom/.
[2] Uzziah, Jotham, Ahaz, and Hezekiah—listed in 1:1—were all good kings of Judah.
[3] Jeroboam II, who was followed by Menahem, Pekahiah, and Pekah.

only worshipped false gods, they mixed paganism with proper Yahweh worship, like the kings of Judah who would follow after God but not cast down the "high places" of pagan worship.[4] The rebuke of these sins is central to the book, and we must be vigilant to apply the repeated rebuke to our own forms of idolatry and syncretism. Idolatry is not just people bowing to statues of wood, stone, or other. That does exist and is sin, but that is not how *we* most often encounter idolatry. In our own lives and in this era, there are some obvious forms of religious syncretism, but there are subtler forms that even claim to be genuine Christianity.

Men are ever prone to make an idol in their own image and call it God rather than be confronted with the God of Scripture. Indeed, the golden calves were meant to be representations of Yahweh but were violations of the second commandment nonetheless. Jeroboam I: The Idol Menace repeated this sin by casting two golden calves and mimicking Aaron's cry from Exodus (1 Kings 12:25–33). God addresses this in Hosea 8:5–6. Men today rarely cast golden calves and call them Jehovah, but they paint portraits of the mind that portray God as humanistic, fickle, incompetent, and impotent. People form a god in their own image from man's dust. It is to these that God's words sound forth, "You thought I was altogether like you?" (Psalm 50:21, author's translation).

Yet our most frequent encounter with idolatry is described by Calvin:

> Man's nature, so to speak, is a perpetual factory of idols. . . . Man's mind, full as it is of pride and boldness, dares to imagine a god according to its own capacity; as it sluggishly plods, indeed is overwhelmed with the crassest ignorance, it conceives an unreality and an empty appearance as God. To these evils a new wickedness joins itself, that mainly tries to express in his work the sort of God he has inwardly conceived. Therefore the mind begets an idol; the hand gives it birth.[5]

One of the best tools for identifying idolatry comes out of Paul's self-description that he is able to be content in all circumstances (Phil. 4:10–13). We have to identify what we "must-have" to be content, what we cannot bear God removing from our lives. I told the congregation I shepherd that my personal test for idolatry is to pray that God would do what is necessary to conform me to Christ. Whatever my heart poses in objection is usually my idol. I have come to call this "the hardest prayer." This is what David does in Psalm 139:23–24. Someone somewhere once said that the difference between idolatry and proper use is the difference between considering a thing a want and a need.

---

[4] 1 Kings 15:14 is just one of many examples
[5] John Calvin, *Institutes of the Christian Religion* (Louisville: Westminster John Knox, 1960), I.XI.8.

Hosea 1:1–5 [6]

> The word of Yahweh, which was to Hosea son of Beeri in the days of Uzziah, Jotham, Ahab, Hezekiah kings of Judah, and in the days of Jeroboam son of Joash, king of Israel.
>
> The beginning of the word of Yahweh with/in Hosea, and Yahweh said to Hosea, "Go! Take to yourself (marry) a wife of harlotries/prostitutions/adulteries and children of adulteries/prostitutions because the land/earth whores adulteries from after Yahweh."
>
> And he went and took Gomer, daughter of Diblaim, and she conceived and begat to him a son.
>
> And Yahweh said to him, "Call his name Jezreel because still a little (while) and I have appointed punishment for the blood of Jezreel on the house of Jehu, and I will bring an end of the kingdom of the house of Israel.
>
> And it will be in that day, and I will break the bow of Israel in the valley of Jezreel."

God prophesied against Israel's sins through his servant Hosea in a most unique way. There are specific instances, like Ezekiel 4, Jeremiah 27, and Isaiah 20, where the prophet of God was called to act out the ways God would bring about judgment. Still, Hosea's specific assignment is far more intimate, grievous, and challenging.[7] God came to His servant Hosea and commanded him to take a wife of whoredom and bear children of whoredom.

People struggle with how God could call Hosea to marry a prostitute.[8] Some claim she was just involved in cultic rituals of Baal or would be unfaithful in the future, but this is meant to represent God's relationship to His people, who were covenant-breaking idolaters before and after this. As we will see, the reality of the sign, not just the thing signified, is important.[9] It is a foreshadowing of Christ, how He would come and be God to the people. What the prophet did as God's voice to the people, Christ would do in coming as God in the flesh and literally be God with His people, Immanuel. We

---

[6] The translations for this chapter are my own. Where there are multiple meanings for a word, I have used a / symbol to connect them, hopefully without creating confusion. The parenthetical words are not present in the Hebrew but are inserted to help make sense of the text.

[7] Personally, I'd rather eat Ezekiel's fecal bread than be married to an unfaithful wife.

[8] It would be a disqualifying sin for a priest to marry a prostitute, but the principle might carry over for the office of prophet. See Leviticus 21:7.

[9] This is also congruent with the divine modus operandi, i.e., David as both historical figure and type of Christ. We are accustomed to typology only occurring in fiction, especially when it is perfectly orchestrated, but God writes real history and embeds foreshadowing of redemption therein.

see this unfaithful Bride as Old Testament Israel prior to His coming, but the same unfaithfulness also arises in the church.[10]

Hosea takes for himself a wife with the unfortunate name of Gomer. He marries her, she conceives, and she bears a child. The original text of Hebrew says she bore *lo*. This *lo*, spelled *lamed-waw*, clarifies that "she bore *to him*" (have no fear, you do not have to know the Hebrew to get the point here). It is a Hebrew idiom to state she bore his child, a child of Hosea's own blood. To understand the significance and gravity of this, we have to see the historicity. Hosea held a child of his own in his arms. God speaks to him and says, "You will name him Jezreel because in a little while I will visit the bloodshed of the valley of Jezreel on the house of Jehu." The story behind this is that Jehu initially did what God said, cleansing out the Baal worship and destroying Ahab's house in Jezreel. Once he had done that, however, he took the power to himself but did not follow after God.[11] He followed in Ahab's footsteps, so God promised to visit Jehu's household with the same kind of judgment. The last king of Jehu's line would soon be cut off for someone else to resume the throne, perhaps as soon as within a year of Hosea's prophecy.

This in and of itself serves as a lesson to the prideful legalist. There is a temptation to look down on others whom we view as more sinful than us, when it is only God's grace that keeps us from such sin. It is a short distance from zealous works to our own fall when we do not put pride to death.

The bow would be broken, and Israel would be left defenseless. The northern kingdom allied with Assyria in exchange for tribute but was then caught trying to make a new treaty with Egypt, and the Assyrians conquered them. The record for all this is found in 2 Kings 17.

The name Jezreel also denotes sowing, as God would "sow" Israel to produce His New Testament church. We will revisit this when we get to verse 11 and even more in 2:22.

Illegitimate Children

Hosea 1:6–11

And she conceived again and bore a daughter, and he said to him, "Call her name Lo Ruchamah (no-mercy/love/compassion) because I will not add again Ruchamah to the house of Israel because I will not ever lift/take for them (their sin).

---

[10] We are not really less sinful, but we are in an age of fuller revelation of the covenant of grace.
[11] 2 Kings 9–10. Though he wiped out Baal worship, he continued the worship of the golden calves.

But for the house of Judah, I will have Ruchamah and deliver them in Yahweh their God, but I will not save them with bow or sword or war with horses or in horsemen."

And she weaned Lo Ruchamah and conceived and bore a son.

And he said, "Call his name Lo Ammi because you are not my people and I am not for you (or I am not I Am to you).

But the number of the sons of Israel will be as sand of the sea which is not measured or counted. And it will be in that place where it was said to them, 'Lo Ammi,' you will call them 'sons of the living God.'

And the sons of Judah and the sons of Israel will be gathered together, and they will set on themselves one head and they will go up from the land, because great will be the day of Jezreel."

When the next two children are born, they are each given names with this prefix of *Lo*. This time it is not the *lamed-waw* that means "to him," but the *lamed-aleph* that means "no." Their divinely appointed names are *Lo-Ruchamah* and *Lo-Ammi*. These are both illegitimate children, signaled by the replacing of the "born to him" idiom with the negation. Therefore, God signals to the reader that these are children of whoredom, fulfilling God's command/prophecy of verse 2. This is a very difficult, painful, sorrowful, and beautiful love story being played out in Hosea's life. In a little vignette, we are seeing what takes place in the greater narrative of redemptive history.

The overarching theme with this is Christ's relationship to us. So as we look at this story, who is the Bride? It is the church. It is Israel, which is the Old Testament church. This is the environment through which the children of God are born. We receive the salvation of Christ through the church, like the Old Testament Saints through Israel. Faith comes by hearing, and hearing the Word takes place in and through the church. Christ works through His church, His Bride through the preaching of the Word, to accomplish salvation in the elect. That is why we speak of the church as the mother of the people of God. It is a continuation of this image of the Bride of Christ. Christ is married to the church, He is the head of the church, and through the church are born His children.

But when God is creating these images of *illegitimate* children, He is exposing those Jews who claim to be children of Abraham on the basis of their bloodline but have no faith. In John 8:39–59, Christ speaks to the Pharisees who are accusing Him of being an illegitimate child. They claim to be Abraham's children, heirs to the promises of God, but Christ says they are not, or they would do what Abraham did. He says they are children of the devil. They are not children of God; they will not be heirs of the kingdom. We have to understand that this is why Hosea is called to raise illegitimate children. They are symbolic of the unbelievers of Israel, children of Baal, named for their benefactor. They do not follow Yahweh; they claim Baal and the gods of other nations but still want the benefits of God's people. These are not true believers but tares among the wheat, believing themselves to be wheat.

In verse 6, Hosea tells us that Gomer bore a daughter and called her *Lo-Ruchamah*. It means No-Mercy. There will be no mercy, no compassion, no love. This is a dark and foreboding note in the proclamation of God against the people of Israel. God is saying there will be no mercy for spiritually illegitimate children, for the nation as a whole. Through Gomer's adultery, God gives her a real, living little girl, and God commands Hosea to name her No Love, No Mercy, No Compassion. It is meant to break our hearts. Because of sin in this world, because of the necessity of the proclamation of the law and the gospel and showing the holiness and sovereignty of God, a little girl went through life with the name No Mercy. God says to call her this because, "I will not add again Ruchamah to the house of Israel, because I will not ever lift/take for them (their sin), but I will have mercy on the house of Judah." It is a difficult and terrifying thing to think of this holiness of God.

For Israel, what does this bring to mind? God has repeatedly proclaimed judgment on them. If you read from Exodus to the end of the Old Testament, Israel's history was an unending cycle of Israel's whoring after idols. God proclaimed judgment, Israel wept and expressed repentance, and then God drew them back. He always had mercy. Hosea is proclaiming judgment on the people of Israel like the prophets that came before, but it is not going to stop there this time. They are hearing this Judges-type condemnation that they are going to be cast down and conquered again, but with an assurance that mercy will not follow. All of the long-promised curses of the Torah are coming to bear (see Deuteronomy 31:16–18 for an example).

What is terrifying about this is these words are coming from the one who always saved Israel. Romans 8:31 says, "If God is for us, who can be against us?" I prefer the translation, "If God is for us, who is against us?" In high school and college, I had a friend we called "little Rob." Small as he was, Rob thought he was invincible because all of his friends were big guys. He was fearless so long as we were around, knowing we would never hurt him and were there to bail him out of trouble. In a similar way, if we have God on our side, who can pose a threat to us? If God is sovereign over all things, then nothing can endanger His children. We encounter trials, but those things are being worked together for our good and God's glory. The terror of this passage is inverting the Romans concept. If God is against us, who could be for us? Who will restrain the hand of God's judgment? It is as though God says, "Do you think these other gods, these other supposed lovers, can save you?"

Verse 7 turns to gospel promises with one of the most vivid proclamations of the deity of Christ and the promise of the new covenant in the Old Testament. There is love and mercy for Judah. He addresses the southern kingdom, a physical nation whose safety depends on armies and soldiers, men capable of wielding sword and sling, chariots, and all other like implements. God tells the nation of Judah that He is going to save them and have mercy on them, but not by any of these things that He has used before. There is not even going to be a battle for them to fight. "I am going to save you by Yahweh your God." Yahweh, Jehovah will save them. He promises to save them by His holy name, by His own hand. *God will save them by God.* It should send chills down your spine to read this. While there was a partial fulfillment in Hezekiah's reign with the slaughtering angel, God is prophesying the Son coming in the form of a man to save them, and they would have nothing to do with their own salvation. It is a prophecy that they would have no claim on their redemption. It would be Sola Gratia, Solus Christus.[12]

This is so much bigger than national security and the physical nation. God is allowing it to be shrouded in shadow. He is allowing them to perceive it as the salvation of a physical nation, providing for them to stay on a piece of dirt in Palestine, but it is so much bigger than that. It is the proclamation of a salvation that even applies to us, in this time, in this age, thousands of miles away and thousands of years later, receiving salvation by faith. We have no involvement in it. We did not do anything, but it is provided for us. We are saved, not by human means, but by Yahweh as the Christ.

Then we move on to Lo-Ammi. Once Gomer had weaned No-Mercy, she returned to her whoring and conceived a son, the second child of Gomer's whoredom whom Hosea must name and raise. This is one of the darkest passages of Scripture in the OT. We see over and over again where Israel transgressed against God, worshipping other gods of other nations. He would chastise, they would repent, and He would remember them as His people and provide for them. He would restore the nation to where it was before; God would remove the oppressors for the sake of His people, His church. They were the means through which Yahweh showed His grace and love in salvation, but a proclamation like this verse never took place before, which is why it is so terrifying. God says to call his name Lo-Ammi. This translates to "not my people." "For you are not my people and I am not your God," or, more literally, "I am not I Am for you." This is the same name for God found in Exodus 3:14 when God enters the scene to free Israel from their captivity to Egypt. They have sinned in presumption, with a "high hand," and though every time prior God had shown mercy, He will do so no more. They are "stubborn and rebellious" sons who will not heed discipline and are fit only for death (Deut. 21:18–21).

---
12 Grace Alone, Christ Alone.

In terms of God's covenant lawsuit, presented by His prosecuting lawyer Hosea, this is the filing for divorce of Sinai. Calvin says it is "as though he said, 'Your origin has nothing commendable in it; ye think yourselves to be very eminent because ye derive your descent from holy Jacob; but ye are spurious children, born of a harlot: a brothel is not the house of Abraham, nor is the house of Abraham a brothel. Ye are then the offspring of debauchery.'"[13] This is the death blow. Isaiah 50:1 makes reference to this same act of God giving Israel a certificate of divorce.

Because we are looking at a covenantal divorce, it is important to take into consideration the context of the Mosaic law because Israel was dealt with nationally as a bride under the Mosaic covenant. The law is an expression, in part, of God's holiness, righteousness, and justice. It is an expression of the divine character. This is why the moral law carries on beyond the dissolution of the covenant with Moses, and precedes it as well.[14] The judicial law holds what we call "general equity" even beyond national Israel, meaning there are principles that transcend that national law.[15] So if the judicial law deals with something as immoral, then it remains immoral, even if we are not required to hold the same repercussions for that action in government.

Deuteronomy 24:1–4 deals with what we might consider an obscure case. If a man marries a woman and finds her to be indecent or adulterous, he may divorce her. If she marries another and then is divorced again, the first husband cannot remarry her. This is said to be an abomination before the LORD. Here in Hosea, God finds national Israel to be adulterous and divorces her. National Israel, as history tells us, is wed to all forms of secularism and Christless Judaism. We have already seen how this northern kingdom tied herself to Baals/husbands. Some dispensationalists have claimed that God will bring Israel back to her original place under the law with the rebuilding of the temple after this "parenthetical age" of the church. This cannot be on two accounts. One, the law was never meant to accomplish justification after the fall, only Christ (Gal. 3:10–14). Second, for God to remarry national Israel would be a violation of that very law and would be an act abominable to God Himself. In this same theological context, Jeremiah 3:1 records God saying that after the divorce, He will not return to her because the land is polluted. So also, in verse 8, God proclaims that He has divorced her for her adulteries. Israel, as we shall see shortly, must die and be born as something new.

Covenant divorce is something Israel has never heard before, but no sooner does He make this statement than He makes a promise.

---

13 Calvin, *Commentaries Vol XIII*, 54.
14 The moral law, which we find summarized in the Ten Commandments, applied before it was instituted at Sinai. It was always sin to commit adultery, to worship false gods, and to murder.
15 WCF XIX.4, 2nd LBC XIX.4.

Paradoxical Promise

Just like Eden, where curse and blessing are joined, no sooner is their condemnation proclaimed than the promise of the new covenant is made. This is God as holy *and* as love. It is the paradoxical promise where Israel is cast off and drawn near all at once. Because of His merciful and gracious love that is unconditional, not based on us, He can make such promises. They will be like the sand of the sea. Where it was said "*lo-ammi,*" it will be said, "you are the children of the living God."

This is not God restoring the covenant of Moses. There is something polemically different between what we see here and what was seen in the Mosaic. If you read through Exodus as the covenant is presented, it is desperately different from the Abrahamic.[16] They barely receive the covenant, Moses returns to the mountain, and they cast the golden calves, breaking the covenant. They constantly transgress and are constantly given mercy, but now it is done. There will be no more mercy under Moses because God is no longer "I Am" for them under that covenant.

But a new covenant will be established. This is the Jeremiah 31 covenant, the covenant of grace, which has been working as a promise throughout the Old Testament thus far. There are no longer conditions for man because we cannot fulfill them. When God makes conditions, He knows we will fail them. That is why His covenant of grace, which provides for us to be saved and enter into rest with Christ, has nothing to do with what we do. It is a paradoxical promise because it seems to be the same promise as before, when it is not. They will not just be called *children of Israel* or *children of Abraham*, but *children of the Living God*.

As for the immeasurable nature of Israel, it cannot be of the bloodline descendants. A simple internet search could give you a rough number. Only in the church can we say the number of the sons of Israel, the true sons of Abraham, are beyond measurement and counting, fulfilling the promise God made to Abraham in Genesis 15.

"And the children of Judah and Israel will appoint for themselves one head." He is going to bring Israel and Judah back to Palestine, not to fix the Mosaic covenant, but to provide for the coming of His son as federal head, the fulfillment of the promises. This is about Christ, not Moses. God spares the nation for this purpose (and the sake of the believing remnant). Here we see the shift necessary for all the Gentiles of the church to be saved. God provides for His salvation to be spread beyond those national boundaries as the people will be "sown" in the diaspora (Acts 8:4). It is because of the horrors of Hosea that we have hope of salvation. The driving force here is

---

16 This is the running theme of Galatians 3.

the proclamation of divorce and the reforming of the bride. Without this, there would be no hope for the Gentiles. He has been so merciful, and even in this, even as God is proclaiming divorce on an idolatrous people, He still pronounces love in the gospel.

As for "great will be the day of Jezreel," in terms of a single day, our best point of reference is Pentecost. The gospel sowing went out to the nations and continued to go out thereafter. Today, the church spans the globe on every continent.[17] Truly we can say, great is the day of God's sowing.

Chapter 2

Up until this point in history, God's elect, with rare exception, have been within the physical nation.[18] Ever since Abraham, there has always been a *spiritual* people with a *spiritual* circumcision awaiting a *spiritual* inheritance embedded within the *physical* people with *physical* circumcision claiming *physical* inheritance. So you wind up with guys like Ahab who are Jews but not actually saved. The challenge of the prophetic idiom in Hosea and the Old Testament, as I said before, is figuring out whom God is addressing. In Romans 9:24–26, Paul quotes this passage[19] as proof the Gentiles would be called alongside the Jews. We have divinely inspired commentary to tell us of ultimate significance of our passage. The Holy Spirit recorded through Paul the meaning of what the Holy Spirit recorded through Hosea, that a transition would take place from Israel to the church, wherein the Gentiles would be grafted in to the true Israel. See also Romans 11:16–24.

God commands in 2:1, "Say to your brothers, 'my people' and to your sisters, 'you have found mercy (*ruchamah*).'" The audience changes back and forth as we progress through these chapters, a cycle of judgment and promise. This is the final word of promise before returning to the judgment material, and it is addressed to the elect. They are the ones who hear and heed God, and they are called to exhort one another as brothers; though they will suffer with the reprobates in the nation, they are still God's people and have received mercy in eternal things. When a saint enters glory, regardless of ethnicity, he comes face to face with the saints from all of history, and the elect Israelites of Hosea's day can say to them, "You are my people, because in our God there is mercy, there is compassion, there is Ruchamah."

Hosea 2:2 says, "Contend with your mother. Contend because she is not my wife and I am not her husband, that she turns aside for her harlotries from before her and her adulteries from between her breasts." This is God striving

---
17 This apparently includes Antarctica, believe it or not—people and penguins both declare the glory of God in their own way. See https://en.wikipedia.org/wiki/List_of_Antarctic_churches.
18 You have outliers like Melchizedek in Abraham's day, Job, Naaman, and others.
19 The quotation combines passages from 1:10 and 2:23 that address the same theme.

with the nation. The Mosaic covenant is broken, but there remains a people, a remnant that includes the genetic line for the Messiah; they are part of God's plan. God is charging the individuals, the elect who hear His voice, to bring charges against the mother because she is not the wife anymore. He is still working through the nation to bring out the elect. He is still going to bring the nation into the land, and His elect will still be constrained to that nation up through the ministry of Christ. God says that national Israel is not His wife. But within that nation, God will still be faithful to His elect. My-People are still within Not-My-People.

He is calling upon the true children to continue the call for repentance within that nation because the Abrahamic/Davidic/grace covenant is still at play in Israel. In that covenant, man is not required to fulfill anything, so the covenant is not broken, and the elect will not be cast out. There will still be the offspring like stars and sand, there will still be the son of David to rule forever. God says, "It only depends on Me, therefore it *cannot* be broken." He is still calling for repentance through His elect, the individual saints whom Christ begets through the labor of the church (or, in this case, Israel). This is how sinners are made children of the living God. God calls upon the individual members of Israel who have been called, who have been saved, and who hear His voice to plead with their nation and fellow man. God says to bring charges against their mother/nation because she is no longer under the Mosaic protection. He says to call her to put away her adulteries from between her breasts, those idols she clutches and refuses to abandon. The nation cannot rely on her lineage to receive blessing; the people will not receive mercy and grace by genetic default. They must be born again as legitimate children to receive God's covenant-faithfulness. As idolatrous children of whoredom, they cannot be children of God unless they are born again.

To understand God's people within Not-My-People, we can examine Daniel in exile. He is both *lo ammi* as part of the nation, but he is *ammi* individually as called and saved. We too are nationally (and Mosaically) *lo ammi* with no promise of land in Palestine, but under the covenant of grace, we are made children of the living God with an inheritance of "land" in glory. Ultimately, we receive the new heavens and the new earth with the True Israel.[20]

In verse 3, God speaks of stripping Israel naked as her birthday and exposing her. We are focusing on shame, on concepts of intimacy undone. God is saying He must remove all these adornments and clothing stained by her adultery, those markings of her other lovers. She has to be without defense,

---

20 I have long been fascinated by the way OT books, particularly the Psalms, seem to play on the semantic range of *erets*, which can mean either "land" or "earth." Translators have played on this same concept in translating Psalm 37:11 as "the meek will inherit the land" and Christ's reference of it in Matthew 5:5 as "they will inherit the earth."

exposed, and aware of the shame of what she has done. Like Adam and Eve, she must be naked and ashamed because there is intimacy in the resulting vulnerability. He is exposing her so that she can feel the shame of her sin and become vulnerable before her true husband.

". . . kill her with thirst." As a native Arizonan, I can attest to the danger of being left in the wilderness without water. God is using the imagery of the desert wasteland, and says He will take her out and set her like a dry land and slay her with thirst. So why is God using imagery of death? This seems to be an abrupt change of direction. He has spoken of divorce and exile, showing her the promised land no longer belongs to her, but why switch from punishment/divorce to death/execution? Because she must be reborn. When we enter into that sacred rite of baptism, it is an image of burial and resurrection. We must die to the world, sin, and self and be reborn in order to be called children of God. For Christ's church to be His, for her to be recast, she has to die and be reborn. The nation is lost, sent into exile, but He will recover His Bride from that remnant. It will never again be just about the physical nation. At this point there is still a bloodline and national identity, but now God is going to remove her to such an extent that she will never fully regain that identity. It will be as though the nation has died like the mythological phoenix, and from the ashes will rise the church, God's people.

". . . for sons of harlotry are they." Once again this really strikes us as merciless because of the literalism. The mother has committed the sin and now her children will be punished? Here, though, the children and the mother are one. The point is that these are national children. As national children they will no longer receive mercy. Like Daniel, they will not be given national blessings in exile. He was removed from the land, unable to call it his own. He suffered the curses of Sinai but had the blessings of the covenant of grace.

In this concept of striving with the mother and bringing charges, there is an exhortation embedded for us. We look at Israel and see the remnant within that is faithful to God. They are seeking God's will and striving to be faithful amidst a group that bears the same name, claims the same things, but is unfaithful and does not seek after God. It is the same with the church today. How many do we see in the world who claim the name of Christ and presume to be under the blessings of Scripture yet go seeking after idols that have only changed in name from Hosea's time. They seek after gods of wealth, health, and prosperity, and claim to be under the gospel. We must strive with the visible church to be faithful, to lovingly and humbly challenge those who claim the name of Christ to seek after the God of Scripture, to work out their salvation with fear and trembling, to return to the love shown in Scripture.

In understanding these concepts of intimacy, vulnerability, trust, and how quickly that can all be lost, it is important to see the use of marital imagery in the Scriptures. There was once a *Weekly World News* article[21] about a man studying and following every known religion, just in case one of them was right. Laughable as that may be, our daily practices are not so far off. Many presume that if they are part of a church, it does not matter what other gods they follow because grace covers everything. So often we presume that if we are following after God along with our idols, all is well with our souls. A large part of the marital imagery is that when there is adultery, that intimacy is lost. Even with repentance, it takes time and labor to rebuild that intimacy. We so often presume that there are no repercussions for our sins. If we are truly saved, God will preserve us to the end, but that is no license to sin. It is ludicrous to presume that within a covenant marriage, earthly or heavenly, we can sin without ramifications. We must be faithful. When we sin, stumble, and fall, there is recovery, but there are repercussions. There is a loss of intimacy. As Thomas Watson says,

> Sin is the peace-breaker. It is like an incendiary in the family that sets husband and wife at variance. It makes God fall out with us. Sin is the birthplace of our sorrows and the grave of our comforts. But that which may most of all disfigure the face of sin and make it appear abominable is this: It crucified our Lord! It made Christ veil His glory and lose His blood.[22]

It is a uniquely Christian mindset that allows us to view sin in a new way. We should not see sin in terms of absolute condemnation and hell any more than good works as merit that earns a place in heaven. To quote Lloyd-Jones:

> How do you regard your sins and your failures? What is the first thing that comes into your mind when you sin? Is it fear of punishment? If it is, you are still under the law in your thinking. If it is rather a feeling that you have grieved the One who loves you, then it is Christian thinking.[23]

On the earthly level, this serves as a serious caution to husbands and wives. The sanctity of the marriage must be carefully guarded. Intimacy is easily lost and painfully regained.

If you wonder why you lack significant growth in your Christian walk and love for your Savior, then I ask, have you sought to be faithful and grow intimate with your Savior? Our salvation is not something that comes by our works. Even our sanctification is something God accomplishes through us,

---

21 For those who do not remember this, it was a fake black and white tabloid printed for humor's sake. I am still wondering what happened to bat-boy and the shaved monkey Saddam Hussein adopted with Bin Laden.
22 Thomas Watson, "The Mystery of the Lord's Supper" in *The Puritans on the Lord's Supper*, ed. Don Kistler (Morgan: Soli Deo Gloria, 1997), 145.
23 D. Martyn Lloyd-Jones, *Ephesians 2*, 92.

but sanctification does not come apart from the labor of the Christian. I urge you to seek after your Savior, the holy and sovereign God, as a spouse whom you desperately love. Seek Him in worship, study, and prayer. As Proverbs 5:18–20 tells us, "Rejoice in the wife of your youth. . . . Let her breasts fill you at all times with delight; be intoxicated always in her love. Why should you be intoxicated, my son, with a forbidden woman and embrace the bosom of an adulteress?" Likewise, we ought to seek after the Bridegroom who loved us when we were yet unlovable.

Hosea 2:5–8: Little did she know

In Charles Dickens' *Great Expectations*, we meet Pip, a lower-class apprentice to a foundry worker. A lawyer comes and says Pip is going to be sent to school and prepared for great things. Pip assumes the secret benefactor is the grandmother of a childhood crush, and the eccentric widow seems to feed this assumption. But at the end, Pip discovers who the real benefactor is, which turns everything upside down for him.[24]

Israel has been greatly blessed, and she is attributing her glory, her bounty, her wealth, to false gods.[25] Where God took pity on His elect within the nation, that national ease emboldened sinners to further rebellion. All this fulfills Deuteronomy 31:20. She has behaved shamefully in pursing after her other gods, her lovers, while the individual bastard children are the result of national infidelity. She says she will go after her lovers. She believes other gods, like Baal and Dagon, have given her all her things. In this BC agrarian society, you would pray to your national gods to bless you, give rain for crops, cause animals to reproduce, stave off locusts, and so forth. Israel has come to believe that through sacrifices to false gods she has prospered. This is her fatal misperception.

People tend to be shortsighted. When I was growing up, my family had a dog named Sam. When visitors came, my parents would give them a dog treat. Once Sam took the biscuit from the guest, she would follow them around and dote on them for this great display of affection. The visitor had done nothing significant, and it was my parents who suggested and paid for the dog biscuit in the first place. The dog, however, in her shortsightedness, did not figure this out; she only saw the person giving the biscuit. We often do the same thing. We look with praise to our employers, our talents, our whatever, and fail to see the source from which these things come.

God saw Israel attribute all her blessings to these false gods when He gave them to her. Because of her sinful ingratitude, He promises to hedge her way

---

24 No spoilers here. You are welcome.
25 Under Jeroboam II, electric boogaloo, the broader borders of Israel were restored. See 2 Kings 14:23–26.

up with thorns. "She will pursue her lovers but not reach them, and she will seek them but not find." When God's people make idols out of good and beautiful providence that should have been used to praise God, sometimes God makes it painful and difficult to pursue after them. He makes this wall of thorns so that when she tries to pursue the idols, He can teach her not to go that way. How often do we do this ourselves with our idols? Even when we find ourselves entangled in thorns, we still strive after them. We pursue sin so violently that we are hurt ourselves in the process.

Now we shift back to the church within the nation. At Hosea's time, the church is found within the nation of Israel. In her frustrated efforts, we are seeing God's harsh providence for His church. This is the bride who will return to her husband after chastisement. Not all of national Israel would do this (some even remained in the Assyrian diaspora, as well as those of Judah later taken to Babylon), but the redeemed remnant did. She must be utterly destitute to return, and what is more incredible, the husband takes her back.

Verse 8: "She did not know that I have given to her ..." These gifts described as grain, wine, and oil seem like repetition at first, and God did provide Israel with these literal things as the staples of life. The gravity of these three things, however, are as images of Christ presented in types and shadows through the Old Testament economy. Whenever Hosea uses these three together—grain, wine, and oil—they are the images of the Lord's Supper representing Jesus.[26] The nation is disregarding the gospel of salvation (to the extent that God has revealed it). There are even extravagancies of gold and silver, but she lavishes it on other lovers, even "gold she made for Baal" possibly playing on the language to say that she not only gave to a false god, but she literally made the idol from it. Instead of laying up her treasures in heaven, Israel has squandered God's gifts on false gods and temporary nations.[27]

It is a shame that so few people in the church take the time to read Ecclesiastes because it puts everything in perspective. *Hevel hevelim*—"vanity of vanities"—recurs over and over again in Solomon's sermon. All of life is vapor and nothingness, mist and smoke. You pour everything you have into this world, then you die, and someone else gets it. Israel invested herself in that which would pass away, and we spend our lives pursuing the temporal to the neglect of the eternal. Just as church attendance is a reflection of our hearts, when we neglect the eternal for the temporal, our heart shows.

What do you pursue in your life that is fruitless or idolatrous? What do you not do to the glory of God? Where you spend your time and effort, there

---

[26] This is true for much of the Old Testament as well. There's even a proto-Lord's Supper with Melchizedek and Abraham.

[27] Israel had paid tribute to Assyria for protection, but then sought to do the same with Egypt and wound up being conquered by the Assyrians who they thought would protect them.

will your heart be also. Are you giving your best to the world and giving the last, if any, to God? What God has given us, we often squander on our idols until we find ourselves on the ash heap.

With young men in our era, a predominant sin is pornography. One thing that they often miss is that not only are they sinning in their lust, but they are using God's providence as means to pursue after sin. They take God's blessings (time, energy, financial investments of computer and internet) and lavish them on idols. Where do you spend your blessings? We need the glasses of Scripture to cure our short-sightedness and understand who it is from whom all blessings flow.

Chastisement or Condemnation

Hosea 2:9–13

> And she will pursue her lovers but not reach them, and she will seek them but not find. And she will say, "I will go and return to my former husband because better for me was then than now."
>
> And she did not know that I have given to her grain and new wine and oil and much silver to her and gold she made for Baal.
>
> For thus I will return and take my grain in its time and my new wine in its season and I will save my wool and my linen to cover her nakedness.
>
> And now I will uncover her shamelessness (genitals) for the eyes of her lovers, and a man will not rescue her from my hand.
>
> And I will cease (shabbath) all of her rejoicing, her feast of her month and her sabbath and her appointed time/meeting.

The question arises, "Is God chastising national Israel in love or is He condemning her in wrath?" It is actually both. It is condemnation to Israel as a whole, but chastisement to the elect within Israel.

The first concept is reclaiming. In verses 9 and 12, God declares a removing of providence. As we saw before, God gave her all these things, food and wealth, but she attributed them to false gods. Baal is specifically mentioned here because of his connection to fertility and agriculture, which are essential to prosperity in Israel. They want kids, cattle, and crops, and Baal seemed to be the guy to ask. They made sacrifices to Baal of what God had given to them, and God is using this extended metaphor of lover, of husband and wife, to show the deep level of betrayal. We do not always sense this in our sin of idolatry against God, but our God is a jealous God. He says He is our Husband, and to seek another god is equivalent to adultery. This helps us see the gravity of our sins. It is not just undone by saying sorry. Though God promises that

He is faithful to forgive if we are faithful to repent, it does not mean that it is not costly. There is a great cost, Christ just pays it on our behalf, and all we see is chastisement perfectly measured to accomplish grace in us. God often chastises and teaches us by removing those things we turned into idols.

God is watching His Bride praising her lovers for God's blessings and then spending those blessings on them. After He expresses the depth of betrayal, He promises to show just how much the false god is able to help. God says He will take back His wine and grain, wool, and flax, and uncover her nakedness. Again, this is not to be erotic but to expose sin and shame. In Lamentations 1:8, we see this expression of shamelessness until nakedness is exposed. Sin may seem comfortable, especially sexual sin, as long as it is hidden. Once it is brought into the open, the burn of the shame appears. God is saying that He will go in to where she is, take her out into the open, expose her sin, and then she will realize the gravity. Specifically, she is being exposed "for the eyes of her lovers," meaning that she is left defenseless before their exploitation.

Then God speaks of the end of mirth and Sabbaths in verse 11. It peaks the compounding offense. Israel attributed God's blessings to other gods, praised them, and used God's providence to make idols of those gods. Finally, she used festivals, feasts, and Sabbaths which that should have been to honor Yahweh to worship false gods and engage in pagan debauchery.

There is actually a pun here. The word *sabbath*, which means to cease, comes in verb and noun form. Before Christ's resurrection, the Sabbath ceasing came at the end of the week. Here God is saying that He will cease their ceasing, end the resting from toil. This is not about abolishing the principle of Sabbath-keeping but about removing the times of festivals and feasting. God gave her more than she needed. So Israel kept what she needed, gave the glory to false gods, and gave the abundance, the excess, to those gods. She held these feasts and festivals that should have been in Yahweh's honor and dedicated them to idols. She used them as opportunities to be drunk and unfaithful. She abused the grace, so He promises to bring an end to her seasons of rest.

The Jewish Sabbath was an image and shadow of what Christ would secure.[28] It is an eschatological image. The Jews have been brought into the Promised Land, and the Sabbath combined with that creates an image or shadow of glory. Now God is promising to drag them out of the Promised Land and its rest. There is no Sabbath rest for Assyrian or Babylonian slaves.

There is a second dimension here that is more positive, though. God would take away the Saturday Sabbath that they imperfectly labored toward through the week in the time to come. As the Jews rested on Saturday, they saw all their incomplete works that symbolized their insufficiency under the law.

---

28 The Christian Sabbath still is an image of heaven, but in a different light now.

That Sabbath is taken away and replaced with a Sunday Sabbath, a Christian Sabbath that is earned by Christ on their behalf. There remains a Sabbath rest for God's people under the new covenant (Heb. 4:8–11) that foreshadows heaven, where we rest in Jesus' work and then labor in gratitude (Matt. 11:28).

He is going to take this land that she cultivated and make it wilderness. Everything she considered the blessings of false gods will now produce fruit for the animals because she disregarded God.

She adorned herself with rings and jewelry, meaning God's riches being spent on idols. This is like the wife wearing the husband's gifts of jewelry in order to seek out a new lover.

In verse 13, there is another pun about Baal. We think of Baal as just the false god, but it also meant "master." It literally says, "I will visit her the feast days of the Baals." It means, "I will punish her the days of Baals," and "I will appoint over her the days of the masters." She says that she wants *Baal*, not Yahweh, so He says that if that is what she wants, He will give her all the days of the *masters* she can bear. He is promising Assyrian masters and slave-drivers over her because she has forgotten her husband.

All this condemnation is based on Israel's failure under the Mosaic covenant and law. Israel responded to the reading of the law and said she would do those things (Ex. 24:3). As one party, the people promised to uphold the stipulations and exalt God over all things. God always fulfills His portion of the covenant, but God told them, "When you fail, these are the curses." He says "when" because He knew they would.[29] We see the Mosaic is in large part a covenant of works, though there is grace in there too.[30] There is grace in the covenant, especially in how God honored the covenant after they broke it. Just as Adam broke the original covenant of works, Israel has broken the Mosaic, but now it would no longer be extended. To find grace, they would have to come to the new covenant in Christ.

Not only is this a historical record, but there is application to us. God has given providence to all of humanity in common grace as well. Any man that has any thing has it because God has given it to him. Every thing that lives lives because of God. All people, in one sense, are guilty of this sin of which Israel is being condemned. People will attribute their blessings to anything but God, especially to themselves.

---

29 Deuteronomy 4:25–26: "When thou begettest sons and sons' sons, and ye have become old in the land, and have done corruptly, and have made a graven image, a similitude of anything, and have done the evil thing in the eyes of Jehovah, to provoke Him to anger:—I have caused to testify against you this day the heavens and the earth, that ye do perish utterly hastily from off the land whither ye are passing over the Jordan to possess it; ye do not prolong days upon it, but are utterly destroyed" (Young's Literal Translation).

30 The Mosaic covenant is portraying in miniature both covenant of works and covenant of grace. So it's both covenants and neither altogether.

God has given you all that you have in possessions, relationships, health, etc. How do you use them? How often do we fall short of using them to God's glory? What sins do you harbor for the sake of your own mirth? What sins do you hide away and assume that all is well? Rest assured, your sins will find you out, and God will bring an end to the mirth for which you harbored them. This is actually grace, though, for God's people. It functions differently for us because we are not under the Mosaic covenant but the covenant of grace. In the Christian life, in our harboring of sins for mirth, God seeks us out in chastisement and brings those sins to an end for our own good as we are being prepared for glory. As Spurgeon said, "The hardest blow that He ever laid upon his child was inflicted by the hand of love."[31]

For the reprobate, they will find the end of their sin unto mirth in the day of judgment. We need to fear the God of providence. We do not like the concept of fear of God, but it is crucial, and our souls should be "trembling at the threatenings" as well as "embracing the promises of God."[32] It is fear in the sense of respect and understanding. When we look upon the God who has made all things and sustains all things, we ought to fear. He requires justice for sin, and that should make us fearful. We should find rest and peace in Christ because of this, not in spite of it. So often, as Christians, we often like to treat our sin lightly, but all the pain and sorrow of the husband scorned, cheated, and mocked were absorbed by Christ. All the punishment due to the Bride, the suffering of divorce, Christ absorbed on our behalf. We should feel sorrow for our sin *and* joy that it is paid for in full.

The Wooing Husband—Hosea 2:14–18

This passage begins with a "therefore," which we would expect to be followed by condemnations, like God's statement to Moses about wiping out the people and beginning again (Ex. 32:10). But God promises to allure Israel, woo her, and speak tenderly to her in the wilderness. It helps us gain a little glimpse of the master plan wherein God seeks after an unfaithful people *because* it is the best way He can show His steadfast love. Because she has done all these things, He will take her out and woo her. He will recast her as His Bride. He will take her to the wilderness and speak comfort.

The wilderness is about dire circumstances, with limited access to water and food. The desert imagery portrays both isolation and exile here. When God took Israel out of Egypt in the Exodus, she was isolated from the world. He led her through this long route wherein He spoke to her, established covenant with her, and made her His people. There is exile in this passage, and

---
31 Charles Spurgeon, "God's Thoughts of Peace, and Our Expected End," sermon, May 29, 1887.
32 WCF XIV.2, 2nd LBC XIV.2.

there is fearful trial here, but there is positive purpose as well. This is the process by which He establishes His people. Sometimes God has to isolate us in order to woo us.

We ourselves exist as a people in exile. We function more like Joseph in Pharaoh's house, or Daniel in Nebuchadnezzar's, than David in Jerusalem. This is part of the two-kingdoms doctrine.[33] As an American, I live and interact with my nation, knowing that God has not made covenant with my nation. Israelites would function this way while in exile. The only promise that remained, because it was unconditional, was that the Messiah would come through David's line and be born in the land. The nation would never be what it once was, and the blood of the sacrifice would not be placed on the mercy seat of the ark, though the bulk of the ritual would limp along until it found its fulfillment in Christ.

New Vineyards

God promises vineyards to her in the wilderness. In dry ground, He will give her bounty. He is going to take her out of the land of milk and honey, leaving it to the wild animals, but He promises vineyards to her in the wilderness. It is bounty from the unlikely ground. The vineyards are also inherently permanent. They take years to tend and cultivate. One does not plant vineyards outside the hotel room. When they are outcast, despairing, and isolated, when they are incapable of providing for themselves, God will give them vineyards and fruit He has long cultivated in that desolate place. From unlikely grounds, from unlikely vines, He will bring forth fruit. God will use the wilderness to provide for His people in the heat and turmoil.

Israel, as such, never really returned from the exile. Northern and southern kingdoms were cast out to sojourn in the wilderness and be wooed. In that sojourning, even with a physical return to Canaan for many, the elect were awaiting a greater promised land and city built without hands, like their ancestor Abraham (Heb. 11:13–16). Yet God had already been growing, pruning, watering, and sustaining the bloodline for Christ. It is out of dry, desert ground that God will bring the root and young plant of the Messiah (Isa. 53:2).

The valley of Achor will become a door of hope. Achor is named in Joshua 7:24–26 through the stoning of Achan and his family as punishment for violating God's command for *herem* warfare. They were to cleanse the land with a vengeance and keep nothing for themselves. Achan kept spoils, and this resulted in Israel's defeat at Ai. Achor means "trouble," and God promises

---

[33] For this, I would highly recommend VanDrunen's book, *Living in God's Two Kingdoms: A Biblical Vision for Christianity and Culture* (Wheaton: Crossway, 2010).

to make it a door of hope. This is to say that through trial and tribulation on account of sin, God will bring hope. For the southern kingdom, there would also be an end to the exile and a return in the hope of the Messiah. But there is something even better embedded here. In the Valley of Achor, we see a place associated with punishment, suffering, and death. It becomes a doorway of hope, just as Golgotha and the cross were a place of suffering and death but became symbols of our hope.

God says that she will answer as she did in her youth. The word here can mean either *answer* or *sing*, and given Hosea's frequent wordplay before, it is no stretch to assume he is using both meanings. She will respond in faith to God's work in her life, but she will also sing as she did in her youth, specifically after she escapes from Egypt. In Exodus 15, we encounter the song of Moses and the song of Miriam after the crossing of the Red Sea. Moses has another song in Deuteronomy 32. Deborah and Barak sang in Judges 5, and Hannah sang her prayer in 1 Samuel 2. David sang before the Lord in 2 Samuel 6:5 and 2 Samuel 22, and, of course, we have all the psalms that precede Hosea. In Psalm 33, 96, 98, and 149, the writer exhorts the audience to sing a new song, and Psalm 144 is a declaration that the psalmist will do so! Even Isaiah calls for the singing of a new song (42:10), though it would be a long time before that would be fulfilled. Hosea couches these songs of praise and adoration in terms of the love songs of a beloved and loving bride. There will not be new songs of redemption recorded until Mary sings at the coming of Christ.[34]

From Baali to Ishi

God says that on that day Israel will no longer call Him *baali*, "my baal," but *ishi*, "my husband." As *ish* is the counterpart to *isha*, which is "wife," the counterpart to Baal or "master" is "servant." This is in part to address Israel's religious syncretism. They formed a false god that partly reflected Yahweh and partly reflected Baal. But if that was all Hosea intended, he would contrast Baal with Yahweh.

Israel was a theocracy under Mosaic covenant, wherein God primarily related to the people as Master. This concept is repeated in Jeremiah 31:32, where it says, "though I was *Baal* to them." The author of Hebrews in 8:9 translates that phrase as "I disregarded them,"[35] which is equally true. God disregarded them, showed no concern to them, because they had broken the covenant of Sinai with their *Master* in many ways, part of which was this religious syncretism where they tried to worship Yahweh as Baal. Now, Israel's

---

34 Luke 1:46ff. The possible exception to this is in Nehemiah 12, but the song itself is not recorded and may not be a new song, but is likely the singing of psalms already written. Psalm 137 (and possibly 44) is written in Babylon, but it is a song of lament, not a song like Israel sang in her youth.

35 The author of Hebrews follows the Septuagint Greek over the Hebrew on this point.

relationship is moving from master/servant to husband/wife. It is true that there will always be a sense of Christ as our Master and Lord. He will always be King as much as prophet and priest. But as Israel is being reborn, the emphasis shifts from master to husband. Transcendence was emphasized over immanence as God spoke from Sinai in darkness, fire, and earthquake. But in the new relationship, a new level of immanence and intimacy will be discovered through Christ, the sympathetic mediator. As Owen succinctly put it, "God dwells no more on Sinai."[36]

Like the annoyingly loud late-night infomercial, "But wait, there's more!" We saw that *Baal* has this dual meaning of Baal and master. *Ish* also has two translation options. It means both husband and **man.** This is a prophecy of the incarnation! God says, "I will come to you, and you will know me as a man!"[37]

Christ will be more intimate to His people than a spouse through the incarnation and because He will be perpetually close through His Holy Spirit. He will labor in their hearts, and they will not even remember the idols they once served.[38] In the new heavens and the new earth, He will make her His own, remove the names of the Baals/masters from her mouth, and she will remember them no more.

He will make a new covenant, the covenant of grace. It is a new covenant and yet an old covenant. God presented it in Genesis as a promise, but it will be ratified in Christ's blood. Hosea uses a synecdoche (where a part represents the whole) to denote all of creation as affected by this work when it reaches its final fulfillment. God will establish eternal peace for His people. When God reigns as sovereign king over the new heavens and new earth, He will abolish bow, sword, and war from earth and make His people lie down in safety. There will be eternal peace, as Isaiah 11:6–9 prophesies. This is essentially the same image of the impenetrable city walls with perpetually open gates in Revelation 21.

Again, we must see ourselves as exiles, as sojourners, and remember that this life is temporary. Our isolation and exile are for a time, and we ought never to cease to pray for Christ's return. As we pass through the wilderness,

---

36 Owen, *Hebrews*, 313.
37 It could be argued that this is even the primary meaning, because *baal* can mean husband as well. So the overall sense is God saying, "You will call me man and intimate husband, even the Son of Man, instead of Baal and knowing me as masterful husband." There may be another reference to this concept in Psalm 49:2, where a distinction is made between "Sons of Adam" and "Sons of Ish." Translators and commentators alike rightly recognize this as those of low estate and high, but it could also be about unbelievers still under Adam's headship contrasted to believers under the headship of the bridegroom. Augustine landed at this conclusion on 49:2, but by a different vein of reasoning.
38 We will not see the fullness of this until glory, but that is pretty common for OT prophetic literature. Christ's first and second comings are often related in the same breath.

waiting for that day, we must remember that it is through the wilderness that God brings forth fruit in us.

Do you relate to God as distant master or as intimate spouse? Do you seek Him as one would cast a message in a bottle upon the waters, or do you appeal to Him in prayer as Father and Husband?

Betrothal and Vows—Hosea 2:19–20

> And I will betroth you to me forever, and I will betroth you to me in righteousness and in justice/judgment and in covenant-faithfulness and in mercies/Ruchamah.
>
> And I will betroth you to me in faithfulness/integrity, and you will know Yahweh.

In *The Bride of Christ*, Claude Chavasse explains Christ's earthly ministry as the act of marrying the Bride, and it is only through Christ's work that these verses before us make sense.[39] God says "betroth" (covenantal engagement) instead of "marry" because while Christ's work functions as the vows and marriage contract, it is only betrothal until the individual believer has responded in faith. We are not eternally justified or justified at the cross, but Christ engages us to Himself there.[40]

Here we see some contrast between the metaphor of marriage and the reality of the covenant of grace. We might speak of earthly betrothal in terms of faithfulness and love or use a poetic hyperbole to say the marriage is forever. It would be awkward to speak of marriage in integrity, but we would never use this language of judgment, mercies, and righteousness. It would not bode well for a husband to tell his wife that he married her out of mercy.

We are seeing aspects of Christ's marriage to His church. He betroths her forever, in a covenant of grace that is perfectly designed to provide *unbreakable* salvation. He marries her in a way that she cannot be divorced from Him. He betroths her in righteousness because He accomplishes righteousness and imputes it to her to clothe her for the wedding. He betroths her in justice/judgment as He expiates her sin and propitiates her.[41] He turns away the wrath of God from us by absorbing it on the cross. He marries her in covenant faithfulness, in *hesed*, the steadfast love that endures forever. He marries her in mercies and grace, loving her when she is unlovable and loving her perfectly

---

39 Chavasse, *The Bride of Christ*, 65.
40 Jesus accomplished our salvation at the cross, but that salvation is not applied until we respond in faith to the gospel. That is when justification is accomplished for us.
41 Expiation is the removing of our guilt, while propitiation is about satisfying God's wrath, turning it from us to Christ who absorbs it on our behalf and making us acceptable through His righteousness.

to the uttermost. In all these things, He betroths her in faithfulness, declaring His marriage vows on the cross. He paid the greatest cost to betroth an unfaithful bride to Himself. As Spurgeon once put it:

> Are you satisfied with what you have been towards the Well-beloved? Are you content with your conduct towards the Bridegroom of your souls? I trow [think] that you are not. . . . He loves, He loves on, and He loves still. Many waters cannot quench his love, neither can the floods drown it. It is indeed "marvelous lovingkindness." Can you think of a better adjective than that? I cannot, yet I am conscious that even it does not fully express the miraculous character of this all-enduring love which will not take our "No" for an answer, but still says, "Yes, yea I will betroth thee unto me in righteousness and in judgment and in lovingkindness, and in mercies . . ." Oh, this wonderful, this matchless, this unparalleled, this inconceivable, this infinite love![42]

Call and Response—Hosea 2:21–23

> And it will be in that day, I will answer/be afflicted, declares Yahweh, I will answer the heavens and they will answer the earth.
>
> And the earth will answer the grain and the wine and the oil and they will answer, "Jezreel" (or "God sows").
>
> And I will sow her to me in the earth and I will have compassion on Lo-Ruchamah and I will say to Lo-Ammi, "You are my people" and he will say, "You are my God."

God says He will answer the heavens, the heavens will answer the earth, and it will answer with grain. Unless we take this in the context of Hosea's wordplay, it will be seen as nothing more than God providing harvest for man's survival. God does indeed decree rain to provide crops for man to eat and live. The earth produces grain and grapes, but Hosea is using language that is too peculiar to just convey agriculture.

There is a second layer here. It says God will *anah*. This can mean God will answer, or something else entirely. It can be rendered that God will be afflicted, and answer the heavens, and respond to the earth's need. The earth will have grain, wine, and oil, and the people will answer that God sows. Prophesying the incarnation, Yahweh will be afflicted as Christ, God in flesh, and answer the heavens, God's requirement of justice.[43] The heavens will answer the earth, which entombed the Christ, God incarnate, by sending a messenger from the throne to roll back the stone. The earth will answer by giving up her

---

[42] Charles Spurgeon, *Treasury of the Old Testament* (Grand Rapids: Zondervan, 1968), 404.
[43] Of course, it is not God Himself who suffers and dies, but we are using the Communicatio Idiomatum. See the 2nd LBC VIII.7, WCF VIII.7.

dead (parallel to Revelation 20:13) as the first fruits of the resurrection and the vindication of the Savior. From the earth will come wine and bread (made from grain and oil), the images of the sacrifices, as well as the elements of the Lord's Supper sacrament that give joy and strength. Christ will be afflicted to become the bread-and-wine Savior, and the people will answer, "God has sown" and "God provides."[44] Through this, they who believe will be His people, and He will be their God.

The last line of verse 22 is that God's people will answer, "Jezreel." This takes us back to chapter 1 with Hosea's first son and the day of Jezreel/sowing. Jezreel means "scattered" or "sown." In John 12:23–24, Christ speaks of His own death as a seed sown to produce grain. Christ uses the same basic metaphor for sharing the gospel, but here it says the Bride will be sown into the earth. We have also seen how God uses this as a term for the scattering of Israel, the diaspora of exile. Jezreel is also nearly identical to the word Israel. Israel will be Jezreel, and it is God who sows. God will sow her for Himself in the earth. Israel will "perish" as the unified, physical nation as she is scattered, but through that sorrow, a church will emerge that will be far greater. At its core, that church will always be from the seed of Israel; it will always contain the remnant. The acorn may not resemble the oak tree, but it contains all the coding for the oak tree.

Hosea then returns to the second and third children's names, *Lo-Ammi* and *Lo-Ruchamah*. God told national Israel that they will not be pitied and they are not His people. The Holy Spirit that worked in Hosea worked in Paul to write Romans 9 to tell us this is not about national Israel. God is predicting His church, a spiritual Israel, mixing Jews and Gentiles. Those who were *lo ammi* will be *ammi* and shown mercy.

Chapter 3

Picasso's cubism was about showing the same object from multiple perspectives. In a similar way, Hosea's cycles become shorter as the same themes and events of indictment, charges, condemnation or punishment, and promise through the gospel are revisited in different ways. In chapter 3, there is a prologue, condemnation, and promise.

PROLOGUE

God tells Hosea to go again and love a woman (this is still Gomer) who is loved by someone else. He is called to go, find, and bring her back, even though she has been adulterous. He is commanded to love a girl who is loved

---

[44] There is a parallel here to the description of God (Jehovah Jireh) declared by Abraham after Isaac's near-sacrifice experience in Genesis 22.

by another, which will bring shame. This is what God does for His people; Christ endured the shame He despised (Heb. 12:2). Hosea must love her who loves raisin cakes. Raisins are not intrinsically evil, but these raisin cakes were associated with Baal worship.[45]

This is love in motion as command. This is not raw emotion but selfless seeking after another and her well-being. God shows love not as an *emotion* but *in motion*. When we are commanded in Scripture to love our neighbor, or even our enemy, it should function this way.[46]

Hosea bought Gomer for silver and barley in an amount that would roughly total thirty shekels of silver,[47] prophesying the blood price Judas received for betraying Christ. This price was also foreshadowed by Zechariah 11:12, where Israel paid the prophet thirty shekels as wages. It was the price of a slave (Ex. 21:32). This is further implied in Hosea by the original text, which literally says, "And I traded her for myself . . ." This shows us two things. First, this is all that Gomer is worth to the lovers whom she chose over Hosea. All we are worth to the world is the price of a slave. Second, Hosea is willing to pay for his own bride in addition to the cost of his shame. Our value to God is the blood of the incarnate deity, symbolized by thirty shekels. Christ, the creator, the sovereign God of the universe, humbled Himself to take on the form of a man, live a perfect life for us, and endure the hell we deserved so that we could be saved. He did all of *that* because *that* is what we are worth *to Him*. We are defined by that value, not the world.

Condemnation

God calls Israel to live as single or celibate for a season. Hosea and Gomer are to live as such in prophetic symbolism. In the exile, Israel will not have a temple or priests, but they will also be without those idols of the Canaanites. It will be a season of physical exile, but even in their return, the blood of the sacrifice cannot be put on the ark. There will be a waiting in the interim until Christ comes. It is similar to the way in which we are waiting in exile without new prophecy for the return of Christ, the Prophet, Priest, King, and Bridegroom.

---

[45] A case might be made though that oatmeal raisin cookies can bear false witness to being chocolate chip.

[46] There's some complicated theology here, but I'll try to keep it brief and simple. God chooses to love from His own will (what we call *ad intra* to *ad extra*), whereas we normally love in a reactionary way to character and experience (*ad intra* to *ad extra*). As Christians, we are called to draw nearer to the image of God, in which we are created and choose to love people as God chose to love us.

[47] This claim is made by the editors of the Reformation Study Bible in a footnote on the passage.

Promise

Afterward, they will turn to seek God. They will seek David their king, meaning the Davidic line. This is about the true Israel seeking Christ in the days of His incarnation. They will come in fear to the Lord and to His goodness. Most literally, it is, "They will fear the Lord and His goodness in the latter days." This is not fearful retreating or retraction, but fear to or toward the Lord. J.M. Neale describes the four kinds of fear of God, the final and greatest of which is "filial, when we fear, only and entirely because we dread to offend that God whom we love with all our hearts."[48] They will come, approaching the Lord, His goodness, and His holiness in fear. This is not paralyzing fear but an awareness of His holiness and goodness. Because God has called them, they will come.

The Rest of the Book

It does well for us to accelerate a bit, as this book is not intended to be a comprehensive commentary on Hosea. Others have done that work and done it well. We also revisit the same material as we progress through these cycles, as is common for the prophets. If this material feels rushed, that is because it is. I would love to carry you through all the eloquence of this book, but that would be a different literary undertaking.

Chapters 4–5 are the presentation of law before the comfort and hope of the gospel. As the rest of Hosea plays out, the Bride of Christ references become more scarce, so we will address these in a more rapid-fire format, viewing individual vignettes and their significance for God's people.

In 4:6, God again proclaims the destruction of Israel, meaning the nation under the Mosaic covenant, specifically in connection to the Aaronic priesthood that must be replaced by Christ's Melchizedekian priesthood where the priest never dies. *The children will be forgotten*, that is, unless they are born again through Christ's Bride of the church. This new priesthood under Christ will not profit from sin or be greedy, unlike the priests of Hosea's time (4:8).[49] Indeed, the judgment is greater for those who are called to a sacred office, as it is for church leaders today. Notice the source of their destruction: "lack of knowledge" (v. 6). This might seem strange, but it strikes upon an essential truth of Christian life. We could summarize Christian life as the gaining of and trusting in knowledge.[50] God is rejecting the Mosaic priesthood of the nation because they have not faithfully taught the truths of Scripture in which the people must have faith. Faith requires knowledge.

---

48 Cited by Charles Spurgeon in *Treasury of David* (Grand Rapids: Kregel, 1968), 167, on Psalm 34.
49 They eat the sin (which can also mean sin-offering) and their soul's desire was Israel's iniquity.
50 The Puritans described faith in terms of knowledge, assent, and trust.

He shows the ludicrous nature of Israel's whoredom in verses 12–14 as they talk to and listen to wood. God speaks of handing them over entirely to their sin, Romans 1 style, wherein the women will even escape punishment (individual but not corporate) for adultery and prostitution because it is no greater a sin than that which the men commit toward God. It is the men of Israel who are paying them as cult prostitutes! He denounces their false oath swearing in 4:15, even speaking of the once-beloved Beth-El (meaning house of God) as Beth-Aven (house of iniquity). Verse 19 speaks of a wind or spirit that has wrapped them in its wings. It is a spirit of prostitution that brings shame to them.

Jumping ahead to chapter 11, God calls Israel out of Egypt. This is where the metaphors become mixed and confusing. The immediate reference is to national Israel, referred to as one person through their ancestor, the patriarch formerly known as Jacob. God called the nation out of their slavery in the land of Egypt through Moses (as a type of Christ). This calling sets them aside as a holy people. Then God laments their turning away to idols, despite the loving and protective upbringing God provided.

This is, at the same time, a prophecy of the Messiah. Christ, the only-begotten Son, would come and be taken away to Egypt until God called Him back to Canaan with His earthly parents. In doing this, Jesus identified with God's people, retracing the steps of His Bride. Although Christ certainly never committed the sins of idolatry, those sins of God's elect were imputed to Him so that He might absorb their punishment on the cross. This runs parallel to the Davidic covenant that is also ultimately about Christ, where we see punishment doled out for sin. One of my favorite metaphors of the Torah is in the grain sacrifice, where the whole mound is anointed. Then one portion is cast into the fire, representing God's judgment, and by this the remainder is made holy. This is Christ, identifying with His people to take their sin on Himself, anointed, then cast into judgment in order to render His people holy.

We also see how we are called by God out of Egypt, a symbol of our slavery to sin.

There is an interim section that deals with the promise of exile, but then we see the Lion's roar. Given the persistent connection between Judah and the lion image, even the Old Testament Jew would have seen this as the Messiah's call. What is in shadow, however, is that the Lion's roar would be made in grief first: "My God, My God, why have you forsaken me?" Secondly, the roar would be a cry of victory in what appeared to be defeat: "It is finished." The roars of the Lion slain would call out God's people. This is more than just the return of national Israel from exile. God's children come from both east and west, even though God has just promised not to send Israel back under Egypt (though some did wind up in Egypt, like Jeremiah's captors).

God's elect come from all over the world. They come trembling, humbled, and devastated by their failure of the law, to be embraced by their Father. The immediate fulfillment is Israel's return from exile to their homes in Canaan, but spiritual Israel is called home to Christ.

In 12:12, we catch a glimpse of Christ as the Bridegroom amidst the record of Jacob. It says that Jacob fled to the land or field of Aram where he "served" or "was a servant" for a wife. Aram is a proper name for a region, whence Aramaic comes, and also is a root word for "fortress" or "citadel." It says he kept watch for a wife. Jacob was a type of Christ, who would go to the place where Aramaic was spoken, to the fortress of Jerusalem, and tend sheep as the Good Shepherd to obtain His wife. "And Israel served in/with/for a wife, and in/with/for a wife he kept/guarded." Obviously, for Jacob's context, the translation options are reduced, but for Christ, we can say that He served for His Bride, but also within and with His Bride. Christ kept His sheep in His earthly ministry, but He also kept and guarded His Bride. The subsequent record of Moses as the Prophet also foreshadows Christ, who brings the true Israel out of the Egypt of bondage to sin and guard her.

Hosea 13:11 recounts Saul being anointed king to replace Samuel as judge. God gave Israel a king in anger (for her rebellion and desire to be like other nations, per 1 Samuel 8:7–9) and took him away in wrath, speaking to the death of Saul after his rebellion against God. Yet we see Christ here as well. "I gave you a king from my anger and I took (him) in my wrath." The Father provided that King of kings to satisfy the divine justice, the holy wrath due to sinners.

In 13:13, we return to bridal/children imagery. At the time of calling for rebirth, Israel refuses. This is about the majority of Israel rejecting Christ when He comes. The pangs of childbirth will kill, in one sense, the mother and child. Verse 14 furthers this, with the passage quoted in 1 Corinthians 15:54–55. Again we have inspired exegesis. God poses a rhetorical question of whether He should ransom them from the condemnation of the law in Christ. Through Jesus, the plagues and sting of death are gone, but God's compassion is hidden for much of national Israel (not being elect).

Hosea 15–16 is a prophecy of Assyria (and Babylon for Judah) coming like the hot east wind to strip her of her treasures. Again, if God is against us, who can be for us? She will bear her guilt under the law. This is what sin has wrought in the world: war and sorrow. As Owen said, men can thank themselves for death and hell.[51]

In 14:1–4, Israel is commanded again to return to God in repentance and faith. This faith must be in God alone and no other thing. Then Hosea says

---

51 Owen, *Hebrews Vol 1*, 409.

that in God, the orphan finds mercy. This is in light of the killing of the mother, national Israel. The elect in the nation will find mercy, though the nation overall is lost from under Mosaic covenant. God will heal the apostasy of His chosen people in the covenant of grace. Love will flow; anger has turned away. Their hope will be in God, not Assyria or the idols their hands have made. It would actually be Assyria under the banner of those idols that would come and destroy the nation. To spiritual Israel, true Israel, God will be dew. Verse 2 is referenced by the author of Hebrews (13:15) in the context of how sacrifices will no longer be bulls and goats, but praise.[52]

Of course, this statement that the orphan finds mercy in God will be extended beyond the Jews. All of mankind is "orphaned." All of humanity is alienated from the Father. Every human being has sat beneath the cold shadow of night and cried out in their hearts for that meaningful connection they cannot find in humanity, longing for someone who truly understood them and loved them. Through Christ and the covenant of grace, these orphans find mercy.

Hosea 14:5–6 uses a masculine pronoun, showing Christ as the root of the plant, the vine onto which the branches are grafted. Verse 7 transitions to plural, showing how each believer participates in flourishing and blossoming under the canopy of God's grace. Verse 8 is one final exhortation against idolatry because it is not idols, but God, who gives them their fruit, their growth, their life.

Closing Thoughts

The greatest difficulty of dealing with Old Testament Israel is not judging them. We read through the Old Testament and see all their sins laid bare on the pages. When Israel seeks after other gods, other means of salvation, it is easy to sit back and wonder why they never seem to learn. Looking at this promise to Judah about monergistic, man-free salvation, how many of us seek our own salvation and providence to live by? We may trust our eternity to God, but trust ourselves with daily providence. So often, we place our trust in everything but God for life. We have different names for our idols, but they are still sex, money, and fertility. Thank God our salvation does not rely on us. We are an idolatrous people who are loved in spite of ourselves. This is why we must work out our salvation in fear and trembling, learning to trust in God alone for our salvation. If it were up to us, to our works, we would hear, "Depart from me for I never knew you, *lo-ammi*." It is only by His grace that we are His people, His children.

Idolatry sets anything over God. Idolatry was present in the first sin, and in every sin thereafter. Pride is idolatry of self over God. Gluttony is idolatry

---

[52] The author of Hebrews uses the Septuagint rendering of "fruit of our lips"

of food or drink over God. Paul tells us coveting is idolatry (Col. 3:5). One of the best-masked idolatries is homosexuality. Homosexuality is impossible to rend from paganism; the core concept is monism, in contrast to Christianity's dualism. Christianity has man and woman, man and God, sin and righteousness. Homosexuality and its polysexual variations declare that *all* people are simultaneously masculine and feminine. If there is no dualism in sexuality, only monism, the other categories are to be merged as well. Paganism presses not only to merge or dissolve genders but also to dissolve distinctions between man and God as well as sin and righteousness.[53]

Whatever your idols are, the only thing that truly separates you from the Israel condemned in Hosea is Christ. We must strike the balance of standing in opposition to whatever idols culture presents to us without forgetting that only the grace of God distinguishes us from them. It is not hate that we proclaim but the love of God for sinners. If the world is not told that condemnation comes, then how can they repent? How can they be saved? The law that reveals sin is not the theme of redemptive history, but it is an essential preface.

---

53 For more on this subject, read Peter Jones' *The God of Sex: How Spirituality Defines Your Sexuality* (Colorado Springs: Victor, 2006).

VII
Emperor Seeks SWF
Esther

Purim

"The lot is cast into the lap, but its every decision is from the LORD" (Prov. 16:33).[1]

Life is often not what we expect. The Christian life is a cognitive balancing act of the nature of probability, the fallenness of this world, and the sovereignty of God. Probability exists, and creation is fallen, but God is still sovereign over both. The casting of Urim and Thummim (Ex. 28:30; Num. 27:21) was probably similar to the casting of lots or dice within a sacred context. God is in control of every aspect of His creation, and within a divine institution, God would reveal His will through the roll of the dice, so to speak. [2]

The narrative of Esther is the foundation of the Jewish festival Purim. The name comes from Haman casting lots, or *purim*, to schedule his genocide of Israel. No doubt, he thought his gods would determine the outcome, but the God of the Israelites controlled it instead. Observation of this festival continues to this day with pastries called "Haman's ears," noise-makers to "blot out" Haman's name when the book is read, costuming, and other merriment.

Haman's date for the genocide of the Jews is perfectly timed for Esther to have risen to power and influence. When we look at the festival of Purim, it is essentially celebrated by Christians every Lord's Day. Just as we celebrate Christ's birth (every Sunday, not just Christmas), His resurrection (not just Easter), God's divine providence during sojourning (the feast of booths), God passing over us because of atoning blood (every Lord's Supper), and others, so too we rejoice in God working through means to save and preserve His people.

Chance and luck are major elements of the book of Esther. There is suspense and a *seemingly* undetermined outcome at multiple points. From the

---
1 This is necessary to understand passages like 1 Kings 22:29–35 and Ecclesiastes 9:11.
2 This does not mean playing craps or roulette are acts of religious worship, though, just to be clear.

one-thousand-foot view, we see God's sovereignty over every element of creation. That sovereignty is essential to the plot in tandem with the absence of primary causes (or direct motions) of God. Esther is a study in the nature of secondary causes (Gen. 8:22).[3] A friend once told me a story of God's providence. They found an anonymous gift of money in the mailbox with only the words "from God" on the envelope. He knew that God did not create currency *ex nihilo* with the words "United States of America" on it, place it on an envelope, and sign His name in English. Yet we understand God works through events of history and desires in the hearts of His people to bring about extraordinary providence. It is not a miracle, but it does warrant praise for our God.

In particular, exile narratives like this apply to us as we wait for our arrival in the promised land. The same can be said of the wilderness narratives of the Torah. As a Bride in exile from Eden, we are waiting for the promised land of the New Heavens and New Earth. We observe God's work almost exclusively through secondary causes. Esther has unique application and encouragement for us, despite the historical distance.

Summary

In case you have not read Esther recently, here is the CliffsNotes version. After a marital spat at a party, Ahasuerus kicks out his wife and sets out to find a new one. Esther was just a small-town Jewish girl living in a Babylonian world who took the beauty pageant train going anywhere. She becomes Queen, and it is a Babylonian Rhapsody.[4] Meanwhile, Haman hates Mordecai and decides to kill all the Jews by a cunning plot. Mordecai convinces Esther to intervene for her people, and she bravely comes into the throne room without a summons. Esther wins over the king through the clever use of dinner parties, a new decree allows the Jews to defend themselves, and Haman is hung on his own gallows.

Remaining Jews

An important element of the context for Esther is the time period. After the Decree of Cyrus, Jews were permitted to go back to Israel. The Jews in Esther are those who assimilated to some degree into the Babylonian/Persian empire and chose to remain instead of return. This is crucial to understanding the book. These are believers who have grown comfortable in the world.

Note that these are children of the promise, descendants of Abraham. There were other pagan people groups who had been brought into Babylon

---

[3] This promise in the Noahic covenant shows God as the first cause behind the natural processes of history which carry out His decree and purposes.
[4] I know, it should be Persian, but Babylonian is way closer to Bohemian.

(then transferred to the Persian empire), conformed and assimilated, but they were never were threatened with genocide. The Jews were unsettled and persecuted because they were not meant to be content in Babylonian lands. In a similar way, God chastises and stirs up the consciences of His people when they become comfortable in the world, especially when they are comfortable in sin.

God is curing the sleeping, prayerless people. The lack of reference to Adonai and Yahweh is not problematic in this book, but it is pedagogical. We are not just seeing God in secondary causes; we are seeing the alienation these people had from God. They are practical atheists whose lives have become so egocentric that God's name has faded out of their vocabulary. What we see in Esther is a lethargic, prayerless people being shaken awake by God through trial. God often does the same to us.

Benjamites and Agagites

The next theme in the background we want to understand before diving into the Bride of Christ aspect of Esther is the heritage of Haman versus Mordecai. If we go back to Exodus 17, we see how God promised to blot out the Amalekites from under heaven (v. 14) and yet they would contend with the Israelites from generation to generation (v. 16). However, when we reach 1 Samuel 15, the line should have been wiped out. Saul was called to contend with the Amalekites and destroy them, especially the leader Agag. His failure there is recorded, and Samuel himself kills Agag, but the extent of Saul's failure is evident when we see that Haman is an Agagite. This is why Mordecai refuses to bow down to Haman, even though he was bowing to Xerxes.

Sin has a way of revisiting us when it is not dealt with. It grows and develops until it comes back stronger and with a vengeance. As Shakespeare said, it is easier to kill the serpent while it is yet in the egg.[5]

Comparing Kings

As has been our pattern in this book, we take a comparison/contrast approach to husband figures for typology of Christ, like Adam being a federal head. When we dive into Esther, there are a handful of parallels between King Xerxes/Ahasuerus[6] and Christ; each aspect is greater and more beautiful in heaven than in Persia. Xerxes had power and authority as the emperor of the Persian world; he was not one to be disregarded or disrespected. He was also jealous for that glory and pride. Yet Xerxes' power and authority only pretended at being absolute. His will was frustrated by his own wife, which "troubled" the entire empire.

---
5 William Shakespeare, *Julius Caesar*, Act II Scene 1.
6 These are two names for the same man. This was not uncommon for the era.

Christ's authority, however, is absolute. Job's statement is as true of Christ as the rest of the trinity when he says that no one can frustrate His will.[7] He is also jealous for His glory, but righteously so. Isaiah 42:8 says, "I am Yahweh; that is my name; my glory I give to no other, nor my praise to carved idols."

The book opens with Xerxes in his display of opulence, decadence, and authority. The description of golden couches and mosaic floors rivals the most indulgent of modern celebrities. He even seeks to display his wife as part of his wealth.[8]

Xerxes was insanely wealthy by human standards, but he had nothing in comparison to our Savior. What we see as foolish exorbitance in Xerxes' parties pales alongside Christ's kingdom in heaven. Just a glance at Revelation 21–22 shows us gold used for paving stones and precious jewels for gates. We see it as foolish in Xerxes because there were poor who needed relief, and the storehouses of wealth were vast but ultimately limited. Christ, on the other hand, owns all that creation holds, giving both generously and wisely according to the needs of His people. Indeed, even if the world were to run short of supply, Christ has the authority to speak riches into existence *ex nihilo*. As Xerxes brought out the wealth of his storehouses to display before the princes of the provinces in Esther 1:2, so, too, will Christ bring out the wealth of His glory in heaven when He has gathered in all His saints alongside the angels.[9]

Xerxes only had those things which God had provided for him, so he was intrinsically poor. His authority, power, and wealth were only temporary and gifted to him. Because he only pretended at divine authority and his jealousy was tied to a capacity to lose everything, we find Xerxes to be fickle and selfish. "It is clear that, from the point of view of . . . Xerxes, good and evil are defined by how they affect the interests of the king and the dynasty."[10] Even his own life would be taken from him in 465 BC after failing in the war against the Greeks.[11] One of the reasons we refer to Christ as King instead of Emperor is because an emperor's authority (like Xerxes') was largely ill-gotten by unrighteous conquest, whereas Christ rightfully owns all.

His power, wealth, and authority not only vastly exceed Xerxes, but they also are never diminished, nor can they be taken away. And though Christ is jealous for His glory, He willfully surrendered it, after a fashion, and left the

---

7 Job 42:2; see also Daniel 4:35 and Isaiah 14:27.
8 It is likely that when Xerxes called for her to dance before the men, he did not intend her to be clothed for the dance. He was objectifying her in front of the leaders of his kingdom, further displaying his need for Jesus.
9 Goodwin, *Ephesians*, 173.
10 *Civilizations of the Ancient Near East*, 523.
11 *Civilizations of the Ancient Near East*, 1020.

beauty and peace of heaven in order to come and woo His Bride, to declare His vows, and to accomplish the marriage. While Xerxes was assassinated after military defeat, Christ went to His death willingly and purposefully to gain victory over death itself. Xerxes gave nothing for Esther, but Christ gave His life for His Bride.

Despite all of Xerxes' authority and wealth, Queen Vashti, who is busy with her own decadent party, refuses to come. So we see a pagan bride refusing the summons of her lord, which results in her banishment. She is never again to come into the presence of the emperor.

In the first chapter, we are already being presented with a parallel to God and Israel. As we saw in the prophets, Israel, in her paganism, rejected the wooing call of her rightful husband. As a result, she is in exile. Yet while Xerxes cast out Vashti and simply looked for a new bride to replace her, God transformed His Bride into a new creation.

Part of the palace drama is the teaching purpose of Vashti's banishment. The nobles are concerned that Vashti's rebellion will incite other women to follow her example. So, too, we see how the record of Israel's exile cautions us as believers. It shows how we are worthy of being exiled from God's presence, even to condemnation in hell, and that drives us to Christ. Only there do we find the unconditional marriage wherein we are never cast out.

Here we are introduced to the Persian "immutable" decree. I place that in quotation marks because it only pretends at the kind of immutability we see in Christ. This is not the only time we see unchangeable decrees in the Old Testament, perhaps the most famous resulting in Daniel's one-night stay in Hotel Leo.[12] We see three of these decrees in Esther.

As part of the triune God, Christ participated in the decree of all history and engaged in its fulfillment to the minutest detail. Christ's decree is immutable. It is *truly* immutable. It cannot be frustrated by powers below or even above. The "immutability" of ancient Near Eastern decrees were often problematic, but we rejoice that God's decrees of election and love do not change. They cannot change because Christ Himself does not change. As Hebrews 13:8 declares to us, Christ is the same yesterday, today, and forever.

Xerxes was dependent on fallible counsel. We see him regretting his "immutable" decrees and lamenting his inability to change them. Because he is selfish, we also see that he only accomplishes good when someone else leads him to it, independent of his own desires.

But Christ is never lacking wisdom, nor does He heed poor counsel. He is, in and of Himself, the infinite wisdom of God (1 Cor. 1:24)! Christ's decree is

---

12 This account with King Darius is in Daniel 6.

not only genuinely immutable, it is formed by perfect wisdom and cannot be any greater, any more glorifying to His name, nor any more beneficial to those who serve Him than it already is.

Preparing the Bride

Once Xerxes gets over being mad at Vashti, he gets lonely. The young men suggest he find a new sweetheart from the beautiful virgins of the land, and Xerxes decides that is a solid plan. So the beauty pageant begins.

The first thing we note here is that he was concerned only with the external aspects of his bride. Esther did not need to be wise, kind, gracious, or even loving toward her king. She just had to be beautiful and submissive.

On the other hand, Christ chooses His Bride according to His good pleasure. He chooses the weak and simple things of this world to glorify Himself. His delight in her is not regarding the external things but the internal.[13] First Samuel 16:7 says, "But the LORD said to Samuel, 'Do not look on his appearance or on the height of his stature, because I have rejected him. For the LORD sees not as man sees: man looks on the outward appearance, but the LORD looks on the heart.'" Christ not only delights in love, joy, peace, patience, kindness, goodness, faithfulness, gentleness, and self-control in His Bride, but He brings those things about as fruit in her through the work of the Spirit that proceeds from Him (Gal. 5:22). He does require submission from us, but He gives us all reason to willingly submit.

When Esther is chosen as a bridal candidate for Xerxes, we see his extravagance again come into play. Her skin is scoured, and she is bathed in perfumed oils. This changed the texture and scent of her skin.

A diet was imposed upon her. This is not like the fad diets we see of our day, intended to reduce body fat and pursue a contemporary ideal of skinniness. In the ancient Near East, being skinny was for the working class, and this diet was to fatten Esther up for the ideal of that time. She was also clothed in fine cloths and adorned with jewelry.

Essentially, Esther was prepared for the bridegroom inside and out. She was fattened, perfumed, softened, and dressed to make her presentable, to make her fit to be a queen of the greatest emperor of the time.

Christ, too, prepares His Bride. He takes each of us and scours us of the grime and defilement of this world as well as our callousness. He makes us to be pleasant in sight, "touch" (sensitivity to His workings in us), and "scent" before himself. He "fattens" us on a diet of the Word of God and the meal He presents to us in the Lord's Supper. He clothes us in His righteousness and

---

13 God did not choose either Martin Luther or me for our good looks. Of course, even these aspects of "inner beauty" are the workings of God in His people, and we'll get to that in a moment.

adorns us through the good works He prepares beforehand for us to do. He transforms us into a fitting Bride, finally bringing us into glory. As Edward Pearse said, "For, indeed, Christ marries not any for their beauty, but those whom He marries He marries to make them beautiful."[14]

Summons by Messenger

Xerxes sought out his bride by messenger. He prepared her by servants, primarily his eunuch Hegai, then summoned her by messengers. So also does Christ use His people as messengers, especially the ministers of the Word. He seeks out His Bride by believers testifying to the grace in them and by preachers proclaiming the gospel. He even sends the Holy Spirit to prepare His Bride. The general call to repentance and faith is made by a pastor, while the Holy Spirit makes the effectual call in the heart to summon the Bride to the Bridegroom.

Even after we are saved, Christ uses the means of grace, especially preaching, to summon us to the banquet, to instruction, and to intimacy with our Savior. Have you ever thought of church this way? And when our earthly journey is done, God sends His angels to bring us safely to Him into glory.

One of the most striking contrasts to the Bride of Christ is that Esther always had to wait on Xerxes to summon her. She risked her own life to come before him un-summoned.

I need to be clear about the way we approach God in Jesus. Christ is not pure immanence without transcendence. Strictly speaking, sinful men cannot come to God on the grounds of their own works. We see the Son as God on Mount Sinai in the context of the law. There, the people tremble at His authority, His glory, His holiness, and cry out for the voice of God to stop lest they die. They plead with Moses to mediate for them. Yet within the new covenant marriage, the dread of the condemnation of the law is taken away as Christ comes to His people by the Holy Spirit. After salvation, we can approach the throne through our union with Christ *without* summons. We do not risk life by coming to God in prayer, but rather we are made able to approach the throne with boldness (Eph. 3:12; Heb. 4:16).

Contrasting Mediators

Though it is slightly outside the purview of our work on Christ and the Bride, it bears noting the ways in which Esther herself compares and contrasts to Christ. Just as we are to reflect Christ to the world, God used Esther to foreshadow Christ for us as a mediator, while displaying her insufficiency to fulfill His role.

---
14 Pearse, *The Best Match*, 111.

Esther was indeed a mediator who accomplished salvation for her people. She was raised up by God in God's perfect timing, but the comparison really does not extend much beyond that. Let us examine these contrasts point by point.

Esther was of common birth and raised up to palace life. She was a common, exiled Jew, whereas Christ was divine and humbled Himself to be like us in all ways but sin.

Esther was consistently passive until the crisis point, and even had to be coerced by her uncle into intercession, but Christ was actively pursuing His role throughout His earthly life, accomplishing righteousness. He then set His face toward Jerusalem for the crucifixion (Luke 9:53). Esther was fearful and reluctant to accept her role, but Christ chose to be our mediator and Savior before the world began.

Esther's work was tainted by self-serving fear of someday being persecuted herself, but Christ's labor was purely of love and self-sacrifice.

Esther was disregarding the law. Her diet from Xerxes' eunuch was certainly not kosher. She bowed before a pagan king. She even married a pagan. But Christ was perfectly obedient to the Father.

Her mediation ultimately cost her nothing. While Esther did risk her life in order to mediate for her people, it ultimately cost her nothing. Christ gave Himself for us, dying on the cross under the outpouring of God's wrath.

The mediation accomplished by Esther was temporary and short-lived. It would only last for that generation and only against death from the threat of men. There were Jews who were "saved" by Esther who would eventually be condemned to hell for their sins if they did not repent and believe. Christ's mediation is eternal and saves us from the wrath of God.

As we compare *ourselves* to Esther, we can easily spot the application of her story for those in authority but miss its breadth. Each of us has a place in this world, even if it is a low station, with friends, family, co-workers, and neighbors.[15] Your place in this world provides you with opportunities that are unique to you. You are the Bride of Christ with access to the throne of the God of all creation. He hears you and loves you as His Bride. Your position in life is not accidental. These are opportunities for living Christ, bearing witness, and praying specifically. You can stand in the gap between God and those who would be condemned and make intercession. As one Christian put it, there is an unbroken line of intercession by Christ's people pleading for those who

---

15 As Garth Brooks said, "I've got friends in low places . . ."

were saved. Mordecai's words are for you as well as for Esther. Perhaps you have been brought to this place for such a time as this.

Haman, Paul, and You

It is comfortable to put the "villain" label on Haman and dismiss him. He was under the condemnation of God for both his heritage and his own grievous sin. He was divinely denounced along with all the Amalekites.

Yet look at Paul, a Benjamite like Mordecai, who sought to wipe out God's people (Christians) from under heaven under the guise of zeal. While both of their lives ended in execution, Paul went to heaven, and Haman went to hell. So what is the difference between Haman and Paul? It is not their heritage; it is Christ. God called Paul and saved him by grace through faith in Christ alone.

Haman was hung upon a tree, like the Canaanite kings (Josh. 8:29; 10:26), as one who is accursed (Deut. 21:22). Christ was hung upon a tree as accursed by God, though He was righteous. He was accursed for our sins so that we might be saved.

We as humans are under condemnation for our works as well as our heritage from Adam. We would be blotted out from under heaven for it. If we have only our works and not Christ, a fate far worse than hanging awaits us. Rest in Christ and Christ alone for your salvation.

VIII

Husband in the Flesh

The Gospels

"A LOVER USUALLY (his heart being enflamed with love and ardent affection to the person, though she being in another country, very far off) takes a journey resolving to give her a visit; and in order thereunto he suits himself in a fit garb, and clothing, that so he might every way render himself a person acceptable, and meet, likely, and capable of winning and enjoying her. Jesus Christ after this, such was the greatness of his love, and strength of his affection, resolved to take a journey to give poor sinners a most gracious visit; the journey he took was long, as far as it from heaven to earth. And that he might accomplish his blessed purpose, he fits himself with a garb accordingly, laying aside his heavenly robes, he clothed himself with our flesh, or did assume a man's nature, that so he might every way become a meet object for the sinner..." – Benjamin Keach[1]

"Where do I start reading the Bible?" As a pastor, that is a question I love to hear. My stock answer that I stole from my father (who probably stole it from somewhere else) is, "Start with the gospel of John, then go back and read Genesis and Exodus. After you finish those, we will figure out where to go." John gives them enough of the law to show them they are sinners, along with the good news of the gospel. Then they can go back and see how it all started. I have had Christians tell me that they tried to read the Bible straight through but got bogged down in Leviticus, Numbers, and Deuteronomy. At that point, they normally skip ahead to Joshua or give up and go back to familiar or happy books like the Psalms.

I have often wished that I could somehow go back and read the Bible with fresh eyes, starting in Genesis straight through to the end. That may sound strange to you, but the Scriptures are primarily the unfolding of redemptive history. Starting in the gospels is like opening a book a few pages before the climax. You would not start Tolkien's *Lord of the Rings* trilogy with the third

---
1 Keach, *Preaching from the Types*, 324.

book because you cannot fully appreciate all the characters and their journey. Some would say it is wrong to even start with *Fellowship of the Ring*, but that you need to begin with *The Silmarillion* and *The Hobbit*. I hope the preceding chapters on the Old Testament have given you a sense of the background for the gospels' account of Christ's incarnation, the climax of not only the Scriptures, but human history itself.

Much Ado About Mary

In the history of the church, there has been almost as much issue over the mother of Christ as Christ Himself. One of the earliest controversies in the church over Christ's deity centered on a title for Mary, *theotokos*, or "mother of God." Protestants have an awkward relationship with Jesus' mom because Rome idolizes her. It is almost as if we fear that saying too many nice things about Mary is a gateway drug to popery.[2]

As it is with much of Christian life, a balance needs to be struck. Mary is not a demi-god to be prayed to and adored. She was a sinner in need of a Savior, like every other Christian, but she was an exceptional woman. She did not co-author salvation but, among believers, she had incredible faith. God used Mary to bring Christ into the world and serve as a flesh-and-blood image of Israel and the church. When most of the disciples ran away from Christ's crucifixion, Mary stood at the foot of the cross. She is a heroine of the church and should be remembered as such. All that to say, if you like Mary, you do not have to be ashamed of it.

When Gabriel came to tell Mary she would carry Jesus, we find an interesting tie-in to our bridal metaphor. In Luke 1:34, she asks how she can be a mom without a man knowing her that way. Gabriel tells her that the Holy Spirit will come upon her and the power of the Highest will overshadow her, therefore the one begotten will be holy and called the Son of God. When Gabriel gets to verse 37, he says that "nothing *will be* impossible with God."

That phrase confused me for a long time because God has been doing the impossible quite literally since time began with creation. Waters parted, axes floated, donkeys spoke, and an emperor sent an exiled people home.[3] We saw back in Genesis where the angel asked Sarah, "Is anything too hard for the Lord?" (Gen. 18:14).

The most important impossibility is the salvation of sinners, where the perfectly just God, who will by no means clear the guilty, has somehow been transforming said sinners into righteous saints. Now Jesus is coming in an impossible way to solve the impossible problem of salvation for sinners. Through

---
2 Roman Catholicism, not the dried flower stuff.
3 The decree of Cyrus is a straight-up miracle, if you ask me.

this child, nothing *will be* impossible with God because He is going to accomplish redemption for sinners past, present, and future.

What does this have to do with our metaphor? Mary parallels the church, and Jesus is making the way for the regeneration of sinners. This is how the church works. She is unable to produce life alone, but when the Holy Spirit comes over her, and the power of God Almighty overshadows her, sons and daughters are born unto holiness as children of the living God. Now that Jesus has come, nothing *is* impossible with God.

But that is the second layer to Gabriel's statement. God is literally coming into the world in the form of this child. He uses a future tense because the God-man has not yet arrived. Nothing will be impossible with God because nothing will be impossible with Jesus.

Announcing the Bridegroom

In period films, there is a ritual of announcing the guests. Lord and Lady Wilhelm of Worcestershiresauce are introduced at the grand ball as a herald as they descend a winding staircase to join well-dressed British people and corseted women gasping for air. But what of the High King of Heaven?

His debut in this broken and fallen world was in a feed trough. The first heralds of Christ were a host of angels, which is fitting for God in the flesh, but they announce His arrival to shepherds instead of the aristocracy of Rome or Israel. God did this to show the kind of people for whom Christ came. His Bride was not first found in Caesar's court but on the shores of Galilee and the fields where shepherds tended flocks. John speaks almost poetically of how Jesus came to His own, and they did not know Him (John 1:10–11).[4]

When we do find a human herald of Christ, the Bridegroom, it is not the decorated servant of the court. It is a homeless guy who eats bugs and wears camel hair, which has yet to gain momentum in the fashion world. In John 3:28–30, John the Baptist makes clear that he is not the Christ, but the friend of the Bridegroom who rejoices at His coming. John was the prophesied herald, a kind of returning Elijah who prepared the way. He was the last of the Old-Testament-style prophets, uniquely called and blessed as the herald of the bridegroom to the bride.

We learn an important lesson in seeing John the Baptist as the friend, minister, and herald of that Bridegroom. John directs all glory to Christ and away from himself. In 1 Corinthians 1:13, Paul rebukes those exalting Paul's name

---

[4] We can apply our metaphor here too. The language of "know," as we have seen already, is often used to denote marital intimacy. Israel as a nation saw Him, many even embraced Him as a prophet and potential earthly king, but they did not know Him as the bride knows the bridegroom. The nation did not have that intimacy of the soul with the Messiah.

rather than Christ, who was crucified for their salvation. Even as regenerate Christians, we retain a "bentness" to our nature that skews our inclination to worship like a shopping cart with a bad wheel. It is appalling that Christians idolize preachers and theologians, dead or alive, and it is even worse when those idolized do not denounce it. What an offense it would be for a bride to look longingly at one of the groomsmen while at the wedding banquet!

Christ Himself would attest to the bridegroom aspect of His coming. Matthew 9, Mark 2, and Luke 5 all record the same event wherein Christ talks about feasting with His disciples. He says that the Bridegroom has come, the climax of the greatest love story ever told, and that is why the disciples do not mourn, but rejoice!

This raises an important issue in understanding how the whole of the narrative fits together. Some people claim that national Israel was God's Bride and the church was Christ's.[5] Here we see that idea profoundly refuted. Jesus came to the Jews and told the Jews that He was the Bridegroom. He does not say a new or second bridegroom, but *the* Bridegroom. The church is the Bride, but she is also the true Israel that comes from within national Israel. Gentiles like myself are grafted on to Israel, but we do not replace her. Paul speaks to this extensively in Galatians and Romans.

Adulterous Israel

If you have not read through the historical books, and especially Hosea, some of Christ's remarks to the Jews seem a bit harsh and out of place. In Matthew 12, Jesus heals a demon-possessed man, and a debate about Christ's nature ensues. As the conversation continues, some of the scribes and Pharisees ask for a sign, presumably demonstrating Christ's Messianic credentials. We might expect Christ to humor them, but He had just done an exorcism (assuming this is all the same scene). He understands the unbelieving hearts of those who ask. He responds in verse 39 by calling this the request of an "evil and adulterous generation."

This is not an indication that extramarital affairs were more prevalent in the first century than before. Besides, how could high adultery rates play into a request for proof of Christ's role as the Messiah? Jesus is pointing to a recurring problem in Israel's history of spiritual adultery. These men had made idols of their own works, offices, traditions, and nationalism. We might sum up all of this in the idol of pride. The golden calves may have been carried off long ago in exile, but the idolatry of Israel was alive and kicking. It had to be addressed even more so now because the true Bridegroom had finally

---

[5] Admittedly, I've never actually seen this argument in writing, but I have heard it a few times in discussion.

arrived. Their idolatry of self kept them from recognizing the Bridegroom they claimed they were waiting for, when the reality was that they had everything they desired in the adoration of and power over the people.

He says they will receive the sign of Jonah, where the man of God goes into the belly of the fish for three days and comes out again. This is, of course, pointing to Christ's death, burial, and resurrection. Jesus would use the same language again, albeit shorter, in 16:4.

In Mark 8:38, Christ uses the same phrase of an "adulterous and sinful generation" for those who are ashamed of Him. He goes on to say that He will be ashamed of them on the last day. Paul would later describe Christ and the cross as foolishness to the Greeks and a stumbling block to the Jews in 1 Corinthians 1:23. How could the Messiah, this divine conqueror, be some homeless wanderer and teacher from Galilee who eventually met His end in a way that specifically signified God's curse?

Yet this was God in flesh. More than that, He is the Bridegroom of the soul of every believer in history. Christ is revealing Himself as the Bridegroom, as the Husband of Israel, who has condescended to take on flesh and suffer to purchase her out of slavery and death. How could she ever be ashamed of Him? Yet there are times where we, in our flesh, balk or stumble at professing Christ. While it is not full-blown apostasy, it is shameful. May God keep each of us from that "great transgression" of apostasy (Ps. 19:13).

On the lighter, stranger side, Mark 3:31–35 describes Christ's relationship to the Bride in a different way. Mary and her sons arrive, and somebody tells Jesus. Christ responds that those surrounding Him are His mother and brothers. He even speaks of the individual believer as simultaneously brother, sister, and mother. This ties back in to the confusing family tree of the church. In the family of God, sinners are born again through Christ and His church. Through Christ, they are adopted by the Father to be co-heirs with Christ. John 1:12–13 says, "But to all who did receive him, who believed in his name, he gave the right to become children of God, who were born, not of blood nor of the will of the flesh nor of the will of man, but of God." So if we are saved by grace through faith in Christ, the church is our mother, and the saints are our brothers and sisters. Those disciples who surrounded Christ were the embodiment of the church, True Israel. But in order for those relationships to exist, for the gospel to exist, the Son of God had to be born into the church to earn our inheritance by His obedience and reconcile us to God by dying for our sins. That is why Christ calls the church His mother and the saints His brothers. He was in the midst of that work of saving sinners as our federal head (Heb. 2:10–18).

Maternal Discipline

Matthew 18 presents guidelines for church discipline and dealing with sin within the body of Christ. When you are the offended party, you go and speak with the person who has sinned against you to seek reconciliation. Paul adds the importance of doing this in a spirit of gentleness in Galatians 6:1. If that does not work, you take witnesses to again seek reconciliation. Eventually, if that person does not repent, he is excommunicated. Even that is done in hope that through that sorrowful exercise, God will bring about repentance and reconciliation.

As a pastor and elder, Matthew 18 is a passage I am familiar with walking through, step by step. When a person sins against the body of Christ in general, I am called to go as a representative of the church to seek repentance. At every step, the goal is reconciliation. The elders are not seeking justice, vengeance, or even temporary peace within the body. We yearn, pray, and strive for reconciliation that produces real peace.

It is helpful for pastors or anyone who goes through this process (offender or the offended) to see that this is really maternal discipline. God disciplines His children in His role as a Father. We are even called to rejoice that the Father loves us enough to discipline us as sons and daughters to produce "peaceful fruit of righteousness" (Heb. 12:5–11).

But in Matthew 18, Christ is instructing the church, the Bride, how to discipline the children in His physical absence. She is not supposed to wait until Dad comes home. Church discipline cases are the mother's discipline. As such, it is an act of love, not anger. In an earthly family, the goal of discipline is to address the child's heart for the sake of their future, so discipline should not be any more severe than is necessary. The mother does not (or at least should not) discipline in anger to get justice or vengeance. She disciplines because she loves the child and desires what is best for the child long-term.

The Wedding at Cana

John 2 recounts the wedding at Cana and one of Christ's most iconic miracles, turning water into wine. It should not surprise you that this ties in to the bridal image we have traced so far. So, first, let us take a quick overview of the events.

Christ has come to attend a wedding with His disciples early in His earthly ministry. It might have been for a relative, since mother Mary is in attendance. As the celebration goes on, Mary informs Him that they have run out of wine. Jesus seems surprised and tells her that this does not have anything to do with Him; His hour has not yet come. Mary tells the servants to follow His instructions, and Christ transforms water for purification rituals into wine of superlative quality.

This raises two questions. Why does Jesus respond so cryptically? And why does He turn water into wine? Let us address both of these in turn.

When I attend weddings, invariably my mind turns to my own wedding day. We all do this. We think about the emotions, the decorations, the events, the vows, and so on. Even single people think about what their wedding may be like someday. The Son, the second person of the Trinity made flesh, now attends an example of the metaphor He created with Adam and Eve and perpetuated through human history. He is on the road to His own wedding vows and feast that God decreed before time began.

Knowing the authority and ability her son possessed as God incarnate, Mary asks a favor on behalf of the wedding party. She asks Jesus to make some wine. Christ is not responding to Mary in anger over being troubled with petty issues; this is just the human surprise of being interrupted in the middle of a thought. Christ saw the wine as an image of the bitter cup of God's wrath He would soon drink and the cup of His blood He would provide for His own Bride in the not-so-distant future. This is why Jesus responds to Mary, "My hour has not yet come." It was not yet time for Him to provide the precious wine that would be joy to the heart of believers throughout history.

There was probably other dialogue at this point that John did not record. Ultimately, Mary concludes that Christ would indeed help, and she tells the servants to follow His instructions. This brings us to the significance of the purification water He used to make wine for the feast. Remember, this is the Christ, the second person of the Trinity, empowered by the third person of the Trinity, the Holy Spirit. Christ spoke heaven and earth into existence, so simply creating wine out of thin air was well within His capacity. So why does Jesus use the purification water?

In second temple Judaism, purification rites were an important part of daily life before hand sanitizer was invented. In order to remain ceremonially clean, Jews followed certain procedures that required the large quantities of water described here. These rituals originated in Mosaic law, and temporarily (symbolically/ceremonially) made the washer acceptable before God. Shortly thereafter, something would happen to make them ceremonially unclean again, and the ritual would recur. Lather, rinse, repeat. Of course, all of this was symbolic. It could not actually wash away the filth of sin.

So here, in the middle of this wedding feast, is a symbol of the law that cannot save sinners. The law shows us our sin and need for a Savior. Christ has come to fulfill the law on behalf of His Bride and absorb its curse for her. Christ takes a symbol of what would have been her condemnation and transforms it into something else—wine.

We have already seen foreshadowing in the Old Testament of Christ's blood and wine, and there is more that was outside the scope of our brief survey. One of the most important images presented in wine is that it makes the heart "glad" by its intoxicating nature (Ps. 104:15). Christ takes what does not bring joy—water, and the law—and turns it into wine that brings gladness and symbolizes the joy of salvation. Christ's blood washes away the defilement of sin and brings joy to the heart. We will return to this imagery with the Last Supper, but there are a few more elements to address before we move on.

Christ has the servants pour the water and participate in the miracle. Jesus was an able-bodied son of a carpenter, and could have done the work Himself. He calls upon these servants to help for the same reason He calls the church (especially pastors) to labor in evangelism. The real miracle is accomplished by God, but He delights in using His children, His servants, to participate in the miracle that brings joy to the hearts of others.

Finally, the wine was not bargain-basement quality.[6] The MC for the feast remarks how the wine created by Christ was superior to that which came before.[7] There are two important elements in this. One is that the "wine" of Christ's blood is superior to anything found in the world. There is nothing that compares in either the cleansing it provides or the joy it brings to the soul. The second lesson here is that the greater comes last. Note where this is in the history of redemption. For thousands of years, mankind has had types and shadows. God's people have not yet tasted of the fullness of the Messiah and His work. The best wine has been saved for last.

The Wedding Parables

Throughout Christ's earthly ministry, He used parables to teach His disciples and the multitudes who came to hear Him. Many books have been written on the parables and methods of interpretation, which we will not go into detail on here. Suffice it to say, we want to find the richness of these metaphors without over-allegorizing them.

The first parable we want to look at is Matthew 22:1–13, the wedding feast. A king prepares a wedding feast for his son and sends out the invitations via servants. Some simply disregard the invitation without so much as an RSVP, while others abuse or even kill the servants. The king responds by killing them and burning their city. Then he sends out servants to invite anyone and everyone to the feast. They fill the wedding hall. When one of the guests is found without a wedding garment, he is bound and cast into the outer darkness,

---

[6] Jesus does not make Boone's Farm.
[7] This would have been surprising because you bring out the cheap wine last when everyone is already "glad in heart" and less discerning in taste.

where there is "weeping and gnashing of teeth." This runs parallel to another parable about men charged to keep a vineyard (Matt. 21:33–41).

The basic meaning is as follows. The feast is about the new heavens and new earth. National Israel was given the revelation of the Messiah, first in prophesy and then in reality. While there was a believing remnant throughout the ages (not represented here), many rejected the promise and the prophets who proclaimed it. They treated these prophets shamefully and even killed some. Even in Christ's day, the herald John the Baptist was arrested and eventually beheaded. God would bring judgment through Rome on national Israel in AD 70, and the city of Jerusalem would be destroyed.

Yet the gospel would be sent out into the world, first through the apostles and then by others, giving the free offer of salvation by grace through faith. The wedding feast would be "filled out" with Gentiles. Yet there are some who are not regenerated and saved who would *appear* to respond in faith. They are not clothed in the wedding garment that is the righteousness of Christ. These will be cast into the "outer darkness" of hell at the judgment. This is why Christ closes the parable saying that many are called (outwardly), but few are chosen (elect). Thomas Watson connects this to the unbeliever partaking in the Lord's Supper, saying, "So it will be terrible when God shall say to a man, 'How did you come in here to My table with a proud, vain, unbelieving heart? What have you to do here in your sins. You pollute my holy things.'"[8] Or, as Chrysostom says, "Look, I entreat: a royal table is set before you, Angels minister at that table, the King Himself is there, and dost thou stand gaping?"[9]

There are a number of elements in the parable that are simply products of the art of storytelling. God is omniscient and absolute in His decree, unlike the king of the parable. God knew who would reject the invitation and who would accept because He chose them before the world began and applied salvation through the Holy Spirit. The good and the bad invited together does not mean that there are some deserving of salvation, but that all kinds of men are called by the gospel according to God's pleasure, not merit. In a parallel passage (Luke 14:15–24), Christ speaks of the invitation being given to the poor, the disabled, the blind, and the lame. What a beautiful image of those broken by sin who are restored at the wedding feast of glory!

In Matthew 25:1–15, we find the parable of the wise and foolish virgins waiting for the bridegroom. The bridegroom got stuck in traffic, and the oil of the lamps ran low. When he finally arrives, the foolish virgins are running on empty and have to run out and buy more oil. By the time they come back, the door is shut and they are not admitted to the feast.

---

8 Thomas Watson, "The Mystery of the Lord's Supper" in *The Puritans on the Lord's Supper*, ed. Don Kistler (Morgan: Soli Deo Gloria, 1997), 153.
9 Saint John Chrysostom. *Homilies on Galatians, Ephesians, Philippians, Colossians, Thessalonians, Timothy, Titus, and Philemon* (B&R Samizdat Express. iBooks), on Ephesians 1:22–23.

The finer points of this parable are tenuous, but the image of the oil may represent the Holy Spirit.[10] He is the one who produces light and guides the path, especially through the Scriptures. If this is the case, then the refusal to share by the wise virgins is symbolic of how unbelievers cannot participate in the salvation of believers. You cannot ride coattails into heaven. The foolish virgins had a "temporary faith" that was not regeneration and true salvation. There is no redemption by association with any but Christ. Though, to be certain, there are no merchants where you can buy the Holy Spirit, as Simon the magician learned the hard way (Acts 8:18–24).

The central theme is this: We must be prepared for the return of Christ that inaugurates the full wedding feast of glory. We must seek to be "filled up" with the Holy Spirit and the Word of God. We do not know the day or the hour. It is fascinating that Christ in His first coming is prophesying of the second coming, but certainly there is no conflict given His omniscience as God. The same metaphor is used in Luke 12:35–40, with servants replacing the virgins.

Luke 14:8–11 talks about seating charts at a wedding. Christ tells His hearers that it is better to sit in the low-status seats and be exalted than to sit in the seat of honor and be asked to move. Humility and meekness are essential qualities for God's people that flow out of a gospel-centered worldview. We are sinners saved by grace, not merit and works. We do not deserve a seat at the wedding feast of heaven, let alone the seat of honor. Let us each come with humility and the heart of a servant. A dear saint who worked as a janitor once told me that he was ready to enter the gates of the heavenly Jerusalem and be handed the keys to go to work cleaning. Oh, that we would have the same heart!

The Last, or First, Supper

As with many of the subjects treated in this book, the Lord's Supper has been written on extensively. I will briefly touch on some themes and omit others for the sake of time.[11] What we want to focus on here is the nature of the Last Supper, and its continued observation in the Lord's Supper, as a Wedding Feast. In doing so, we move from seeing it strictly as a somber meal of sorrow to seeing the beauty and joy as well. May this enlighten and enliven your own participation in that magnificent, mysterious means of grace.

---

10 Goodwin takes this view. *Ephesians*, 366.

11 Much of this is valuable, like the debate between Radbertus and Ratramnus on the nature of the elements, but they are unnecessary here. This debate would decide the course of doctrine of the Supper in regards to transubstantiation. See Schaff's *History of the Christian Church: Vol 4*, 549-553. For some reason, no one ever takes me up on my suggestion of either of these names for their children. During the long season over which this book has been written, Richard Barcellos has published a book on the topic which I would recommend.

Christ gathered His disciples for a meal on the night before the traditional Passover. The extent of the connection between Christ's meal (with the resulting Lord's Supper observation) and the Mosaic institution is hotly debated, but most can agree that there is some parallel. It is worth noting the Paschal lamb, the centerpiece of the Passover, is not mentioned and may not have been there because Christ was the actual Lamb whose blood was shed for the salvation of the people.

That solemn meal included both the Last Passover *and* the Last Supper of Jesus. Every year, God's people would eat that Passover meal and look back on God's providence in the Exodus from Egypt, but it would now be replaced by the regular observance of the Lord's Supper. This new ordinance not only points back to an event of God's providence (the cross), but forward to a glory awaited. It was an inaugural wedding feast, albeit humble. Like the wedding at Cana, the best wine would be served last.

The Last Passover and Lord's Supper are actually two separate events in one evening. Jesus essentially ended the Passover and began a new tradition, what we call a positive ordinance. The Lord's Supper was after the Passover meal, as we see in Matthew 26:26–29 and Paul's description of it in 1 Corinthians 11:25. The Lord's Supper began when Christ gave thanks for the bread.

We call this the Last Supper because it was the final meal Christ took with His disciples before the crucifixion. One of my favorite passages in *Foxe's Book of Martyrs* is about a pastor named Nicholas Ridley. "Dr. Ridley, the night before execution, was very facetious, had himself shaved, and called his supper a marriage feast; he remarked upon seeing Mrs. Irish (the keeper's wife) weep, 'though my breakfast will be somewhat sharp, my supper will be more pleasant and sweet.'"[12] No doubt he thought of how Christ's breakfast too was far more sharp and painful, yet the final feast with His Bride, which included Ridley, would be glorious indeed!

Christ arrived to the meal with twelve disciples, washed their feet, and observed Passover and the Lord's Supper before sending Judas away to betray Him. He extended the cup to all twelve, even though Judas was unfit to partake. When we come in repentance and faith to the Lord's Table, we identify with Christ and His Bride, but if we do not come repentant and believing, we identify with the guy who did the same at the Last Supper. This is a sobering warning if we partake of the Lord's Supper unworthily and eat and drink judgment on ourselves (1 Cor. 11:27–32). Thomas Watson says, "Christ's blood is like chemical drops of oil which recover some patients, but kill others. Judas sucked death from the tree of life. God can turn stones into bread, and a sinner can turn bread into stones—the bread of life into the stone

---

12 John Foxe, *Foxe's Christian Martyrs of the World* (Uhrichsville: Barbour, 1989), 153.

of stumbling."[13] And in another place Watson , "He that comes unprepared to the Lord's Supper turns the cup in the sacrament into a cup of fury."[14]

Christ arrived with twelve and left with eleven. This connects to Jewish tradition in wedding feasts. The bridegroom would arrive with the whole wedding party, good or bad, but depart with the bride. Those eleven men were uniquely called to represent the Bride of Christ, the church, the True Israel for this momentous occasion. Claude Chavasse writes:

> Outwardly, too, the ceremonies of the Last Supper suggest a marriage of those days. The house was prepared as for the reception of the bridegroom who had absented himself with his friends; at a given signal, he and his party returned to find the room prepared for the wedding feast. The feast itself began with the prescribed hand-washing and benediction. Then the great winecup was filled, and the principal personage, taking it, and holding it, recited over it the prayer of bridal blessing. Then the men seated themselves. Only the men sat at the marriage supper. After the supper the bridegroom left the feast with the bride.[15]

All this raises the question of what, where, and when is the wedding feast? We have seen Christ feasting with the disciples during His earthly ministry and speaking in terms of the wedding feast. The parables speak of the wedding feast in terms of heaven. Yet there are elements here in the Last Supper that point to the wedding feast as well. We revisit those images every time we observe the Lord's Supper in our churches. So which is the true wedding feast?

We find the answer by first going back to Christ's earlier meals with the disciples. He says that the wedding guests should not mourn while they have the bridegroom with them, and indeed, the great bridegroom had come! Christ was with His disciples for those earthly meals, the Last Supper included. When we observe the Lord's Supper in the church in a fallen world with mitigated joy and peace, Christ is present through the Holy Spirit. The nature of heaven (and the New Heavens and New Earth) is the constant presence of our Lord and Savior, Jesus Christ. It is to be with God in joy and peace. So when we ask which of these is the Wedding Feast, our answer is "Christ is present, so all of them!"[16]

---

13 Watson, "The Mystery of the Lord's Supper," 137.
14 Watson, "The Mystery of the Lord's Supper," 152, referencing Jeremiah 25:15.
15 Chavasse, *The Bride of Christ*, 61.
16 Richard Barcellos has a great treatment of this on p. 113 of his book *The Lord's Supper as a Means of Grace* (Glasgow: Bell and Bain, 2013), wherein he describes the Lord's Supper as "linked with the past ... to the present ... but the New Testament also links the Supper with the future ..."

In the Lord's Supper, we see a variety of images that are significant for us as the Bride at the Wedding Feast. Wedding cakes and receptions are costly, but none compares to this one.

The bread represents Christ's body. The seed is crushed in the mill to show Christ's body crushed in death, anointed with oil (showing him as king, priest, and Messiah), and passed through fire (a symbol of God's judgment). Much of this same imagery is found in the grain sacrifices in the Mosaic Economy.[17] Bread provides energy and strength for the body just as Christ quickens and strengthens the soul.[18] Thomas Watson writes:

> Feeding upon Christ sacramentally will be a good preparation to sufferings... Therefore, Cyprian tells us, when the primitive Christians were to appear before the cruel tyrants, they were wont to receive the sacrament, and then they arose up from the Lord's Table as lions breathing forth the fire of heavenly courage.[19]

The wine likewise begins with the grape being crushed. It represents the blood of Christ which was shed for us. It not only quenches the thirst but is delightful in a way that water is not. It revives. It brings an intoxicating joy to the heart. It is a symbol of bounty because grapes are not fermented and aged during a famine. It is a symbol of feasting and celebration. Thomas Watson says, "Well may the spouse give Christ of her spiced wine and the juice of her pomegranate (Song of Solomon 8:2), when Christ has given her a draft of His warm blood, spiced with His love and perfumed with the divine nature."[20] We might even say that as it takes time for the grape juice to become the wine of joy, it is upon Jesus emerging from three days in the grave that His blood becomes the joy of our hearts.

As the Belgic Confession states, "This feast is a spiritual table, at which Christ communicates Himself with all His benefits to us, and gives us there to enjoy both Himself and the merits of His sufferings and death; nourishing, strengthening, and comforting our poor comfort less souls by the eating of His flesh, quickening and refreshing them by the drinking of His blood."[21] Likewise, Herman Bavinck said, "Christ is and remains the acquisition as well as the distributor of grace."[22] We call a husband who financially supports his

---

17 Leviticus 2 records the proper procedure for grain offerings. The grain offerings included incense, and the portion cast into the fire represented Christ which sanctified the remainder, representing God's elect.
18 Keach, *Preaching from the Types and Metaphors of the Bible*, 415–418.
19 Watson, "The Mystery of the Lord's Supper," 156.
20 Watson, "The Mystery of the Lord's Supper," 136.
21 *Belgic Confession* Article XXXV.
22 Herman Bavinck, *Reformed Dogmatics: Holy Spirit, Church, and New Creation. IV*, trans. John Vriend (Grand Rapids: Baker, 2008), 448.

family the "breadwinner." Still, Christ is the breadwinner and both the bread and grace for His Bride in one sacrifice.

Growing up in the church, I had a fairly "Zwinglian" view of the Lord's Supper. Ulrich Zwingli claimed that the sacraments of Baptism and Eucharist[23] (or Lord's Supper) were nothing more than badges of Christianity. This produces a kind of sorrowful meal, in my opinion, as Christians focus only on the cost of their sin. As Michael Horton says, "Instead of celebrating the foretaste of the marriage supper of the Lamb on Mount Zion, we are still trembling at the foot of Mount Sinai. It is no wonder, then, that there is a diminished interest in frequent communion."[24] As a result, the tender-hearted Christian is often hesitant to come and receive grace. To this, Watson says:

> Has Jesus Christ made this gospel banquet? Is He both the Founder and the Feast? Then let poor, doubting Christians be encouraged to come to the Lord's Table. Satan would hinder them from the sacrament.... But is there any soul that has been humbled and bruised for sin, whose heart secretly pants after Christ, but yet stands trembling and dares not approach to these holy mysteries? Let me encourage that soul to come. "Arise, He calleth thee." (Mark 10:49).... Who does Christ invite to the supper but the poor, halted, and maimed?[25]

As we have already seen from Luke 14, the invitation to the wedding feast is given to the poor, crippled, blind, and lame.

On the other hand, Luther claimed a kind of presence in the Eucharist while denying Rome's re-sacrificing of Christ. Roman Catholicism claims that Christ is essentially brought down from heaven, manifested in the elements (called transubstantiation), and re-sacrificed in every observation to atone for sin. That is truly an abomination, as it denies the sufficiency of Christ's sacrifice on the cross for our sin. It is like Moses in Numbers 20 at Meribah striking the rock unnecessarily. The rock was already struck at Massah/Calvary, and now only a petition of words was necessary to receive the waters for life.

Over time I became convinced by Calvin's view. He claimed that by faith the soul partakes of Christ.

> (Christ) doubtless means that his body will be to us be as bread for the spiritual life of the soul ... it seems to me that Christ meant to teach something more definite, and more elevated, in that noble

---
23 The use of this term is a transliteration of Greek for "thanksgiving," pointing to Christ giving thanks in his institution of the ordinance. See Matt. 26:26–29; Mark 14:22–24; 1 Cor 11:23–26.
24 Michael Horton, *God of Promise* (Grand Rapids: Baker, 2010), 160–161.
25 Watson, "The Mystery of the Lord's Supper," 166–167.

discourse on which he commends to us the eating of his flesh. [John 6:26ff] ... We admit, indeed, meanwhile, that this is no other eating than that of faith, as no other can be imagined. ... I say that we eat Christ's flesh in believing, because it is made ours by faith, and that this eating is the result and effect of faith. ... by true partaking of him, his life passes into us and is made ours.[26]

This is in part derived from Paul's language in 1 Corinthians 10:16, where he says that our drinking the "cup of blessing" is participating in Christ's blood, and eating the bread is participating in Christ's body. The soul is fed from Christ's body and blood for strength and joy, receiving grace. As a colleague of mine once described it, we are spiritually taken up into glory to partake of a meal at Christ's table. What a privilege!

There is still a gravitas when viewing it this way as we approach the Lord's Table in confession of sin. As Watson says, "We that have sinned with Peter should weep with Peter."[27] However, once this sin is confessed, the sorrow gives way to joy and celebration as we, by faith, are carried up to the wedding feast of glory. As Sinclair Ferguson puts it, "In the Supper, the Spirit comes to 'close the gap' as it were between Christ in heaven and the believer on earth, and to give communion with the exalted Savior."[28] Christ is not dragged out of heaven to be re-sacrificed in sorrow, but we are raised up to rejoicing in heaven. Here we experience a portion of Paul's claim in Ephesians 2:6 that we have been raised up with Christ and seated in the heavenlies with Him! Richard Muller says, "The glorious body of Christ is not returned from heaven to earth, but rather the hearts and souls of believers through faith and by the Spirit are raised to union with Christ where he dwells, in heaven."[29] As Augustine prayed, "And when you pour yourself out over us, you are not drawn down to us but draw us up to yourself; you are not scattered away, but you gather us together."[30] How much more fitting, then, is the historical term of *Eucharist*, which means "thanksgiving."

The observation of communion is more than a memorial, as Barcellos notes. It is more than a meal. It is a bridal feast. Faith, the connection of love's knowing trust, makes a wedding feast from the poor man's meal.

---

26 John Calvin, *Institutes of the Christian Religion* IV:XVII:5, 1364–1365.
27 Watson, "The Mystery of the Lord's Supper," 156.
28 Sinclair B. Ferguson, *The Holy Spirit* (Downers Grove: Intervarsity Press, 1996), 203.
29 Richard A. Muller, *Dictionary of Latin and Greek Theological Terms Drawn Principally from Protestant Scholastic Theology* (Grand Rapids: Baker, 2004), 242–43. "praesentia spiritualis sive virtualis,"
30 Augustine, *Confessions* 1:3.

Baptism

While we are on the subject of sacraments, it is fitting to deal with baptism. There has been a long history of debate over this ordinance, just as with the Lord's Supper. Misperceptions abound, especially due to the Bible's description of the sign in terms of the things it signified. Paul talks about baptism as if it actually washed away sins (Acts 22:16; Titus 3:5), which led to a false doctrine we call "baptismal regeneration" that claims that the waters of baptism actually take away sin.

Yet it is clear that this cannot be the case because none of the saints in the Old Testament underwent baptism as we now know it,[31] nor did the thief on the cross. There are those who underwent baptism and were not saved, like Simon the magician. Baptism is a sacrament, like the Lord's Supper, and God imparts grace through it in faith, but the act itself does not wash away sins.

The imagery of baptism is two-fold.[32] First, it identifies the believer with the death, burial, and resurrection of Christ in union and submission. Secondly, it portrays the washing away of sins, which has already occurred in justification by grace through faith. Let us deal with each in turn.

In a believer's baptism, a Christian publicly identifies with his Savior to whom he is united by faith. This is why faith is essential to the sacrament's effectiveness, just like in the Lord's Supper. When that believer passes through the waters of baptism, he declares that he has died to the world, been buried to the world, and raised to newness of life (Rom. 6:2–5). It is a humbling act of submission to Christ, and yet it is one of the most joyful experiences of the Christian life. This is a broad-reaching concept best understood through our bridal metaphor. Dying to the world and its offerings is essential to our souls being wed to Christ, claiming His providence as sufficient for us. We say with David in Psalm 23:1, "I shall not want." As Thomas Manton once said, "And therefore true faith makes us dead to the world, and all the interests and honors thereof; and is to be known not so much by our confidence, as by our

---

31 There is a cornucopia of predecessors to baptism in the Old Testament in purification rituals that followed one being ritually unclean, like touching the dead, and we have already touched on this with the wedding at Cana. We see objects being made clean by passing through water, like spoils of war. Perhaps most importantly, we see the purification rituals for the priesthood, which shows how after the baptism of the Holy Spirit we are made fit to approach the throne, the holy of holies that is heaven, in prayer and supplication. Yet, in all this, we must acknowledge that New Testament baptism is an ordinance of Christ, unique from its predecessors, just as the Lord's Supper is unique from Passover. The image of death and burial was not clearly presented in the OT purification rituals. For a preliminary study of these images, I would recommend Exodus 19:10–14, 29:4, 30:17–21; Leviticus 14–17; Numbers 19:7–10, 31:23.

32 2nd LBC presents four, but I am combining three (union/engraftment with Christ, identifying with his death/burial/resurrection, and submission to God) into the first.

mortification and weanedness; when we carry all our comforts in our hands, as ready to part with them, if the Lord called us to leave them."[33]

This functions the same way as a couple reciting marriage vows. What makes a man and woman legally married is not the declaration of vows, but the signing of the marriage license. Likewise, a Christian does not become a Christian by his public declaration of faith in baptism. The vows are a symbolic act that are treated as necessary unto marriage, even though a couple may be married by a justice of the peace without audibly reciting those vows. On the other hand, a pair of actors in a movie may recite wedding vows to one another without actually becoming married. So, too, a baptism performed without the faith that unites one to Christ does not save him nor impart grace. It is just theater. Yet if a woman refused to make vows on her wedding day, it would be suspect whether she actually desired to be married or was willing to submit in the marriage. This is why we see baptism treated as necessary for Christians.[34]

We again see the bridal metaphor come into play in the image of washing away sins. In Ruth, we saw Naomi instruct her to bathe in preparation for meeting the bridegroom Boaz. Esther was bathed and anointed in preparation for Xerxes. Both of these are images of baptism, but they are incomplete. While the physical act of baptism is performed by a pastor (like Hegai was a servant of Xerxes), the actual cleansing of the Bride is done by Christ through the Holy Spirit, who cleanses her with the washing of the water of the Word (Eph. 5:26).

For proper bathing to occur, every part of the body is washed, as I have often reminded my kids. So, too, every member of Christ's body is called to participate in the image of this cleansing in baptism. Yet the baptism is in the sense of the whole of the church. Ephesians 4:5 has been used to argue that baptism should only be undertaken once, as it speaks of "one Lord, one faith, one baptism." While I agree that baptism is not a repeated ritual, that is not what Paul is presenting.[35] As the Bride of Christ, all of God's people together

---

33 Cited by A.W. Pink, *Hebrews* (New York: Start Publishing, 2012), 788.
34 As I respectfully disagree with my paedobaptist brothers and sisters in Christ, I desire to see them come to an understanding of baptism to be done after a profession of faith. Yet I have pressed my church to allow those baptized as infants who believe their baptism to be valid to be accepted as members of our congregation. The reasoning is this: They have publicly acknowledged Christ as their Savior and believe they have been obedient to that declaration in their infant baptism. This is the essential nature of baptism, and therefore I treat them as misunderstanding the ordinance, though not in rebellion against it. Spurgeon himself once said, "I can make great excuses for brethren who do not see (believer's baptism); I think they might see it if they liked—but if they do not discern the precept, I can understand their not obeying it." (Spurgeon, "A Triumphal Entrance," *Treasury of David*, 472.)
35 For the principle of once-for-all baptism, I always go to Christ's words to Peter at the washing of his feet in John 13:1–10. As baptism is tied to justification, it is a one-time event.

have one Lord. We all have one and the same faith. We all have one corporate baptism, even if it is observed individually.

Before moving on, there is one final note I would like to make about baptism. In the early days of the church, the baptism candidate would disrobe, go down into the waters, and be baptized. When they came out on the other side, they put on a clean white garment. I cannot recommend this for modern practice, but I love the imagery here. The bride is stripped of her old garments, washed by the bridegroom (represented by His minister), and then clothed in purity and fit for the marriage. We will visit this image again under Paul's letter to the Ephesians.

Prayer

Richard Barcellos says, "Prayer is both a spiritual privilege and duty of the Christian. It is the breathing-out of the soul its praise to God and its requests for things perceived as necessary for one's own life or the life of others. Prayer is a great privilege. The believer in Christ has God as his audience during prayer. Prayer... is a means through which God brings needed things to souls. Prayer is a means of grace."[36] And Martyn Lloyd-Jones adds that "prayer is, after all, the highest activity of the human soul."[37]

At the risk of redundancy, I must say that prayer is also a subject well-exposited by many a theologian. Yet my task in much of this is not to give an authoritative, scholarly treatise of complex subjects, but rather to humbly pass these subjects under the lens of the bridal metaphor and draw out an appreciation of the beauty therein.

Prayer is, to put it rather simply, communication with God. It is Trinitarian, as we speak with the assistance of the Holy Spirit to the Father by the mediation of Christ. We are exalted as we exalt God in praise. We are unburdened and reconciled as we confess our sins. We are reminded of His goodness toward us as we express thanksgiving. We unburden our hearts as we entrust our cares to the one who is able to do everything He pleases above and beyond whatever we ask of Him.

The metaphor of bride and bridegroom is essential in this because it saturates the whole event in love and makes it understandable without evicting the mystery and grandeur. It draws us to the truth of Lloyd-Jones' words, "You (after salvation) will long to be so intimate with God that you would sooner spend time speaking to God than anyone else."[38] When my wife talks to me,

---

[36] Richard Barcellos, *The Lord's Supper as a Means of Grace: More Than a Memory* (Glasgow: Bell and Bain, 2013), 74.
[37] Martyn Lloyd-Jones, *God's Ultimate Purpose: An Exposition of Ephesians 1* (Grand Rapids: Baker, 1978), 326.
[38] Lloyd-Jones, *Ephesians 2*, 92.

there is beauty in it. I know that she loves me and appreciates me, but hearing the words make me happy. When she thanks me for everything I have done, it is not only a delight to me but causes her to pause and consider my love for her. She is encouraged as she considers what I have done for her in love.

As for petitions, these are done best in love and faith. When the wife comes and asks things of her husband in love, he is prone to execute them speedily and joyously. When she makes her wants and petitions known, trusting his ability and wisdom, the husband is free to fulfill them to the extent and in the fashion that he perceives is best for her. Then she is able to rest in his love and wisdom. He may even tell her no if he sees that it is not best for her and their marriage. If the Lord's Supper brings the Bride into the banquet hall to taste of the feast, then prayer brings the Bride into the armory and treasury to receive what Christ has already purchased for her in His blood.

One benefit I have found from this metaphor is how it affects the style of prayer. When the relationship is established in grace and love, a husband and wife generally communicate with ease and familiarity. I have had a recurring conversation with an older woman in my church over her fear of being unable to pray eloquently. We all have been tempted to think God will hear us better and be more prone to answer our prayers if they are verbose, especially if we use King James English complete with uses of "thou" and "thus." That is how Paul prayed, right?

I have told her that the point is not to be eloquent but sincere. To pray the Lord's Prayer, it begins with an address of "Our Father who is in heaven." This is not the "hocus pocus" that turns on the divine radio so that He will hear you. It reminds us to whom we are speaking, our Father. He is in heaven, and we are on earth, meaning that He is able to execute His will and perceive our needs better than we. Christ and the Father love to hear from the Bride (corporate prayer) and the children (individual prayer), and it is Christ's mediation and sacrifice that make those words of our prayers precious to them both. Our adoration in prayer should be about affection, not formality.

The Crucifixion

In the Celtic mythology of the Isle of Man, there is a story known as Y Chadee. A young, handsome prince named Eshyn was cursed with ugliness, so he left his father's kingdom. He journeyed to the Otherworld, where, by bravery and wisdom, he succeeded in regaining his previous glory. He also finds a beautiful bride he loves, the princess Y Chadee, the daughter of Orion, who loved him while he was still ugly.[39] Despite its pagan origin, such a narrative resonates with the believer. Our daily meditation is the prince who voluntarily took on

---

39 Peter Ellis, *Celtic Myths and Legends* (Philadelphia: Running Press, 2002), 164–178.

the ugliness of a fallen humanity, though without sin, and became accursed so that He might win His bride. The climax of the gospels, redemptive history, and all of history itself, is the cross and resurrection of Christ. It is no surprise then that the crucifixion where Christ wed His Bride is central to the Bride of Christ narrative we are tracing through redemptive history.

In Luke 9:53, we are told that Christ was not received at a Samaritan village because His face was set toward Jerusalem. In Luke, there is already a record of Christ prophesying His death twice. He strengthened His countenance, and "for the joy that was set before Him" (Heb. 12:2) began the journey. As Calvin puts it, "But as he was neither devoid of feeling, nor under the influence of foolish hardihood, he must have been affected by the cruel and bitter death, or rather the shocking and dreadful agony, which he knew would overtake him from the rigorous judgment of God; and so far is this from obscuring or diminishing his glory, that it is a remarkable proof of his unbounded love to us; for laying aside a regard to himself that he might devote himself to our salvation, through the midst of terrors, he hastened to death, the time of which he knew to be at hand."[40] He had set His mind and path for the cross, wherein He would redeem His Bride at the cost of His own suffering and life.

When my bride and I visited Ireland, we toured Kilmainham Gaol and were told the tragic story of Grace Gifford and Joseph Plunkett. Plunkett was part of the Easter Rebellion in the early 1900s, and Grace was his fiancée. They were married in the jail the night before his execution. Perhaps this comes closest to what we now examine, wherein Christ weds His Bride to Himself not before His execution, but in it.

The Bride's vows and her signature of the wedding covenant are scattered through history and into the future. They are as much in Abraham trusting in God's promises as in John Calvin's heart's response to a sermon in a barn. The bridal vows are the individual responses of the elect in faith to the gospel. In confessing Christ as Lord and Savior in faith, we marry Christ as the Bridegroom. Our wedding vows are secured by identifying with Christ and the cross. To put it another way, *the signatures of both the Bride and Bridegroom on the marriage covenant are written in Christ's blood.*

Christ's vows, however, are declared in the cross. Rather than being surrounded by family and friends, Christ is abandoned by nearly all of those who professed to love Him. His witnesses are Roman soldiers and jeering crowds. His mother weeps at the altar in sorrow rather than joy because it is an altar of sacrifice as well as marriage. He does not proclaim that He *will* love her in sickness and health, in poverty and riches, for worse or better, but

---

40 John Calvin, *Commentaries Vol XVI.*

He sacrifices Himself for her at her sickest, poorest, and worst. He does not come finely dressed to the wedding but is stripped of earthly clothes to suffer shame on her behalf. He is crowned but with the thorns of Adam's curse. In order to hold her hands in matrimony and walk the aisle with her, His hands and feet are nailed to the cross. In place of the reassuring embrace of a father, the Father's face of love is turned away, causing Him to cry out, "My God, my God, why have you forsaken me?" Instead of hearing the joyous words of the Bride, "I do," He cries out, "Father forgive them, for they know not what they do."

The heart of the ceremony is three hours of darkness, wherein Christ is made sin for His Bride and suffers the damnation deserved by His people. Yet He declares the victory, the fulfillment of the vows, while yet on the cross. "It is finished!" In these words, we find our greatest comfort. All that is necessary for us to be found righteous and freed from the bondage of sin has been done. All that remains is for the Holy Spirit to apply for that work, Christ's vows, to the Bride through history and bring her safely to the bridal chamber of glory.

In Matthew's record of the crucifixion, when Christ had accomplished redemption, He yielded up His spirit in death. Then, in 27:51, we are told that the temple veil was torn in two, from top to bottom. This was a vastly symbolic event. Throughout the economy of Moses that spans the Old Testament, the veil separated the Holy of Holies from God's people. In 2 Corinthians 3:12–15, Paul also speaks of the veil that Moses wore as a symbol of the gospel's obfuscation in the Old Testament, which is now removed for those who believe in Christ. "Only through Christ is it taken away" (3:14).

When a bride is presented at the altar for marriage, she wears a veil.[41] It obscures her face and separates her from the fiancé. After the vows have been made, the veil is lifted or taken away for the bridegroom to kiss the bride for the first time as his wife. Christ has removed the veil of His Bride. And to show that the veil could never be put back in place, the veil of the temple was torn.

Resurrection and Ascension

I was in the middle of pursuing my master's degree when I married my bride. As I finished up the semester before the wedding, I was frantically trying to write papers, study for finals, pack up the room I had been renting for the past two years, and fill out paperwork for a new apartment. I was closing out my life as a bachelor and preparing for a new life as a husband.

In Christ's earthly ministry and its culmination at the cross, Christ accomplished redemption for sinners and wed the Bride to Himself. So how then,

---

41 James M. Freeman describes this as "a very ancient custom" in *Manners and Customs of the Bible* (Plainfield: Logos, 1972), 32.

in this running metaphor, are we to view the resurrection and ascension? It is the preparation of the new life in union.

Christ rose again on the third day after His crucifixion. The Father sent an angel to roll away the stone of the tomb, declaring that justice had been satisfied. It affirmed Christ's declaration that "it is finished." A.W. Pink compares this to the guard opening the prison cell door to legally release the inmate and declare him innocent.[42] The price of the wedding and union had been met, and the marriage was established. Unlike the sorrowful marriage of Plunkett, the Bridegroom was alive, never again to die.

Jesus then set about visiting His Bride at the first day of the week, establishing a new era of Sabbath. The former observation was about the Bride "ceasing" preparations for a wedding and seeing her ineffectiveness. Now the Sabbath was about the Bride rejoicing in the presence of the Bridegroom that the preparations and the wedding itself were done. He prepared the Bride for His absence and promised the Comforter who would attend to her until His return. At last, the day came for Him to leave her.

Christ went to prepare for her in heaven. He would spend the next few thousand years interceding for her at the throne of grace, all the while speaking to her by His Spirit and sending His servants, the ministers of the Word, to attend to her needs. He would send her gifts, especially in samplings of the great wedding feast by the Lord's Supper. These were not only tokens of love but foretastes of heaven and promises of what she would have in glory. The wedding has taken place, the vows declared, and the future secured, but the marriage bed of perfect intimacy yet awaits.

This is why we must have that sense of urgency. The honeymoon awaits. I can remember the two-hour drive from my wedding to the honeymoon, the clasped hands and loving glances as I tried to focus on driving. Yet that is where I am today as a Christian. As Bunyan described, I am on the King's highway, journeying to the Celestial City. We, the church on earth, have felt the kisses of the Bridegroom, exulted in His embrace, but we know that it is nothing compared to the consummation of the marriage. Sex remains a taboo conversation topic for many Christians, but the marriage bed is the closest thing we have on earth to the experience of eternal glory. That is what sex is meant to be, unimpeded covenantal intimacy, and that is what heaven is. Ray Ortlund Jr. writes:

> Marriage is not just another mutation of human social evolution, like democracy. It is a divine creation, intended to reveal the ultimate romance guiding all of time and eternity. This is the real reason why

---
42 A.W. Pink, *The Gospel of John* (Grand Rapids: Baker, 2006), 1071.

premarital sex is wrong; it toys with the biblical mystery. The moral imperative is concerned with more than the folly of risking a sexually transmitted disease. God offers a theological rationale in Christ. This is why extramarital sex is wrong; it violates the mystery. This is why same-sex marriages are wrong; they pervert the mystery. And this is why every faithful and loving marriage is precious to God; it shines with the light of Christ's love for his people, and of their devotion to him in the darkness of this present evil age.[43]

The marriage bed is the love and the ecstasy of covenantal union and trust where the two become one flesh, "this mystery is profound, and I am saying that it refers to Christ and the church" (Eph. 5:32).

---

43 Ortlund, *God's Unfaithful Wife*, 173.

IX
PAUL AND THE BRIDE I

Ephesians 1–3

Paul is undeniably a significant mouthpiece of theology and doctrine in the New Testament. Matthew, Mark, Luke, and especially John make their contributions in revealing Christ's narrative and doctrines therein. Peter is a major figure as well, by both his part in Christ's ministry and leading the church after the ascension, in part through his letters. Yet when we want to understand the significance and ramifications of Christ's work, Paul is most often the writer to whom we look. He is the inspired commentator who pulls the Old and New Testaments together and applies the truths of God's self-revelation.[1]

Of Paul's letters, Ephesians is the broadest survey of these principles and deals most with themes that correlate to the bridal metaphor we have been examining. So rather than dealing with each letter piecemeal, I will examine Ephesians and draw in texts from the rest of the epistles as we go.

Orphans Adopted[2]

A world of orphans
 Alienated.
Long lost sinners
 Isolated.
A global orphanage
 And angry mob
Of shaking fists
 And attempts to lob
Stones of furious words
 Like "God is dead",
Hoping to drown out
 Existential dread.
Heaving bricks through windows
 Of their own intellect,

---

[1] Especially if the ancient church was right in crediting him with Hebrews.
[2] This is an original piece of spoken-word poetry.

Shouting "follow us"
>   To every tribe and sect
"We will tear down God
>   like twisted iconoclasts
And replace Him ourselves
>   And we will stand fast
On the day of judgment
>   That will never come
Compile our numbers
>   To a powerful sum",
But yet there are some
>   Who hear the truth
Later in song but
>   At first uncouth;
First, the conscience
>   That screams out the Law
Breaking facades
>   And leaving them raw
Exposing unrighteousness
>   Revealing unworthiness
The calling of "lawlessness"
>   Shows them their life's a mess.
Broken and destitute
>   Like Rahab the prostitute.
Pleading for mercy
>   They cannot deserve.
Pleading for grace
>   From the one they don't serve
Like dogs for crumbs
>   From the master's table.
Drowning in guilt
>   They know they're unable
To earn love
>   From their God.
Since their ancestor
>   Was formed from the sod
Breathed into life
>   Yet broke the law
Tore fruit from the branches
>   And finally saw
What evil was
>   Within himself.

And though once high
    On sacred shelf
He fell, with his wife,
    And all posterity
Fell broken and bent
    From that prosperity
Creating the orphans
    Lost from their God.
Repressing the truth
    They ever applaud
Their works
    To drown out the noise,
Clinging to riches
    Their lusts and their toys.
Yet there are some
    Who from past eternal
God chose to save
    From fate infernal
And sent His Son
    In the fullness of time
To clothe them himself
    In His works sublime,
To turn away wrath
    And absorb it alone.
Now cursed was the one
    Who once sat on the throne
Cursed by their sin
    Through imputation,
Drinking the cup
    For their salvation,
That orphans convicted
    Could now be adopted
By grace through faith
    Their salvation allotted.
For they are made heirs
    Through redemption applied,
Eternal inheritance
    Through Christ now supplied.
Calling, "Abba, Father"
    Who wipes away tears
And approaching the throne
    With boldness, not fear

Pitied,
    Protected,
        Provided for,
            Chastened,
Sealed to that Day
    By everlasting salvation -
Not of themselves
    What they've done
        Or will do -
No man can stand
    To receive his own due,
It's not what they've done
    But what they have heard
Of what Christ has done,
    And salvation assured
In the Gospel of Peace
    To orphans long lost
Through faith we now see
    That adoption's cost
In the cry, "It is finished!",
    Made from the cross
And now He is risen.
    In Heaven he waits
For when angels carry us
    Past those pearl gates
To glory eternal,
    New heavens, new earth
Changed out like a garment
    In cosmos' rebirth,
Where the children adopted
    By faith and by grace
In the arms of their Father
    Will then know their place.

ADOPTION—EPHESIANS 1:3–6

After his standard introduction, Paul proclaims blessing upon God. God is worth blessing just for being God, but Paul adds all the spiritual blessings in heaven that we have received in Christ. He then goes on to describe how those blessings come from God's predestination and election, which is a major theme of the letter.

In Genesis, we saw predestination as an arranged marriage, though Paul focuses here on the products of that salvation, namely sanctification, where we are made "holy and blameless" (3:4). While it is forensic justification[3] that makes us categorically blameless, Paul is speaking of the progressive sanctification process. *Sanctification* comes from a root word meaning holy, just like *saint*. As Christians, we are initially set apart and made holy, but there is a progression of holiness over the course of our lives. We become more and more like Christ and less and less like the world. This holy-fication process is like the journey of a marriage wherein a husband and wife become more like one another, bit by bit. In the Christian life, though, we are only conformed to Christ (Rom. 8:29) because He has already been made like us in all ways except sin in order to be our High Priest (Heb. 2:17–18; 4:15).

In the midst of all this, Paul addresses the *adoption* of those elect in Christ. As many commentators observe, there is a seemingly redundant emphasis on "in Christ." We are predestined in Christ. We are adopted in Christ. Everything that happens to us for the praise of God's glorious grace is in Christ. At the end of this passage, he specifically refers to it as "in the Beloved."

It is generally thought that the reference to Christ as "the Beloved" is to the Father's love for Him. The Father calls Christ the beloved Son in whom He is well-pleased in Christ's baptism and transfiguration (Matt. 3:17; 17:5). Yet there is another dimension to this that is easily overlooked. Christ is not only the Father's beloved as Son, but *our* beloved as Bridegroom, drawing us back to the language of Song of Solomon.

Christ married the Bride, the church, the *ekklesia* of called-out-ones, by His life, death, burial, and resurrection. Through this Bride, children are born to their Father, who is God-in-flesh, as well as to His Father, who is God the Father. It is by these means that we are called "children of the living God."

Here is where it becomes a bit tricky. How can we be adopted if we are born again as God's children? If our regeneration, or second birth, comes before the response in the faith that produces justification, why does John 1:12 describe the sequence as to "as many as received Him," meaning in faith, to those "He gave power to become the sons of God" (KJV)? Why do theologians describe the order of salvation, or *ordo salutis*, as regeneration—response in faith—justification—adoption—sanctification—glorification? Now we have struck upon the key for the lock.

Regeneration makes us children of God, children of Christ, by means of the new birth. Peter said, "Blessed be the God and Father of our Lord Jesus

---

3 Forensic justification is not a distinct thing from regular justification. When we refer to it as "forensic," we simply emphasize the legal aspect of us being declared just in the sight of God on account of Christ's work alone.

Christ, which according to his abundant mercy hath *begotten us again*" (1 Peter 1:3 KJV, emphasis added). Christ told Nicodemus he had to be born again in order to see the Kingdom of God (John 3:3). This is where the Holy Spirit draws us out of death and into life.

But adoption is something different. The word we translate as "adoption" is *huiothesian*, which is related to the word for son, *huios*. In the Greco-Roman world where Paul wrote, this was a term that focused on inheritance rights. This son-making act gave the adopted person rights to inherit titles and wealth from the one who adopted him. So when Paul and the rest of the New Testament speak of adoption, it is the covenantal promise of inheritance of the blessings in heaven through Christ.

In a sense, it is covenanting the inheritance to us, the children, under the umbrella of Christ's marriage to the church. Thomas Goodwin says, "Even as a woman comes to be a man's daughter-in-law by marrying his son, or by his son's betrothing himself to her; so are we sons-in-law unto God,—as the word 'adoption' plainly signifieth,—even by a positive law; and this by marriage with his Son, which makes the relation nearer and stronger than those kind of adoption among men do, when marriage with a child is not added to it."[4] So when Christ married the church, He established the grounds for our adoption, which was impossible before justification. In adoption, what is His by nature is then promised to us, covenanted to us. John Stott says, "God put us and Christ together in his mind. He determined to make us (who did not yet exist) his own children through the redeeming work of Christ (which had not yet taken place)."[5]

There is a chain reaction here. Regeneration makes us sons and daughters of Christ and produces faith (a gift of God) by which we participate in Him. God uses that faith for justification through the blood of Christ to whom we have been united. Our sin is imputed to Him while His righteousness is imputed to us. In justification, the offense between us (Christ's children) and God the Father is taken away, and we are adopted as "Sons of God." This makes us legal heirs of the Father through the Son, just as a grandfather might name his grandson in a last will and testament. Spurgeon reminds us, "Adoption is not an after privilege, granted only to assurance or growth in grace; it is an early blessing and belongs to him who has the smallest degree of faith, and is no more than a babe in grace. If a man be a believer in Jesus Christ, his name is in the register-book of the great family above, 'for here are all the children of God by faith in Christ Jesus.'"[6] In fact, there are many

---

[4] Goodwin, *Ephesians*, 96.
[5] John Stott, *The Message of Ephesians: The Bible Speaks Today* (Nottingham, UK: InterVarsity Press, 1984), Eph. 1:4–6.
[6] Charles Spurgeon, "Adoption—the Spirit and the Cry," Gal 4:6, published as a tract (Grand Rapids: Inheritance).

instances wherein the term "father" is used for a male ancestor instead of strictly the father/son relationship.

In 1 Corinthians 15:45–49, Paul describes our relationships to two Adams. According to the flesh, the first Adam is the one from Genesis, our ancestor and federal head. Adam 1.0 is the origin for our physical life, along with Eve. Because he is our federal head in the flesh, all of us fell in his sin because he represented us. According to the Spirit, the "final Adam" is Christ, our spiritual father/ancestor and federal head. Christ is the origin of our spiritual life, along with the church. Because He is the federal head in the soul and spiritual life, those born again into Him are made righteous by Him, atoned, and made acceptable before God. So Christ became our brother under the first Adam and the law, making the Father His God (Eph. 1:3, 17), in order for Christ to be the last Adam and our Father. We are taken from Adam's family to Christ's family. Hebrews 2:13 quotes Isaiah 8:18 speaking of the children God has given to Christ, pointing both to Christ as our Father by regeneration and to the Trinitarian work behind it. Among the titles ascribed to Christ in the prophecy of Isaiah 9:6–7 is "Everlasting Father."

This emphasizes that our sonship depends on Christ's sonship. A grandchild's inheritance is through and by virtue of his connection to his father, and a bride's inheritance from a father-in-law is dependent on her marriage. As John Stott once said, "The sonship of God is 'in Christ'; it is not in ourselves."[7]

This is the point at which the bridal metaphor is stretched to its limit, and we have to acknowledge the mystery of God as well as the limitations of metaphor. We want to prevent falling into a kind of modalism or partialism as we view the Trinity.[8] Part of this is done simply by seeing that predestination, redemption accomplished, regeneration of the believer, justification, adoption, sanctification, and glorification are all Trinitarian acts. One person of the Trinity may be highlighted in an event, but all three are active in it. All of Scripture's language is the lisping of God to mere mortals. God talks to us like a father to a child in metaphors and similes so that we can grasp an ectypal, finite version of the archetypal reality. So when I say that Christ is our Father and the Father is our grandfather, I am only employing a metaphor Scripture uses to describe how creatures are brought into an incredible relationship to their creator where they are loved and glorified without human merit.

When all of these images are united, it shows how predestination reveals the glory of God the Father and God the Son as Christ and Bridegroom. Thomas Goodwin notes, "God first made Adam; and then, seeing it was not

---

[7] John Stott, *The Message of Ephesians: The Bible Speaks Today* (Nottingham, UK: InterVarsity Press, 1984), Gal. 3:25–29.

[8] Modalism and partialism are heresies that deny the orthodox doctrine of the Trinity. If you do not know these heresies, that is ok. I included that line for the people who know what they are and might be freaking out a bit by what I wrote before.

fit for Adam to be alone, he brought Eve as a companion for him. So did God bring the Church unto Christ as a meet companion for him, for it was not meet that he would be alone; and so we were chosen *for* him."[9] So in election, the Father prepared for the Son to be married. In justification and adoption, the God-in-flesh reconciled us to the God-without-flesh.

All of this is actually communicated to us by the Holy Spirit, primarily by the means of grace. All these graces are planned by the Father and accomplished by the Son. Still, they are directly applied by the Spirit in the chronology of our lives, first by preaching, then further enlarged by the sacraments (baptism and Lord's Supper), preaching, and prayer.

The Bride and the Spirit—Ephesians 1:11–14

As Paul reaches the end of his breathless sentence that spans verses 3–14, he deals with redemption applied in light of redemption planned and accomplished. In other words, these verses are about the Holy Spirit applying to individual saints what the Father planned and Jesus accomplished. These verses are important for our narrative for a few reasons. First, Paul is showing us that the Jews are saved in the same way (and to the same degree) as the Gentile Christians, which shows the unity and singularity of the Bride of Christ.

For the second, allow me to weave a story for you. A long time ago, in a blighted fiefdom, a woman was debilitated by illness to such a point that she was in a coma. We will call her Anastasia. Anastasia had broken countless laws of criminal negligence of her children, theft, perjury, treason, murder, and more. For all her crimes, she was imprisoned and awaited, unbeknownst to her, execution.

A surprising father-son conversation took place within the royal palace in the land where Anastasia lay condemned. The king had arranged a most unusual marriage for his son, not to a daughter of a king or ruler, but to a daughter of poverty and wickedness, in order to show kindness and grace. The prince asked where he might find her and came to the prison hospital. When he found her upon the hospital bed, she was decimated by the illness, emaciated, filthy, and ugly. But having the same heart as his father, Joshua set his love upon his betrothed, Anastasia.

He then set to work, first by disguising himself as a commoner of the kingdom, then traveling through the land and repairing the damages wrought by her crimes. He called upon the royal doctor to revive her from the coma and attend to her until she was fully healed. He persuaded his father to grant her a legal pardon. With all this done, Joshua purchased a beautiful dress fit for a queen to replace the rags of her imprisonment. She remained in the

---
9 Goodwin, *Ephesians*, 99.

prison hospital but now served her former captors and prison-mates with a tenderness and grace she did not have before. The prince came with a pastor to perform the wedding, the pastor giving her each line of her vows to recite. The prince placed a beautiful ring upon her finger that testified that she was the princess bride. He left her in order to prepare a room in the palace for them to be together. Still, in his absence, he sent her a royal messenger with words of comfort, encouragement, and descriptions of the palace where she would live happily ever after. The prince even sent the royal chef with meals fit for a princess to assist her in healing and gaining strength while the doctor continued to attend to her. Each day she became more beautiful. Each day she became more loving like her beloved. Each day she grew in love for the prince who loved her first.

In this thinly veiled metaphor, it is easy enough for us to identify Christ, the church, and the Father, but that is not why I am telling it. In the bridal metaphor, the roles of the Father, Son, and Bride are easily discerned, but we serve a Trinitarian God. Where is the Holy Spirit? The Spirit is the doctor who revives and heals, the pastor who marries the church to Christ, the ring upon her finger, the messenger who comforts and encourages, and the chef who feeds the Bride's soul by the body and blood of Christ. He is the outstretched hand of the prince. Augustine said that the Holy Spirit is the bond of love between the Father and the Son in what we call the ontological Trinity, and He is also the bond of love between us and both Father and Son.[10]

So when Paul describes the sealing and earnestness of the Holy Spirit to our inheritance in Ephesians 1:13–14, we see that royal messenger proceeding from the Bridegroom to give assurance, experience, and hope of the love to be enjoyed eternally. John Stott notes that in modern Greek, the word *arrabon* that we translate as "earnest" or "guarantee" is now used to denote an engagement ring.[11] Beautiful as that is, it is not quite right for our analogy. An engagement ring is a promise that someday the covenant will be made that creates the marriage. We could kind of say that about the work of the Holy Spirit in the Old Testament or the Spirit's work of regeneration before justification. But the outpouring of the Spirit we have after Christ's ascension is something else. It is the wedding ring that testifies to the vows declared and the covenant "cut."[12]

---

10 Cited in Ferguson, *The Holy Spirit*, 77. The whole paragraph there deserves reading, not just the Augustine reference.
11 Stott, *Ephesians*, 48–49.
12 In the ancient Near East, when you made a covenant, they said you "cut" a covenant because you actually cut it into stone, which might be where the phrase "cut a deal" comes from, but I really have no idea. Anyway, when your Bible says "they made a covenant," it is actually "cut a covenant" in the original text. The more you know . . . insert rainbow graphic.

Regeneration—Ephesians 1:19–20

There is a sense in which the whole Bride is being regenerated. In Hosea and Ezekiel, we saw these themes of death for the sake of rebirth. When Paul is writing, this new Bride is emerging from the chrysalis of her metamorphosis as a multi-ethnic Bride, and we will see more of this as we progress. Here, in 1:19–20, Paul is focusing on the individual narrative of rebirth that has more to do with the Bride's children than the Bride herself, but what is true of the parts is true of the whole.

Regeneration is something we have already seen repeatedly in shadow. One of the most vivid presentations in Scripture is Ezekiel's valley of dry bones (chapter 37). Christ Himself presents the concept to Nicodemus in the opening of John 3, where He declares that unless a man is born again of the Spirit, he cannot see the kingdom of God. Yet nowhere is the image of regeneration presented more clearly in terms of its power than in the text now before us.

Paul begins by heaping up synonyms in verse 19 to describe God's power employed. It is a surpassing or "overcasting" greatness of power, meaning it goes further than any other. Even some works of God's power are less than what we are examining. It is an effectual working, the energy of the unstoppable force of God's determination. It is God's "great might," and the word for "great" is often translated as "dominion."

As if this was not enough, Paul goes on to declare that this power is the same kind and degree employed in the resurrection and exaltation of Christ. The power of God is displayed in creation, in providence, in other resurrection events, and even in the condemnation of sinners, but Paul knows that these are lesser by comparison. Christ's resurrection and our regeneration are the fullness of Trinitarian power.

When other people in redemptive history are raised from the dead, like the widow's son through Elijah or Lazarus and the Centurion's daughter by Christ, only one or two persons of the Trinity are "visibly" engaged.[13] The resurrection of Christ, though, employed all three persons of the Trinity. Acts 2:24–36 shows the Father's role in the resurrection, Romans 8:11 examines the Spirit's, and 1 Thessalonians 4:14 the Son's.

It is also the fullness of God's power. That is not to say that God's power was exhausted in this, but that all His faculties were engaged in this miraculous act

---

13 The widow's son is raised by only the Holy Spirit, and some would say the same for Lazarus and the Centurion's daughter being only by the Spirit's power and not the Son's. At the end of the day, these things are hard to parse out. With the unity of the Trinity, it is hard to say that one person's power can be utilized without engaging the other two, but my point is that we are only shown specific persons engaged in an act, to the exclusion of others.

of raising Christ from the dead. In the cases of Enoch and Elijah, they only escaped death. With Lazarus and the others, death was briefly overturned, and they would eventually return to the grave.[14] Only Christ's resurrection was a conquering of death.

So the power we are examining, to sum up, is the *fullness* of surpassing, overcasting greatness of the power, the effectual working of the great might of the omnipotent *triune* God that conquered death to raise Christ and exalt Him. This power is directed at Christ's Bride.

Lloyd-Jones asks, "What is the exceeding greatness of his power to us-ward who believe by virtue of his mighty power working in us? To bring one soul to believe in God and in Christ demands the exceeding greatness and strength of God's eternal might; and without it we are utterly and completely helpless. By the grace of God, and by that alone, I am what I am (1 Cor. 15:10)."[15] The resurrection of Christ is by the fullness of Trinitarian power, and so is our salvation for which Christ died. As Thomas Goodwin said, God has called us to love Him with all our strength, so, too, He loves us with all His strength. Only the power of God can depose Beelzebub the king of self-love and cast down his strongholds to turn a man to faith and salvation.[16] Were all the angels of heaven and all the saints present and past to pour their collective might into changing the hearts of one man, they could not do it. Only by the Father's will in the Son's work applied by the Holy Spirit are sinners saved.

So, first, Paul uses this reference of Christ's resurrection to show the power in regeneration because it is equal in exertion, so to speak. Second, it is appropriate because we are looking at the resurrection of the soul from spiritual death, to which Paul speaks later in 2:1–5. Third, these are conjoined efforts of God's love to accomplish redemption. Goodwin says, "The power that God will shew in glorifying his saints will infinitely exceed the power he sheweth in condemning wicked men. The power that love stirreth up is a greater power than what wrath stirreth up in God."[17]

Our final lesson from the text is the *monergistic* nature of salvation. God intentionally employs metaphors for regeneration beyond human capacity: the open-heart surgery of replacing the Bride's heart of stone with a heart of flesh, raising the Bride from the dead, and being born again. In surgery, resurrection, and birth, no one could claim involvement. So, too, the regeneration

---

14 It is worth noting that in art history tradition, depictions of Lazarus show him to be quite perturbed, because he was dragged out of heaven to a fallen world and knew he would have to die again before returning. I have no citation for this, as I learned it in a college lecture from a professor whose name I have forgotten.
15 Lloyd-Jones, *God's Ultimate Purpose: An Exposition of Ephesians 1*, 410.
16 Goodwin's treatise on Ephesians has been influential on every part of this section spanning pages 323–465.
17 Goodwin, *Ephesians*, 337.

of the lost is the work of God alone. Paul emphasizes this by saying, "This is the power of God toward us." It is not our power to wield or set down, but God's work alone. This is why one of my favorite declarations of the Second London Baptist Confession is that the elect is "thereby enabled to answer this call and to embrace the grace offered and conveyed in it, and that by no less power than that which raised up Christ from the dead."[18]

Exaltation and Union—Ephesians 1:21–23

This passage essentially has two concepts that dovetail into one: Christ in His exaltation and Christ with His church. Paul is praying for the Holy Spirit to reveal to the Ephesians the power of Christ's resurrection and ascension. He wants this for their comfort and growth. So let us examine each in turn along with their connection to our metaphor.

The beauty of Ephesians 1:20b–22 is that it brings together images scattered throughout the Old and New Testaments. We find pieces of dominion/supremacy language in Genesis 1:26–28 (Adam's call to dominion that is fulfilled and furthered in Christ), Psalm 2:7–12, Psalm 8:6 (quoted in Hebrews 2:8 as prophecy of Christ), Psalm 110, 1 Corinthians 15:24–28, Ephesians 4:10, Philippians 2:9–11, Colossians 2:15, and Colossians 3:1. Paul brings all these concepts together in this passage to describe Christ at the right hand of the Father. From His place in heaven, Jesus is ruling over all principalities and powers that can be named, and putting all under His feet.[19] He has even conquered death and will vanquish it in the end! There is nothing in heaven or earth, forces human, natural, spiritual, or angelic, that can overthrow His authority as King.

When we take this in the context of the bridal image, we see the church as the queen that rejoices in the authority and glory of her Husband, the King. She is willingly and happily subject to the King. Christ's conquest of the church does not force begrudging, external submission after battle that masks resentment and a rebellious heart; it is a conquest of her heart. He has wooed her and drawn her to Himself. This places the church in a unique position. As the queen is simultaneously the beloved of the king and a subject, the church lives in the honored position of Bride while remaining subject to her Husband and King. We, the church, have an imputed authority, not intrinsic authority.[20]

---

18 2nd LBC X.2.
19 This imagery harkens back to Joshua 10 and the placing of the foot on the neck of the five conquered kings.
20 Christ has given authority to His church for her functioning, but it is grace. Imputed authority means that it has been transferred to us, but Christ has intrinsic authority by His nature as God.

This is key to understanding the authority of elders in the church as they represent Christ and, more directly, the church to the congregation. Christ alone has legislative authority in and of Himself. He determined the nature of the church and the nature of her worship. The apostles had a kind of legislative authority derived from the Holy Spirit's inspiration, but it was only to declare what Christ revealed to them. Paul did not invent offices of elders and deacons, he only proclaimed them as Christ's prophet. Even less so do the elders hold authority. As a queen may declare the will of the king to servants and subjects, the elders (representing the Bride) declare what God has revealed in the Scriptures. The elders govern the church by the Scriptures, not themselves. Elders and pastors hold *imputed administrative* authority, not *intrinsic legislative* authority.

These are the principles that drive doctrines like Christian liberty and what is known as the regulative principle of worship. The Reformers took great offense, and rightly so, at the pope's claim to have legislative authority that essentially set him as the king of the church. The pope claims that he is the head of the church, a position Scripture ascribes to Christ alone, but we will come back to that image shortly.

We do well to meditate often on the power and authority of the exalted Christ.[21] It is our comfort and security as the children of God as well as the corporate Bride. A queen has reason to be worried if her husband is a foolish king whose authority is threatened because her destiny is tied to his. When we look upon Christ, His perfect wisdom, power, and authority is not only uncontested, it is uncontestable. There we find great comfort as His Bride and children.

Yet all this begs the question, "Why us?" Every believer, when faced with his own sin, asks why God would choose him. Why would God choose the weak and simple people of this world to constitute His Bride? The simple answer is for His own glory. Thomas Goodwin adds to this a beautiful, if not humbling, explanation:

> I will give you the reason why Jesus Christ makes his wife and his spouse of those that are under his feet. . . . What is the reason that kings will not marry so low, they affect to marry kings' daughters, but yet great, absolute monarchs will not do so. Go among the Turks and Persians, read the Book of Esther; they never affected to marry kings' daughters. Why? Because they would acknowledge none greater than themselves, therefore they would marry slaves, such as were under their feet: so Turks do at this day; it is to show their greatness. It is all one to them to choose a king's daughter or a slave; for they

---

21 I say this of exalted Christ because of the context of Paul's work. Christ had, in a sense, all this authority and power even during His earthly ministry as the Son, but it is brought to light especially after His ascension.

acknowledge themselves so high that no king else could come up to them. So it is with Jesus Christ . . .[22]

In other words, Christ chooses such a bride because there is no bride fit for Him as an equal, no princess with comparable inheritance. So He chooses that Bride from the lowest ranks of creatures to display both His greatness and His grace.

Now we return to the doctrine of union with Christ that produces the unity of the church. As I described in the chapter on Genesis, the bridal metaphor gives us the safest avenue by which to approach the doctrine without making it into more than it is. It conveys what Horton describes: "There is union without fusion, communion without absorption, with the covenant people (ecclesia) always in the position of receiving rather than of extending the personal existence and gracious reign of its ascended Lord."[23] In the 1644 First London Baptist Confession of Faith, our bridal metaphor is used to describe "that God the Father, and Son, and Spirit, is one with all believers, in their fullness, in relations, as head and members, as house and inhabitants, *as husband and wife* . . ."[24]

We are revisiting union in Ephesians 1:22–23 because Paul presents the image of Christ as head of the church. There are three different "head" metaphors of Christ. As Goodwin says:

> I come to . . . The Head of the Church. It is a similitude, as all that are made of Christ have the greatest reality in them. A head in Scripture is to be taken in three several senses. There is, first, a political head, a ruling head, as a king is said to be the head of his loyal subjects. . . . Secondly, there is a conjugal head, as a husband is the head of his wife. . . . Thirdly, there is a natural head . . . that is the head of the natural body, as a man's head is of the members of his body. In all these senses is our Lord and Savior Jesus Christ, head of the church in a peculiar manner.[25]

As we have seen already, the political head and conjugal head are not mutually exclusive metaphors for king and queen. The majority of headship instances in the Scriptures use those two, yet this instance in Ephesians uses the language of the natural head.[26] As the body derives its wisdom and knowledge

---

22 Goodwin, *Ephesians*, 532.
23 Horton, *The Christian Faith*, 850.
24 1644 LCF chapter 24. Note, this was removed in the revisions made later, because it was confusing in the way it was written. Italics mine.
25 Goodwin, *Ephesians*, 545–546.
26 Chrysostom's homilies on Ephesians seem to indicate that he took headship to be about husband and wife, specifically in comments on 2:6 he speaks of Jacob's wife bowing in him in regards to Gen. 37:9–10.

from the brain, so does the church from Christ. Movement and coordination begin with the head. Christ is likewise the source of life for the church, which cannot live without Him.

Yet quickly we see how these headship metaphors overlap. The queen is subject to the king and follows the instruction of his wisdom and knowledge.[27] Her life is tied to his. And as a wife's identity is partially derived from the marriage, as Eve's was from Adam, the church's identity is derived from Christ.

Paul tells us that Christ is the head and the church is His fullness. This contains two aspects. The first is that the church completes Christ. While the Son has no intrinsic need outside the Trinity, Christ as the God-Man considers Himself incomplete without the church and saints. Calvin says, "This is the highest honor of the Church, that, until He is united to us, the Son of God reckons himself in some measure imperfect. What consolation is it for us to learn, that, not until we are along with him, does he possess all his parts, or wish to be regarded as complete!"[28] And Hendriksen agrees, "As to his divine essence, Christ is in no sense whatever dependent on or capable of being completed by the church. But as *bridegroom*, he is incomplete without the *bride*."[29] This means that the least member of the church, the weakest and poorest, is still essential to the fulness of Christ.

Earlier, I made the claim that the majority of "headship" passages are about conjugal/royal headship rather than natural, so let us briefly examine those passages. Ephesians 4:3–7 explores the unity of the church body in light of the Trinity. There is one body, Spirit, hope, calling, Lord (Christ as conjugal/royal head), faith, baptism, God, and Father for every saint regardless of ethnicity, geography, or time. The church derives its unity from the Trinity. When we observe the church as the Bride of Christ, we see the Trinity at work and each person thereof concerned with our salvation. The Son is the one Lord and Husband.[30] The Father has arranged the marriage and adopts the Bride and children, being above, through, and in all aspects of the Bride's vitality. The Spirit animates the Bride like circulatory and nervous systems with life-giving blood and electrical impulses. Here, the Scriptures and the pastors who preach them are like nerves and blood vessels.[31] We must, then, have every aspect of this, or we have none of it. We either live in union to the

---

27 The metaphor here is limited, as husbands should make decisions for the household with the combined wisdom of husband and wife. Christ, however, has all of the fulness of the wisdom of God, and needs none of ours, which is only granted by him.

28 John Calvin, *Commentaries Vol XXI*, 218.

29 William Hendriksen, *Galatians, Ephesians, Philippians, Colossians, and Philemon* (Grand Rapids: Baker, 2002), 104.

30 We saw some of this same Lord/Husband language back in Hosea.

31 Matthew Henry, *Commentary on the Whole Bible*. In Eph. 4:16, he describes the Spirit in conjunction with the sacraments, faith and love to be like the veins and arteries of the body of Christ.

flesh, the world, and Satan and are bound to their defeat, or we live in union to the Trinity (with a subsequent *bodily* unity) and are bound to their victory.

At first glance, Ephesians 4:15–16 appears to be natural headship. It speaks of the head and the members (each joint and part working properly). Yet, to look more closely, it is strange to speak of the body growing up into Christ the head. It is possible that Paul sees the early church as being in the stage of infant or pubescent disproportion, with a head too big for her body. It is more natural, however, to see the church here as growing and maturing as the young wife of a mature and wise husband, even though Paul speaks of the mature "man." She is growing into her role. Ephesians 5:23 is explicitly about Christ as conjugal head, but we will leave that until later.

The letters to Corinth are focused on unity because of that church's tendency toward division. We see this in an early church letter: "Do we not have one God, and one Christ, and one gracious Spirit that has been poured out upon us, and one calling in Christ? Why do we mangle and mutilate the members of Christ and create factions in our own body? Why do we come to such a pitch of madness as to forget that we are members of one another?"[32] First Corinthians 11:3 certainly carries that tone for us, declaring God as the head of Christ, Christ the head of each Christian man, and the husband as the head of the wife. First Corinthians 12:14–31 is perhaps the most famous of these "body of Christ" passages, though the reference to Christ as head is absent. Some would assume that this is natural headship, but that becomes problematic when some members are described as eyes, ears, and noses. It is more likely that Paul is taking this long-running and exhaustive metaphor of the Bride of Christ and applying it here again to the church, especially given that reference in the previous chapter.

Colossians 1:18 could go either way. We can attach it to the preceding idea of holding all things together (which would indicate natural head) or what follows about Christ being the firstborn (which would make Him the kingly Husband and conjugal head). Colossians 2:9–10 closely parallels our Ephesians 1 passage but seems to lean more toward the conjugal head image. If we take it in this way, it provides beautiful imagery for how the church participates in the deity. The Bride is known by her Husband in the intimate embrace of the marriage bed and is completed by Him. This teaches that the church and her members participate in Christ without some kind of panentheistic view of ecclesiology.[33] Admittedly, though, Paul may only be speaking of Christ as natural head and filling His church, the body, by His Holy Spirit.

---

32 1 Clement 46:6–7.
33 Panentheism is the idea that God or some divine force is "in" every part of the universe. Rather than the Christian concept of omnipresence, where God is in all places at all times while distinct from it, panentheism would claim that we all have some "god-ness" in each of us. Ecclesiology is doctrine of the church.

Last but not least, Colossians 2:19 is a use of the natural head image.

If we could really understand our being part of the body of the Bride, it would eliminate envy among the saints. We could realize that Jesus loving the eye or the hand of the Bride means loving the Bride. Their gain is ours, as is their love and joy.

A Tale of Two Fathers—Ephesians 2:1–5

It is troubling to open this segment of Holy Writ and only address a minor theme within it. Ephesians 2 is, in my opinion, the most beautiful discourse of the doctrines of grace, especially in terms of total depravity, unconditional election, and salvation Solus Christus Sola Gratia. I cannot imagine anyone reading that text and not falling in love with Reformed theology. These first five verses summarize Christian anthropology, theology, and soteriology by showing who man is (in his spiritual death and depravity), who God is (in mercy and grace), and how man is saved (in Christ).

Thomas Goodwin and Martyn Lloyd-Jones have both written elegantly and exhaustively in commentary on this text, and yet there is a theme at play here that I wish to draw out without denying what these men and others have rightly proclaimed about the passage. To do this, I will first give a painfully short treatment of the text outside the metaphor, and then draw out another layer of meaning through the bridal metaphor we have been using.

The first three verses describe man without the supernatural work of redemption, specifically what the Ephesians were prior to that work.[34] Man is born spiritually dead in sin and pressed on three sides to remain in that state. The flesh labors in its passions, the world with its empty cares, and Satan in deceptions. Man is a son of disobedience, by nature a lawbreaker, and a son of wrath, meaning he is born under the condemnation of God for sin. This triune influence of flesh, world, and Satan can only be overcome by the same Trinitarian work that raised Christ from the dead. As the text declares, "but God..." God's mercy, grace, love, and power come upon sinners and save them.

Paul intentionally uses two genealogy references that tie in to the metaphor we have been tracing since Genesis. We are born sons of disobedience and children of wrath. He is pointing back to the fall and the condemnation passed on to each subsequent generation. Because of Adam's sin and its consequence, spiritual death, which God warned him of in Genesis 2:17, every natural man in his line is spiritually stillborn. So in this sense, we are sons of Adam's disobedience. I say all this to affirm what others have said of the text so that I might then step further out.

---

[34] The same is true of Paul himself.

However, what is most terrifying here is not our role as sons of Adam. In John 8:44, Christ tells the unbelieving Jews that they are of their father, the devil, and following him, as opposed to their claimed lineage of Abraham. Here in our text, we are told unregenerate man is following after Satan, the prince of the power of the air, and under his influence. This influence is said to be on the sons of disobedience. So all of mankind is not only born into death by Adam, but also by Satan. This adds a new dimension to "sons of disobedience" and "children of wrath." Satan was the original usurper and under the wrath of God, and so, too, are his children.

Adam was created into a role of submission, as the initial bride in shadow. He was designed to function in submission to God, but he ate of the fruit, believing the lie of the serpent that he would be like God.

This sheds new light on the concepts that follow in terms of regeneration through Christ. Mankind is spiritually dead to God, born into wrath and disobedience under Adam and Satan. Unregenerate man is spiritually the child of Adam and Satan. As such, he is brought forth in iniquity, as David says in Psalm 51:5. For a man to be saved, he must die to sin and the devil, to the flesh and the world. He must die with Christ to the world and be born again of Christ to eternal life and the kingdom of God. Romans 6:2–10 presents exactly this. God rehabilitates and renovates those saints on whom He has set His mercy, grace, and love. He regenerates man by the Holy Spirit and grants saving faith that unites them to Christ's death, burial, and resurrection. We can no more save ourselves than be born again by our own will. We cannot resurrect ourselves, but God is able.

Unity of Unities—Ephesians 2:11–12

Here is a beautiful discourse on the nature of peace in unity. While Paul is not explicitly using the bridal metaphor in these verses in Ephesians, when he encounters the same concept in 1 Corinthians 12, he explains it through the body metaphor, as we have already seen. In verse 15, he does allude to the body metaphor, albeit male, so it is no stretch for us to apply the bride metaphor here to great benefit.

Paul the Jew is writing to Gentiles about how the work of Christ has gathered the elect out of both and into the church. The Mosaic ceremonial institutions found their end in Christ, and now the two peoples are united in Christ. This goes well beyond shared hobbies and common goals; Paul speaks of the two becoming one in Jesus. It is difficult for us in our era to comprehend how revolutionary this idea was, because each despised the other. William Barclay gives us a glimpse into that divided world:

> The Jew had an immense contempt for the Gentile. The Gentiles, said the Jews, were created by God to be fuel for the fires of hell. God, they said, loves only Israel of all the nations that he had made. . . . It was not even lawful to render help to a Gentile mother in her hour of sorest need, for that would simply be to bring another Gentile into the world. Until Christ came, the Gentiles were an object of contempt to the Jews. The barrier between them was absolute. If a Jewish boy married a Gentile girl, or if a Jewish girl married a Gentile boy, the funeral of that Jewish boy or girl was carried out. Such contact with a Gentile was the equivalent of death.[35]

Paul then shows how this union of believers is really God-ward. These Jews and Gentiles, the near and far off, are not just brought together horizontally, as politics strive to do. They are brought together as they are drawn upward to Christ. It is like a wind chime. Laying down, the various tubes sprawl out, but are tied together by strings into one knot. When that knot is raised vertically, all the pieces are drawn to the center.

Paul employs a handful of metaphors to convey this. They are one man, fellow citizens, one household, and a temple of living stones. The citizenship image is unique for Paul's circumstance, a Jew and yet Roman citizen who had specific privileges other Jews did not as mere conquered peoples under the Roman Empire. Paul was writing this letter from Rome because he had a right to appeal to Caesar!

With all this in mind, I would like to draw the individual concepts of Ephesians 2 together under the bridal metaphor to its own union. God's people come from a variety of backgrounds, ethnicities, classes, and experiences. We can even say they come from different eras of human history into one universal church. All this is displayed to us in the Bride.

We are one body under Christ's headship and animated by the same Holy Spirit. It is cancerous for one part of the body to pit itself against another. Such infighting is pointless, self-destructive, and entirely averse to the newly created nature. Psalm 133 declares the precious nature of the unity of the saints, how good and precious is that unity among brothers (and sisters). Embrace this truth and live it out with eternal perspective. Know that your brothers and sisters in Christ, regardless of their intelligence, politics, ethnicity, or even idiosyncrasies, are one with you in the body. Love one another as Christ commanded (John 13:34–35), for love covers a multitude of sins (1 Peter 4:8). Consider each above yourself in humility, as Paul teaches in Philippians 2:3. Be longsuffering and eager to forgive in kindness, which are fruit of the Spirit

---

35 Quoted by John Stott, *Ephesians*, "A Single New Humanity (2:11–22)" and in a blog post at Langham.org, November 18, 2016. http://us.langham.org/bible_studies/18-november-2016/.

(Gal. 5:22). Do this in the church, with your spouse, your children, and even strive for this in your relationship to unbelievers who may yet be saved.

We are designed for unity, which is why isolation is a destructive path. Many people claim to be Christians yet willfully isolate themselves from the local church for a variety of (illegitimate) reasons. It is baffling that people do this because it is essentially self-excommunication. The severest degree of discipline in the church is the removing of a person from the membership, yet many do this to themselves! Returning to the bridal body concept, isolation is like attempting to cut off your own arm and then artificially keep it alive by oxygenating a blood supply and pumping it through. You could use electrical impulses to stimulate the muscles and reduce atrophy. It is possible, through modern science, but it would be painful and pointless, as the arm no longer serves a purpose for the rest of the body. The body of the Bride is meant to be united and laboring together in love for the Bridegroom.

The Bride, by marriage, changes citizenship and household, as do her children. Imagine, if you will, the son of Caesar in Paul's day taking a bride from Ephesus. She would be given Roman citizenship by right of the marriage, and any children born from her by Caesar's son would have that citizenship as well. They would all become part of Caesar's household, and privileged in ways that other Ephesians were not. True, any Ephesian had general benefits from Rome, like road systems and protection by the Roman army, just as all people are granted common graces by God, but Caesar provided for his own household far beyond what he gave the conquered peoples.

This is important for our perspective in life, as we are often distracted with the cares of the world and even allegiances to it. We are no longer citizens of this world. We live here; we engage with the politics for the sake of our livelihood, fellow man, and our children. Yet we must remember that our citizenship and household has been changed. The words of Psalm 45:10–11 are for us as that daughter and queen to heed. We are to forget our people and our father's house, and the king will desire our beauty. Because He is our Lord, we must bow to Him.

One of these privileges, and perhaps the greatest of them, would be access to the throne room. If the wife or child had some need or great desire, they could come to the foot of Caesar by the introduction of Caesar's son saying, "This is my wife" or "This is my child, please hear what he has to say." This is what Paul conveys to us when he says that through Christ we all have access by the Holy Spirit to the Father. When we come to God in prayer, we are heard not as mere creatures, or even just citizens of heaven as Philippians 3:20 tells us, but as members of the household of God. The author of Hebrews tells us that we have boldness to approach the throne of grace with our petitions

(4:16; 10:19–22). Paul's Roman citizenship did not spare his life, but heaven was secure because he was not only a citizen of heaven through Christ, he was a child of the household of God.

The Suffering Bride—Ephesians 3:1

One of the great recurring plot lines is the underdog tale, most commonly in sports films. If you have ever watched the *Rocky* movies, you know what I am talking about. You may have noticed that writers almost always include a love interest for the main character because it gives depth to the sorrow and magnifies the triumph. You not only watch the main character struggle, you watch the wife or girlfriend suffer vicariously and personally, especially in terms of poverty. Even if their suffering is less than the main character, it is suffering nonetheless. We are sympathetic to the wife because she is willing to identify and suffer with the protagonist.

In Ephesians 3:1, Paul begins a thought on his current prayer life wherein he alludes to his current imprisonment, but he takes a detour to address the proverbial elephant in the room. It would have been disheartening for the Ephesians to hear that the man who preached the gospel to them was now a criminal awaiting trial. So Paul, with that beautiful pastoral heart of his, takes the time to explain why this is no reason to lose heart, but rather something in which they can rejoice. He calls it their glory (v. 13).

We do not even have to go into the parenthetical explanation (which runs up to verse 13) to really understand Paul's heart in this and the grace given to him. Look at how Paul describes his state here in verse 1: "I, Paul, a prisoner of Christ Jesus on behalf of you Gentiles." He knows that he is where he is because he preached the gospel to Gentiles like the Ephesians. He does not try to hide that fact, but proudly proclaims it. This is not resentment, saying, "I would be free and loving life if it was not for you people." It is a statement of fact.

The real treasure here is his self-description, "a prisoner of Christ Jesus." Paul uses similar language in Ephesians 4:1, 2 Timothy 1:8, and Philemon 1 and 9. It is true that Paul was a prisoner of Caesar and Rome, but he looks beyond that to see God's sovereignty in his life. When Paul's life was transformed on the road to Damascus, he did not know that new course would lead him to prison in Rome, but God did. Paul did not even know he would be executed when he wrote this letter, but God did. Paul *did* know that God worked all things together for the good of those that love and serve Him as he wrote to the Romans (8:28)!

The reason I am addressing this in this book is that it is the vicarious and personal suffering of the Bride. What is the question always asked of

Christians? "Why does God let bad things happen?" Or there is the phrasing I really despise, "Why does God let bad things happen to good people?" There are not actually good people for bad things to happen to, except Christ, who suffered for our sake. Yet the question remains, "Why do terrible things happen even to those who love and serve God?"

There are multiple aspects to the answer. Part of it is that we, as humanity, are to blame. As we heard before from Owen, "Men may thank themselves for death and hell."[36] So we might say that in many of those instances, it is bad people (sinners) doing bad things to other bad people. However, the greater part of it is that God is using the brokenness of this world to glorify Himself and to prepare His saints for glory.

All of that is embedded in Paul's declaration that he is a prisoner of Christ. He is part of the Bride who suffers in identifying with Christ but will enjoy the glory of heaven, even the new heavens and new earth with Christ. Just as the underdog hero rejoices in success and riches with the wife who suffered with him through the hard times, so, too, will the saints be included in the ecstasy of eternal life. So the next time someone asks you about why God would put you through a certain trial, you can tell them, "I do not know all of it, but I know that I deserve far worse for my sins, that I can count it all joy to suffer in part as my Savior did in whole, and that it allowed me to have this conversation with you."

In Acts 20, we see Paul speak to the Ephesian church for the last time in person. He told them that he was going to Jerusalem, and he knew imprisonment was a certainty. Yet he was determined to go because he did not count his life as precious, only the mission imparted to him by Christ Himself. That mission, that ministry, he said, was to testify to the gospel of grace (Acts 20:24).

We can see this truth in Paul's life from the clarity of the future. Paul, had he remained a Pharisee, probably would have died in the destruction of Jerusalem around AD 70. We can see how God used his imprisonment to minister to Caesar's household as a steward of grace unto them. We can be especially grateful that Paul's imprisonment gave him time to write not only Ephesians, but Philippians, Colossians, 2 Timothy, and Philemon. Paul did not lament his imprisonment because he knew he was precisely where God meant for him to be. As Lloyd-Jones observes, his reaction is not bitterness over God's providence, stoicism in the face of trouble, or even calm acceptance. He rejoices in it! He does not even count suffering in this world as worthy of comparison to what is to come (Rom. 8:18). We can see these same principles in play in Acts 5:40–42 and 16:25–34. As Calvin observed, "The crowns and scepters of kings, to say nothing of the imposing splendor of an ambassador,

---

36 Owen, *Hebrews Vol 1*, 409.

are less honorable than the chains of a prisoner of Jesus Christ."[37] Tertullian, the early church father, said more broadly of persecution, "But nothing whatever is accomplished by your cruelties, each more exquisite than the last. It is the bait that wins men for our school. We multiply whenever we are mown down by you; the blood of Christians is seed."[38]

When you view your own circumstances as part of the Bride and a child of God, you may be tempted to grumble and complain like the Israelites in the wilderness. You may have less than you desire of wealth, strength, intelligence, wisdom, charisma, or health. Yet you are precisely where God meant for you to be, and you have all that you need to do what God has called you to do. That is what Paul really meant when he said from prison, "I can do all things through Christ who strengthens me" (Phil. 4:13)

The strange reality is that Paul was more free in prison than Caesar, who was in bondage to sin. He was already seated in the heavenlies (Eph. 2:6). Paul had the peace of God that surpasses all understanding as part of that grace given to him as an apostle. My question to you is this: Are you truly free? Just because you are not in a literal prison does not mean you are free. I mean, are you in bondage to your sin that is the slavery unto death, or are you a prisoner of Christ, which is a freedom no earthly court can overrule? Can you sing God's praises while in chains, or do you feel the weight of the chains on your soul that will drag you to hell? If you do not know Christ as your Savior, I urge you to not delay, but flee to the cross in repentance and faith in Christ that you might be saved.

One final note on this section is necessary in terms of occasional grace. We are tempted to think great men like Paul are cut from a different cloth. "I cannot be expected to react to imprisonment with joy. Sure, Paul was brave and optimistic in the face of sorrow, but I am not built that way." This kind of thinking is propagated by the Roman Catholic classification of "saints" as these super-Christians that are a world apart from us. The bridal metaphor teaches us differently, however. We are part of the same body, the same Bride as Paul, David, Noah, and the rest. So how do we account for the difference? The difference is what we might call occasional grace. In times of great difficulty, God often gives greater grace. John Lennon was wrong; it is not mother Mary who whispers words of wisdom to comfort, it is Christ by His Holy Spirit groaning within us. If you have need of greater grace, seek it in Christ and through the Bride, primarily with those means of grace: the preaching of the word, the sacraments, and prayer. Seek them in "times of trouble," but seek them in times of peace that you might be ready for the trial.

---

37 Calvin, *Commentaries Vol. XXI*, 247.
38 Quoted by S.M. Baugh, *Evangelical Exegetical Commentary: Ephesians* (Bellingham: Lexham, 2016), 212.

Residence in the Heart—Ephesians 3:17–21

A woman's abusive husband dies, but she is eventually courted by another man. He woos her and loves her, and they are finally married. She already owns a home, so the husband agrees to sell his home and move in with her. Upon returning from the honeymoon, however, she asks him to move into the guest house on the property. She leaves the former husband's clothes in her closet and his things throughout the house. Despite her new husband's allergies, she refuses to give up her dog. When mold is discovered in the basement, she refuses to allow renovations to the home. She keeps a separate set of bank accounts. The intimacy of the marriage suffers, yet she continues to insist that if he loves her, he can adapt.

If such a scenario is troublesome to you, good. It should be. To adapt the famous words of Nathan, the prophet, "You are the woman." To varying degrees, this describes every Christian, and this is what Paul prays against for the Ephesians and for us.

Ephesians 3:14–19 resumes Paul's description of his prayers on behalf of the Ephesian church. Paul prays that Christ would dwell in their hearts through faith. This is not something he is praying for unbelievers, nor is it only for pastors and Uber-Christians. This is what he desires and what is offered to ordinary believers, many of whom were likely slaves.[39] For these, Paul prays that Christ would dwell in their hearts through faith.

That may strike you as strange because whenever someone is saved, he is granted the Holy Spirit by which Christ dwells in the heart (Rom. 8:9–11). So why would Paul pray that Christ would dwell in their hearts? Is He not already there?

The real key to the verse is in the verb for "dwell." There are a variety of words that mean "presence," but this one is emphatic in permanent residence, like "putting down roots." This is about Christ as the Bridegroom of the heart taking full possession of our hearts. It is giving Him reign and right to knock down walls and remove what is odious to Him. We ought to ask ourselves how much we know of Christ's rule in our hearts, and what sins we know He hates that we keep stashed away in the closets. In Galatians 2:20, Paul says that Christ is living in him and through him, that his life is now Christ's.

This permanent residence of the Bridegroom is necessary for deeper communion. Revelation 3:20 is a passage almost exclusively used as a tool for evangelism. The preacher declares that Christ stands at the door of the

---

39 D. Martyn Lloyd-Jones, *The Unsearchable Riches of Christ: Ephesians 3* (Baker Books: Grand Rapids, 1979), 142. Steve Baugh makes reference to this as well. *Evangelical Exegetical Commentary: Ephesians* (Lexham: Bellingham, 2016).

unbeliever's heart and knocks, and if we will just open the door, He will save us. The problem with that is the same as in Ephesians; it is addressed to Christians already saved. Granted, the church of Laodicea is populated by lukewarm Christians who are bearing little to no fruit, but that is really the point. They are saved, but they are trying to keep Jesus in the guest house after their husband of the world is dead to them. They have died to the world, but they cling to remnants thereof.

We ought not be content in the low valleys of the Christian life, but to strive and climb to the peaks. The missionary Hudson Taylor used to pray the same poem daily. "Lord Jesus, make Thyself to me a living, bright reality; more present to faith's vision keen than any outward object seen; more dear, more intimately nigh than e'en the sweetest earthly tie."[40]

Paul also tells us the means by which Christ takes residence in our hearts—faith. We must pray for more faith and more Christ. We must cling to Christ with all that we have and all that we are. Each of us hopes that we will have the strength to stand firm if following Christ requires the giving of our lives, but have we had the strength to do this in our daily lives? As Calvin puts it, "Faith is not a distant view, but a warm embrace, of Christ, by which he dwells in us, and we are filled with the Divine Spirit."[41]

Next, we move to verse 19, where Paul speaks of his prayer for them to know the love of Christ, which "casts beyond knowledge," and be filled with the fullness of God. This is language of immersion. His prayer for the church should be your pastor's prayer for you and your prayer for yourself, to be plunged into the seemingly endless love of Christ. It is beyond our comprehension to trace out the borders or sound the depth, but only when we immerse ourselves in Christ's love do we appreciate its vastness. We most appreciate the love of our spouse and our Savior when we immerse ourselves in it. This often happens spontaneously, but we do well to create the habitat for it. When we actively seek our Savior in prayer, when we search for the Bridegroom in the pages of Scripture, when we come through the church doors expecting to hear the words of our beloved, we step off the boat into the vastness of the ocean of Christ's love.

It is important that we see union, communion, and communication as indivisible elements. This is something we fail to understand in earthly marriage as much as the spiritual. Christians want to feel united to Christ, to feel in love with Him and feel His love for them, without examining the element of communication. As I said earlier, we must seek God in prayer like a bride speaking to the bridegroom if we are to grow in that union. Often, our

---

40 Cited by Lloyd-Jones, *The Unsearchable Riches of Christ: Ephesians 3*, 149.
41 Calvin, *Commentaries XXI*, 262.

conversations with God in prayer become like text messages. A lot of the daily communication my wife and I have throughout the day is like this. When I need to tell her something, but there is not time for deep and meaningful conversation, I will simply send my wife a text. "Please grab milk." "Do you need anything at the store?" "Love you." "Headed home." "Do you know where our son's pants are?" Unfortunately, I find too many of my prayers become the same. "Lord, please fix Doug." "Bless Shorty." Certainly, there is a time and place for that in marriage and in prayer, but we cannot allow it to become the predominant conversational method in either. Take the time to have real conversations without distractions in both kinds of marriage.

This ties directly into the next concept of being filled with the fullness of God. This is not some pantheistic or panentheistic concept wherein we merge with the divine. In Colossians 1:19, 2:9, and Hebrews 1:1–3, we see that Christ is the fullness of God. So what Paul addresses here is really the same thing he dealt with in verse 17; he just takes it further. It is the mysterious union with Christ we have already seen in the marriage metaphor. We are to be filled up with Christ, and, as John the Baptist said, He must increase while we decrease.

As Christ fills up our hearts, we take on His priorities and eternal perspective in our lives. Our work becomes an opportunity to serve others as Christ served men in His earthly ministry. Everything in our lives becomes opportunity to glorify the Father as Christ did.

That is precisely what is presented to us in the following doxology. Paul's doxologies are among my favorite passages of Scripture. Doxology literally means a "study in glory"; they are moments wherein we stand still in awe of our God. Verse 20 reminds us of the incomprehensible power of the Almighty as well as His benevolent gaze upon His adopted children. Verse 21, however, is nigh unto a call to labor. What is surprising, though, is it includes Christ alongside His church in glorifying the Father. What a beautiful reminder of the nature of marriage!

The Husband and Wife stand side by side, church and Christ, as they glorify God. Together, Christ and the church glorify God in a way they cannot alone. As F. F. Bruce said, "The glory of God 'in the church' cannot be *divorced* from his glory 'in Christ Jesus.'"[42] This is something every earthly marriage should strive to imitate. As husband and wife, two sinners are formed into a living metaphor for Christ and His church with a unique opportunity to glorify God. This is why believers ought to be equally yoked as they pull along the plow of doxology, which breaks up the hardened ground of sinners' hearts and create furrows for the seed of the gospel by their testimony. If you are

---

42 F.F. Bruce, *The Epistles to the Colossians NICOT* (Grand Rapids: Eerdmans, 1984), 331.

married, you do well to ask yourself if your marriage is focused on the glory of God. Daniel Rogers said, "Only marrying in the Lord prepares the soul for the work: it has her tools in readiness to fall to the trade, whereas the contrary is still to seek."[43]

---

[43] Daniel Rogers, *Matrimonial Honor*, 22.

X
PAUL AND THE BRIDE II: THE QUICKENING[1]

Ephesians 4–6

The Called and Gifted—Ephesians 4:11–12

As Paul presents the diversity of the church that contributes to its unity, he makes a surprising turn in Ephesians 4:11–12. When we would expect a discourse on gifts of teaching and charity, or even tongues and healing, he begins to describe the offices of the church. We are tempted to jump immediately to the ways God gives officers in the church gifts, talents in things like teaching and preaching. That is part of the passage, but we can miss the main point. Paul is saying these officers—apostles, prophets, evangelists, pastors, and teachers—*are* the gifts. The apostles and prophets are no longer with us, but the Scriptures they penned continue to testify to the gospel as these men hold their office from glory. Evangelist church planters, pastors, and teachers are with us today proclaiming those Scriptures.[2]

Paul describes a three-fold purpose for these officer-gifts. These men are to *equip* the saints. The word we translate as "equip" can mean unite, bind together, mend, make useful, and complete. We do not normally import all possible meanings of a word to a text,[3] but here we can see that all of these fall within the purview of the pastor's office.

God has given evangelists and pastors gifts, as well as gifting them to the church as servants. Many people think of the church as a pyramid with apostles and prophets on top, evangelists below, pastors next, deacons, and the congregation at the base. The abuse of such a mentality has led many to reject Christ's structure for the church altogether, which is equally nefarious.

---

[1] Yep. I made a *Highlander* reference. I almost went with "I Still Know What You Did Last Covenant."

[2] Pastors and teachers are predominantly one office, as we see in 1 Timothy 3 and Titus 1:5–9, but there are some teachers who are not pastors (gifted brothers), or are not primarily pastors, such as seminary professors.

[3] That is called an illegitimate totality transfer.

The truth is that we must turn the pyramid upside down. The Scriptures, evangelists, and pastors are meant to hold up, build up, and serve the congregation to the glory of God. As Edmund Clowney said, the pastorate is not a grand staircase leading to heaven, but a backdoor staircase going down to the servant's quarters.[4]

Finally, we see a very specific reference to the body/bridal metaphor. God has given these officers to build up the body of Christ. Christ has given apostles, prophets, evangelists, pastors, and teachers in order to grow God's children in sanctification and to grow the church in saving sinners. To bring all these elements together, the called and gifted officers of Christ's church are the arteries and nerves by which the life-giving blood and directing impulses of the Holy Spirit are conveyed to every part of the body.

It is then foolishness, as Calvin says, for God's people to not avail themselves of these gifts or to deny the structure which Christ has set for His church.[5] Yet it is likewise foolish for ministers to forget Paul's words in 1 Corinthians 4:7: "What do you have that you did not receive? If then you received it, why do you boast as if you did not receive it?" Pastors are sinners called and gifted to serve the Bride of Christ for a purpose.

Mimics of God—Ephesians 5:1–2

As we have seen before, the image of children of God is tied to the Bride of Christ metaphor, and in Ephesians 5:1, we see a practical outworking of that. Paul exhorts us to "become mimics of God," and the reasoning and catalyst to this is that we are "beloved children of God." John tells us in his first letter, "We love because He first loved us" (4:19). When we connect the concept of beloved children to the imitation of God, we find a beautiful image of the son or daughter imitating their parent.

I love to watch my children imitate me, and there I experience the truth of the old adage, "Imitation is the sincerest form of flattery." Living in close proximity to my own parents, I see my eldest son try to imitate his grandfather as well. I remember the first time my son saw me tying my tie on Sunday morning and asked if he could have a tie to wear too. It was a wonderful moment, wrapping the loops and recalling how I once imitated my father.

We delight our Heavenly Father when we imitate Him. It is not about learning to shave or wearing a tie for Sunday, but what we call the communicable attributes of God. At the forefront of the text is our imitation of God's

---

4 "When the apostles argued about rank in the kingdom, he offered his cup of suffering . . . for patterns of ministry he gave them a basin and a towel. . . . The stairway to the ministry is not a grand staircase but a back stairwell that leads down to the servants' quarters." Edmund Clowney, *Called to the Ministry* (Phillipsburg: Presbyterian and Reformed, 1964), 42–43.

5 Calvin, *Calvin's Commentaries XXI*, 282.

forgiveness (4:32) and His love as it is revealed in Christ. Of course, this reaches beyond those two. One of the best passages to see these imitation-worthy attributes of God is in the fruit of the Spirit in Galatians 5:22–23. Love, joy, peace, patience, kindness (a disposition of grace and eagerness to forgive), goodness, faithfulness, gentleness, and self-control are all things we find in God, in Christ, in the Holy Spirit. They are wrought in us by the Holy Spirit, and they are things we ought to strive to imitate.

One other thing we must note before leaving this passage is the fragrance of Christ as an offering and sacrifice in verse 2, a topic we have only briefly alluded to before now. Paul presents something from the Old Testament in this language that is easily overlooked but important. This description of a sacrifice or offering as a pleasing aroma or fragrance is found many times in the OT, first in a covenant sacrifice that establishes peace after the flood in Genesis 8. It is found with peace offerings, food and drink offerings, and many others, especially those with frankincense. These point forward to Christ, especially in the gifts of the Magi. Frankincense is only fragrant when it is crushed and put into the fire. The language of the fragrant aroma is never found, however, in connection to sin offerings, which also never contain frankincense. The last piece of the puzzle, so to speak, is in Isaiah 53:10, where, in a prophecy of Christ's atoning work, it says "it was a pleasure to Yahweh to bruise him" (author's translation). Some translations downplay this, translating it as "will," even though the word *haphets* means "delight."

So what does all of this mean? God's delight in the Old Testament sacrifices, which prefigure Christ, was in the covenant, the peace, and the reconciliation. God did not delight in punishing Christ for our sin placed on Him, though we might say God was satisfied in His justice. It was *necessary* that Christ be that expiatory sacrifice on our behalf. Yet God's delight was in the propitiation, the way in which the fragrance of Christ's righteousness was "released" in suffering to be transferred to us and to make us acceptable in His sight.

Returning to our bridal metaphor, God delights in the Bride that is "perfumed" in the righteous blood of Christ. This pleasing aroma and fragrance placed upon the Bride never fades, but is carried into the world. Thus Paul describes the saints, especially the apostles, as an aroma of God to the world, and of Christ to God (2 Cor. 2:14–16).

Thanksgiving and Service — Ephesians 5:20–21

It is the nature of marriage that our emotional state is tied to that of our spouse in a kind of lowest common denominator. There is a saying that when you are single, you are as happy as you are, but when you are married, you are only as happy as the least happy spouse.[6] If I have had a wonderful day, but my wife has had a terrible one, my sympathy causes me to grieve with her. There is an element of this in Christ as our sympathetic mediator, as He is described in Hebrews 4:15. It is rarer, in the brokenness of our race, for my joy to raise up my bride to the same exaltation. It is also a truism that the unwise choices of one spouse bring sorrow to the other, while wise choices bring them joy. If my wife manages our finances well or if I am a good and faithful father to our children, it produces joy in the family.

In this passage of Ephesians, we encounter an exhortation for Christians that also describes what a Christian does when filled with the Holy Spirit. Paul calls us to give thanks, always and in all circumstances, to God the Father in the name of Christ, our Bridegroom. We can find this theme of thanksgiving throughout the Scriptures. It is prevalent in the Psalms,[7] which connects to the previous verse on singing. We have already noted how this ties into Hosea's prophecy about the Bride answering or singing as she did in the days of her youth (2:15). This is also a consistent theme of Paul's. The references abound when we realize that thanksgiving to God is tied to praising God.

The marriage of the church to Christ places the believer in the context of the divine family. This means that our joy and peace which produce thanksgiving are anchored in God, and God does not change. God is perfect in His triune independence and self-satisfaction. This means that while Christ does indeed grieve with His people in their suffering, the Trinity can never be diminished in its perfect joy. This emotional anchor within the veil for our souls keeps us from utter despair. The more my joy is dependent on Christ and God, the shorter that anchor line is, and the less the sorrows of this world can devastate me.

To be sure, there is sorrow in this life that warrants grieving. That is the nature of a world broken by sin. Even Christ wept at Lazarus's tomb. Yet when I rise above the storm to see the eternal nature of things, I am reminded that I am perfectly loved by the Bridegroom of my soul. My eternal life is secured in Him, and I can give thanks. As Susannah Spurgeon once said,

> Every heart knows its own bitterness, and every heart has bitterness to know. Sin must bring sorrow, tears are the inheritance of earth's children; but in the city to which we are going, "God shall wipe away all tears from their eyes; and there shall be no more death, neither sorrow, nor crying, neither shall there be any more pain; for the former things are passed away." Blessed be your dear name, O Lord.... Tears may, and must come; but if they gather in the eyes that are constantly

---

[6] Referenced in the pilot episode of the TV show *Rules of Engagement*. I am not endorsing the show, only confessing that I have watched it.

[7] For a survey of these topics in the Psalms, just look to 7:17, 26:6–7, 33:2, 73:25, 86:12–13.

looking up to you and heaven, they will glisten with the brightness of the coming glory.[8]

And this is not even the whole of it. God has decreed all of human history to the finest detail in His perfect wisdom. Christ, the Bridegroom of our souls, is working all things together for the good of those who love and serve Him (Rom. 8:28). Paul goes on in that chapter to describe how there may be much suffering in the Christian life, but nothing can separate us from the love of God. There will be times when you think, "How can I possibly praise God in this trial? I have lost everything that I love in this world! Certainly, Paul did not mean that I should give thanks to God in *these* times." It is then that we turn to Job and see him declare that God has given and taken away, yet blessed be the name of the Lord (1:21). We can turn to Lamentations and see how though there is seemingly limitless sorrow, in the eye of the storm in chapter 3, the author turns his eyes toward heaven to find God's mercies are new every morning. Romans 5:3–5 and James 1:2–4 remind us that suffering is good for us in the long run. Just as each of us can see how past trial in marriage has prepared us and improved us to be a better spouse, so, too, these trials prepare the bride. It is the toning of her muscles and the abrasives that soften her skin.

Job was better prepared for heaven and God's glory was more clearly displayed by the end of the book than the beginning. When I know that all I endure in trial, sorrow, and even chastisement is for my good and God's glory, I can praise Him. My tears may carve furrows through the ashes of this world that cling to my cheeks, yet through pained gasps for air, I have reason to give thanks to the God who has loved me.

Paul then calls us to serve and submit to one another. This is no new concept, even within the book of Ephesians. It is rooted in Christ's living example. We are to be foot-washers. This is essential to the body of the Bride, where the parts serve one another, as we have already seen. What is unique to this exhortation, however, is the motivation Paul cites. This applies to all exhortations we receive, not just mutual submission and service. He says it is for "fear of Christ." While some translations render it as "reverence," it is the Greek word from which we get *phobia*. When we speak of the fear of God, especially in Old Testament contexts, it is often about a consciousness of God as judge, the existence of justice, and a kind of undercurrent fear that keeps even the unbeliever from gross injustice. This consciousness of a higher power and judge is foundational to morality. This is why Proverbs 1:7 says the fear of God is the beginning of wisdom. Paul is not addressing a fear of God in judgment, God in law, God at Sinai. Christ will be the face of that judgment, as we see in Revelation 19:15, with the sword from His mouth coming to

---

8 Quoted in Jessalyn Hutto, *Inheritance of Tears: Trusting the Lord of Life When Death Visits the Womb* (Minneapolis: CruciformPress, 2015), 101.

tread the winepress of the fury of the wrath of God. God in judgment is truly awe-inspiring; it is worthy of our gaze and meditation, but it does not produce song. It does not create thanksgiving in the heart or joyful mutual submission.

There is a reverential fear here, wherein we perceive the might of our Savior, His authority and glory, yet that is not the whole of it. As Lloyd-Jones observed, this is a fear of disappointing or grieving our Savior. For this, we look to Peter. In the garden of Gethsemane, Peter was fearless. Reckless, but fearless. At the trial of Christ, however, the fear of man gripped him, and he denied his beloved Savior three times. Yet when he had done this, the realization of a greater fear hit him. The rooster crowed, but as we see in Luke 22:61, Jesus turned and looked at him. Later, the threefold confession of his love for Christ was required for his restoration, but that fear never left Peter. It was a fear born of love, and it was good and healthy. It was a fear that Peter carried, and that carried Peter past his crucifixion to the gates of glory. Our fear in this is beautiful because it directly represents our understanding of Christ's love for us. In Luke 7:47, we see that the one forgiven little loves little, but the one forgiven much loves much.

Next we will come to our most crucial set of passages for this metaphor. As Ray Ortlund Jr. puts it, "But Paul is the one who lifts our hermeneutical capstone into place by revealing openly what our intuitions may have suspected all along, viz that marriage from the beginning was meant to be a tiny social platform on which the love of Christ for his church and the church's responsiveness to him could be put on visible display."[9]

Church and Bride in Submission
—Ephesians 5:22–24

Sometimes the best parts of Shakespeare are in the subplots. One of my favorites is in *Midsummer Night's Dream* Act 1 Scene 2, where we find a play within a play. A director is meeting with a raggedy group of performers to assign roles. Nick Bottom, the weaver, is the prima-donna of the group. He is assigned the part of Pyramus, the lover, but he immediately begins to wax eloquent on his performance range. When a young man balks at playing a woman, Nick contends to take on that role as his own lover Thisbe, and then again offering to play the lion. As he is offering up his talents, the director Quince responds, "You can play no part but Pyramus; for Pyramus is a sweet-faced man, a proper man as one shall see in a summer's day; a most lovely, gentleman-like man: therefore you must needs play Pyramus." Often in life, we find ourselves pushing back against "playing Pyramus" or at least wanting more than the role assigned to us. This can be good, driving us to do more, but if it remains unsanctified, it can get us into a lot of trouble.

---

9 Ortlund, *God's Unfaithful Wife,* 172.

Before we deal with our passage, we have to understand our intrinsic struggle against authority. We are born rebels, and we are descendants of rebels. Sin came into the world through rebellion against God's authority and structure. In the curse of Eve, we saw the perpetuation of that rebellion (Gen. 3:16). This rebellion is not unique to marriage, though. We are all called to submission in various spheres and falter at each. We are to submit to Christ and the Father. We do this first in repentance and faith, acknowledging our brokenness, sinfulness, and unworthiness, then clinging to Christ as our Savior and righteousness. As we grow, we continue in the submission we saw in Ephesians 1:20–23. We are to submit to the government (Rom. 13:1–7). Paul calls us in Philippians 2:3 to consider one another above ourselves, and Christ specifically prescribed this in Mark 10:43–45. We are to submit to one another as we just saw in verse 21, which shares the "subjecting" verb with verse 22.

In Mark 10, Christ served His disciples to set an example, even though He was in authority over them. Furthermore, Christ submitted to the Father as His head. In John 4:34, Christ said the food that sustained Him was doing the Father's will, and in 6:38, Christ said He came not to do His own will, but the Father's. In 1 Corinthians 11:3, we see the Father specifically described as the head of Christ. This teaches us something contrary to the world and even our instinct: *Submission does not equal inferiority in God's economy.* Galatians 3:28 shows us that all saints are equal in terms of assigned value. There are no second-class citizens, even when one submits to the other. *True submission is an act of love and faith.*

We once sought self-satisfaction and self-actualization in a Darwinian struggle. There is no place for true submission in seeking success in survival of the fittest. But God invaded your life and brought you from death into life. As an adopted child, you received the promise of eternal reward, peace, and joy. God has promised to give you what is best for you. We know Him to be faithful and sovereign. Without understanding that, without that faith, we cannot truly submit.

We are then called to trust God with ultimate justice. Romans 12:19 exhorts us to not avenge ourselves, but to trust in God, because vengeance is His. We are also to trust God with the reward of service and the fulfillment of promises. Abraham brought strife upon himself when He sought promise fulfillment outside of God. We are to submit to Him in faith that He will work all things together for our good and God's glory.

The passage we examine here and its parallels in Colossians 3 and 1 Peter 3 have caused many to dismiss Paul as a product of his time, but these verses actually reveal that the accusers are a product of their time. The principles presented here and elsewhere in Scripture are timeless, and to reject them is to reject Scripture and its divine authority.

God created marriage before the fall, and He alone has the authority to determine those roles. As A.W. Pink said, "What right has the husband to require submission from his wife? None, unless God had appointed it."[10] To be sure, if men selflessly fulfilled their role, we would not see such a drive to subvert and invert these roles. Good authority rarely inspires a coup. Today, we see a public mockery of the patriarchal role, though it has always been a part of fallen man's nature to mock authority. The Pantaloon character back in Commedia Del Arte works of sixteenth-century Italy was designed to ridicule the patriarch. Today, we also see an exaggerated exaltation of women motivated by guilt. Women have been treated as second-class citizens at many points throughout history, so we do what sinful man does best: We overreact. We pretend that there is no difference between the sexes to make up for the abuse of authority, but two wrongs do not make a right.[11]

What we find in Scripture is the elevation of women in their God-given role. They are not presented as male imitators, but complements toward men's completion. The Bible exalts them in their uniqueness and instances of extraordinary faithfulness (like the women at the foot of the cross and near the tomb). This exaltation is not from pity, guilt, or farce, but in love.

Paul is, in a sense, presenting three parallel pairings: head and body, husband and wife, Christ and church. Let us look first at the relationship of head and body. In Monty Python's *Search for the Holy Grail*, we find a giant with two heads rendered ineffective by contest between the heads. Steve Baugh recounts the *Fable of Babrius*, where a snake's tail takes leadership to destructive ends.[12] So, too, Shel Silverstein's poem "Us" shows a man with two faces bemoaning the inability to overcome differences of opinion.[13] All these share the same concept: The body requires one head.

The body informs the head by its senses of pressure, pain, and heat. If you absentmindedly place your hand on a hot stove, you pull away because your hand tells your brain, "Excuse me, but AAAAHHHH!!!" These inputs are essential to our decision making. In turn, the head guides and directs the body in what is best for the body. When the body ignores the head's direction or governs, it is illness and destruction. Seizures are when the body functions independently of the brain, and gluttony is when a man allows the stomach to govern him.

---

10 A.W. Pink, *Attributes of God: A Solemn and Blessed Contemplation of some of the Wondrous and Lovely Perfectison of the Divine Character*, "Sovereignty of God" (Swengel Bible Truth Depot, 1961), 29–30.
11 But three lefts do.
12 S.M. Baugh, *Evangelical Exegetical Commentary: Ephesians* (Bellingham: Lexham, 2016), 481.
13 Shel Silverstein, *Where the Sidewalk Ends* (New York: Harper Collins, 2004), 36.

Now we come to the husband and wife. A wife is called to submit to her husband in life. There are exceptions in unlawful things, sin, or those things against conscience, though not opinion.[14] As Lloyd-Jones says:

> Here, then, is this basic fundamental teaching—the man is to be the head of the wife, and he is to be the head of the family. God made him in that way, endowed him with faculties and powers and propensities that enable him to fulfill this; and so made woman that she should be the "complement" of man. Now the word "complement" carries in itself the notion of submission; her main function is to make up a deficiency in the man. That is why these two become "one flesh"; the woman is the complement of the man.[15]

She is called to do this "as unto the Lord" Jesus Christ, meaning that submission to her husband is submission to Christ. It is not because her husband is perfect or wise. Paul uses similar language in Colossians 3:18, "as is fitting in the Lord."

When she does this, she does her part in reflecting the gospel. Remember, the earthly marriage has served as a living metaphor for the relationship between Christ and His Church since the days of Eden. This is why Lloyd-Jones says, "It is only the Christian who truly understands and appreciates marriage. That is one of the wonderful results of being a Christian."

In submitting, the wife challenges the husband to fulfill his role in completing the image of Christ and the church (1 Peter 3:1–6). He is to be the head and make wise decisions for the benefit of his household. He is also to be her "savior" in protecting and preserving her. The husband of a godly wife is charged with caring for a daughter of the King and doing all he can to ensure her well-being until she enters glory. It is a far easier thing for the wife to submit when the husband loves her as Christ loves His church.

The wife glorifies God by entrusting God with justice and her honor. She also evidences that her reward is not of this world. Her best life is next. Wives, submit to your husbands as unto the Lord, and pray for your husbands to live Christ in your marriage. Your submission is not a diminishing of your value, but an act of love to your husband and your God. You love your husband when you respect and honor him. Titus 2:3–4 shows the calling for older women to teach the younger to love their husbands.

Be his complement, the supplement of his wisdom, knowledge, and strength, and let him be your head. You may be smarter, wiser, or stronger in certain ways than your husband, but "you must needs play Pyramus." God has given you all of those gifts with which you are to glorify Him, not to glorify yourself in rebellion.

---

14 These are largely the same kind of exceptions we have for submission to government.
15 Lloyd-Jones, *Life in the Spirit in Marriage, Home, and Work* (Grand Rapids: Baker, 1973), 105.

Last, but certainly not least, we come to Christ and Church. This passage has application for every one of us, including single women, men, and children. We have the perfect Bridegroom of our hearts. He is all-wise, omniscient, omnipotent, and most-loving. He owns the cattle on a thousand hills. He is selfless and loves sacrificially. There is nothing lacking in Him. He is our Savior, the author and perfecter of our faith, as Hebrews 12:2 tells us.

We are called to submit to Him individually. He has called us to service, and we are to submit to that work with an eye to glory. We must address our rebellious hearts and surrender our lives to Jesus. It is in serving God, and serving one another for Christ's sake, that we find our peace and joy. As Paul tells us in 1 Corinthians 6:19–20, "You are not your own, for you were bought with a price." This can be the most difficult in submission to trial which He has designed for our good. In the convicting words of the Puritan Jeremiah Burroughs:

> Is this not God's hand and must your will be regarded more than God's? O under, under! Get you under, O soul! Keep under! Keep low! Keep under God's feet! You are under God's feet, and keep under his feet! Keep under the authority of God, the majesty of God, the sovereignty of God, the power that God has over you! To keep under, that is to submit.[16]

We are called to submit to Him corporately. It is Christ's church, and He has declared its order and purpose. Let us be about our Father's business as ambassadors in a broken world (Eph. 4:15–16). This is what drives the regulative principle of worship, wherein we worship God and Christ only in the ways that God has prescribed. Christ alone is head of the church, and He determines how the church is to conduct itself. We have no exceptions to this because the Bridegroom of our souls never commands us to do what is unlawful, sinful, or against conscience.

This is also true in the structure of the church, with the appointing of officers. We cannot, we must not, utilize our own criteria for determining who will be an elder or deacon, or we go against the perfect wisdom of the church's Husband. It does not matter if Bob is really handsome, a charismatic speaker, and a visionary businessman. If he does not meet Christ's qualifications that He gave us through 1 Timothy and Titus, then Christ has not called him, and we rebel if we appoint Bob anyway.

Christ and Husband—Ephesians 5:25

In Gary Thomas's book on marriage, *A Lifelong Love*, he tells the story of seminary president Dr. Robertson McQuilkin, whose wife Muriel developed

---
[16] Jeremiah Burroughs, *The Rare Jewel of Christian Contentment* (Carlisle: Banner of Truth, 1964), 33.

Alzheimer's. As a godly husband, he retired early in order to care for his wife. As he was following her in an airport, towing all their luggage from place to place, they paused time and again next to a well-to-do business woman. At one point, the woman commented, "I was just asking myself, will I ever find a man to love me like that?"[17] She actually envied a woman with dementia! She saw something that she lacked in her life, but what she did not realize was that what she admired was Christ reflected in this man's love for his wife.

It is important at this point that we recall our context. Paul is in the application-heavy half of his epistle, wherein we find the answers to crucial questions. How does doctrine affect our lives? Or, to put it another way, how does Christ's love for us call us to love in various spheres of life? What does it mean to love and serve one another? We are also examining what it means to be filled up with the Holy Spirit. This is key because what we are examining is impossible without the work of the Holy Spirit in us. We have also just considered what it means for wives to love their husbands by submitting to them and how that is a testimony to the world that sees submission as weakness.

Now we come to the question, "How should husbands love their wives?" Clearly, there is much application here for husbands, but it goes beyond that. Single men, if you want to get married someday, listen carefully to what God will require of you and for what you must prepare yourself. Wives, hear what is required of your husbands so that you can be their helpmate in these things and see why you do not want their job. Single women who want a husband, hear what qualities you ought to seek in a future spouse over good looks and dancing ability. Believers, see how Christ has loved you, and let that deepen your love for Him. Unbelievers, learn what love is, and consider your need for a Bridegroom for your soul in Jesus.

Let us first examine Christlike love. Paul tells us that husbands are to love their wives as Jesus loved the church. This does not mean that wives are to submit and husbands are to love, as some have claimed. This means wives love particularly in submitting as the church must to Christ, and husbands love in the ways that Christ loves His church. Husbands need to study Christ in order to know how to love and serve their wives.

Christ shows love to all people. This includes but is not limited to sustaining their very existence, as we see in Acts 17:28, "in Him we live and move and have our being," and Colossians 1:17, "in Him all things hold together" or "have their subsistence." Yet Christ loves His elect, His Bride, uniquely and supremely. We often talk about this in terms of common grace versus saving

---

[17] Gary Thomas, *A Lifelong Lover: How to Have Lasting Intimacy, Friendship, and Purpose in Your Marriage* (Colorado Springs: David C. Cook Publishing, 2015), Ch 11. He was president of Columbia Bible College. His book *A Promise Kept* records his journey of caring for his bride.

grace. The Westminster Confession says, "As the providence of God doth in general reach to all creatures, so after a most special manner it taketh care of His church, and disposeth of all things to the good thereof."[18]

Paul first expresses this as, "Christ loved the church and gave Himself up for her," or, more literally, "gave Himself on her behalf." This, as we will see, includes His sacrifice on the cross, but His sacrificial love goes far beyond that.

The love story began outside of time in the covenant of redemption with election (Eph. 1:4–5). The Father chose those who would be saved, and Christ set His love on them. He planned to provide for her eternal security, for our salvation. Galatians 4:4–5 tells us that in the fullness of time, Christ came to be born under the law to accomplish righteousness on her behalf. This was the plan from before creation. So, in that fullness of time, the Son surrendered glory, leaving the "parental" home and comfort, if you will, where He sat enthroned, surrounded by the praise of angels (Phil. 2:5–8). The Son was self-sustained and self-satisfied within the Trinity, but He came to show love to the Bride and set His delight on her. Isaiah 62:5 says, "As the bridegroom rejoices over the bride, so shall your God rejoice over you."

Christ loved His Bride, even when she was unlovable. In the next section, we will get to the details on how Jesus sanctifies, cleanses, and beautifies His Bride. One of the most striking things we see in this is not that Christ loved her because she was beautiful, but His love made her beautiful and pleasing to God (Rom. 8:5–8). He wooed His Bride, not once, but throughout her life, as we saw in Ezekiel and Hosea. It is the dedicated love of the Husband and the ensuing pursuit that sets her apart as the Bride. So a person cannot by mere morality become part of the true church. Christ has to love him or her as part of the Bride.

Jesus suffered injustice when it was for her good. Just read the accounts of Christ with His disciples, not to mention the whole history of the church sinning. Love is patient, longsuffering, and kind, as we see in 1 Corinthians 13, and nowhere do we see this more accurately or abundantly than in Christ. He did not just forgive her, He facilitated her forgiveness.

He taught and raised her up. He sent prophets and apostles, evangelists, and shepherds to help her to grow into the Bride she was meant to be (Eph. 4:11–14). In all this, His headship as husband did not give her a spirit of fear, but of boldness, love, and peace (Rom. 8:14–17; 2 Tim. 1:7). In everything, Christ considered the church above Himself, as we already saw in Philippians 2:5–8. He led her by example. He did not just command her to be humble, but showed her humility. He taught her what love is, what righteousness is.

---

18 WCF V.7, 2nd LBC V.7.

He even gave His life for her. He endured hell on the cross, the wrath of God due to her sins. As we examined in the first chapter, when Adam saw his wife Eve in sin, he joined her. When Christ saw His Bride in sin, He gave Himself for her and accomplished her redemption (Gal. 3:13). He purchased all the graces she would need by His works, sent His Spirit to apply them, and intercedes with the Father for her in glory until she is brought safely to heaven. He is her sympathetic mediator, as we see in Hebrews 4:15.

So how does this translate to the husband's responsibility? First, single men, if you would have a wife, your work begins now in becoming self-sufficient, praying, and seeking to be more like Christ.

Husbands, in marriage, you surrendered the right to be selfish. You are to fulfill your wife's shortcomings, provide for her, sympathize with her, and be steward of this precious daughter of the King until glory. As Chrysostom once said:

> Thou hast seen the measure of obedience, hear also the measure of love. Wouldest thou have thy wife obedient unto thee, as the Church is to Christ? Take then thyself the same provident care for her, as Christ takes for the Church. Yea, even if it shall be needful for thee to give thy life for her, yea, and to be cut into pieces ten thousand times, yea, and to endure and undergo any suffering whatever, refuse it not. Though thou shouldest undergo all this, yet wilt thou not, no, not even then, have done anything like Christ.[19]

Lead your wife, instructing her in the Scriptures and raising her up. It is a common joke that the husband is one more child to raise, but that ought to never be the case. You are not the perfect husband, but you serve the perfect Husband. Point your wife to Christ in the course of life. Facilitate her Christian growth. Love her in such a way that she is bold, loving, and at peace in the marriage. Lloyd-Jones once said, "No husband is entitled to say that he is the head of the wife unless he loves his wife."[20] So actively love your wife. Woo your wife. When Adam was in the garden with Eve, they were naked and unashamed. You must have not just physical but emotional bareness with your wife and be vulnerable to her.

When you fail as a husband and sin against your wife, seek forgiveness. Bring her with you to the foot of the cross in repentance and faith. And when your wife sins against you, facilitate her forgiveness. This is part of leading your wife and nurturing her Christian walk. Remember how much Christ has forgiven you, and see that sin against you as an opportunity to live Christ

---

19 Chrysostom, *Homilies on Galatians, Ephesians, Philippians, Colossians, Thessalonians, Timothy, Titus, and Philemon* (B&R Samizdat Express. iBooks).
20 Lloyd-Jones, *Life in the Spirit in Marriage, Home, and Work*, 132.

to her. Do not be concerned with justice or your immediate reward. Your treasures are laid up in heaven. And remember, you do not actually want real justice.[21] Trust God with the reward, and set yourself to loving your wife.

When you do these things, when you love and serve your wife, you glorify God. God created marriage to proclaim the gospel. Your marriage is an open letter to the world about what love, grace, and forgiveness really are.

Presented Spotless—Ephesians 5:26–27

The history of the world is filled with bizarre beauty rituals. There seems to be no limit to how far people will go for vanity. Countess Bathory murdered women to bathe in their blood. Crushed bugs and crocodile dung, larded wigs, and arsenic hair removal have all been used in the pursuit of beauty. Of course, this raises all kinds of questions about the nature of beauty and its discernment by apiarists (the bee-holders). Ultimately, we are talking about an aesthetic, what is acceptable and pleasing to someone else. In these verses, we come to the most important beauty, that which makes us lovely in eyes of our beloved Savior and God.

As we come to this section, there are three important categories that we have to keep clearly delineated: justification, sanctification, and glorification. We have to know what each of these are and the sequence in which they occur.

The first is justification. This is the cosmic courtroom where God the Father declares a person just, where the balance-transfer of imputation takes place. Our guilt is transferred to Christ and His righteousness is placed on us. This is where the Bride is clothed in the righteousness of the Bridegroom and the marriage contract is signed.

The second is sanctification. This is where we are made holy and set apart from the world. It is an ongoing process of being made more like Christ between our justification and entering into glory or glorification. In Augustus Toplady's hymn "Rock of Ages," he says, "Be of sin the double cure, save me from its guilt and power." Justification removes the guilt, but sanctification removes sin's power and presence in the believer.

The third is glorification, which is where the sanctification is completed, the sinner is fully saint, and he is made unable to sin.

To put it another way, we have examined already what Christ did for us in the incarnation, and now we are seeing what He does in us by the Holy Spirit on the road to heaven.

---

21 Real justice, absolute justice, would be according to God's standard. It would mean eternal condemnation under the wrath of God. We all want grace when it comes to our failures, but we want full reward for something "good" we have done. There seems to be an elaborate pulley system on our imagined scales and balances.

Paul utilizes this Bride of Christ metaphor to warm and humanize these clinical categories. Justification, then, is the marriage. That is what makes us Christ's Bride, as we saw in the gospels.

In Esther 2, we saw Ahasuerus in search for a wife from his kingdom. His servant chose Esther on account of her beauty and then bathed, beautified, fed, and perfumed her to prepare for meeting the emperor. We also saw how Ruth was bathed before going to win the heart of Boaz at the threshing floor (3:3–6). In those instances, we see the expected order. A woman is beautified, by herself or with a little help from her friends, then the man sets his love on her and marries her. The bride is made as beautiful as possible for the day of the wedding, and many brides look back at that day as when they felt most beautiful.

Yet with Christ and His church, this is completely inverted. It is counter-intuitive, like getting dressed up before going to bed or going to the prom and then renting a tuxedo. The church is found ugly and defiled with sin. She is of ignoble heritage. She is even dead in her trespasses and sins. Yet the King of kings, Lord of lords, sets His love upon her, upon us.

He has already declared His wedding vows in the cross. He then brings us to life and weds us to Himself in faith. He loves the unlovable and unites her fate to His. It is with the marriage complete and her unimaginable debt paid in His blood that Jesus sets to making us, His Bride, beautiful. We saw all of this prophesied back in Ezekiel 16:8–14.

Paul says that Christ sanctifies us, purging us, washing by water in Word. There is a lot of complicated discussion we could go into, but ultimately it comes to the same conclusion: the sanctification image in baptism.

Baptism is a visible sign of the rebirth, of our identification with the death, burial, and resurrection of Christ, and of being washed clean of our sins. We see the merging of the sign and thing signified in a similar way in Hebrews 10:22, Titus 3:5, and other passages. Yet it is clear in the Scriptures that a believer may enter heaven without being baptized, like the thief on the cross and the Old Testament saints, and baptism without faith does nothing. When submitted to in faith by a child of God, baptism is a means of grace. The same Holy Spirit that hovered over the waters of creation hovers over the waters of the baptismal today.

As observed earlier, the guilt of sin is removed in justification, but the power and presence of sin is removed by degrees. The flesh, the old man (or woman), is crucified. Galatians 5:24 tells us that "those who belong to Christ Jesus have crucified the flesh with its passions and desires." This means it is condemned to death and dying. Meanwhile, the new Bride and creation are blossoming and becoming more beautiful.

She is being purged of sin, and by the washing of sanctification, every blemish, spot, and imperfection is being removed. This exfoliation, waxing, and scouring is at times unpleasant, but it is always necessary. Its pain is often increased by our lack of cooperation, like bathing a cat. If you are part of Christ's Bride, you will be cleansed one way or another.

Now we want to examine two specific aspects of our text. First is the cleansing water. Chrysostom just assumes this is baptism and goes no further in the examination, but there is more to it. We are atoned, covered by the blood of Christ, and we are washed and cleansed with water. This is the work of God to which the water of baptism points, and with the blood, it is provided or purchased by Christ's sacrifice. Leviticus 14:1–8 depicts the cleansing ritual of the leper where blood and water mixed are sprinkled on him; he bathes and is rendered ceremonially clean. So, too, Hebrews 9:19–22 recounts the ceremony of the law in Exodus 24:6–8 where the people and the book of the law are sprinkled with blood and water. And 1 John 5:6–8 speaks of Christ coming by blood and water and how the blood, the water, and the Holy Spirit agree. The climax of all of this is in John 19:34, when Christ's side was pierced, and blood and water flowed out. It is the blood of Christ that removes the guilt of sin, but His water removes the sin itself. Again from Toplady, "Let the water and the blood from thy riven side which flowed be of sin the double cure, cleanse me from its guilt and power."

But what is the word? It is not the usual term, *logos*, which would indicate Christ or the canon of Scripture. Paul uses a more obscure word, *reyma*, which has a more elusive meaning, "words as distinct from deeds."[22] This is not the Scriptures, but the declaration of Christ Himself. It is His agreement to atone for her outside of time, it is His acceptance of the Father's decree in the garden, and His declaration on the cross that "it is finished." It is the promises presented in the Scripture from the Bridegroom to the Bride. It is the truth that we are Christ's and no longer of the world. In our clinging to these, the world is washed from us and we are prepared for glory. As Christ asked of the Father in John 17:17, "Sanctify them in the truth; your word is truth."

We are between the vows and the honeymoon of the new heavens and the new earth. As composed of all the elect, the Bride has one foot in heaven and one on earth. We are the loved church but not yet the glorious church. This passage points us to the ultimate goal, that "not having spot or wrinkle or any such thing," "holy and spotless," Christ will present to Himself the glorious church at His second coming.

Husbands, remember that you are called to love your wife as Christ loved the church. That is our context here. This means you are to love your wife

---

22 *Theological Dictionary of the New Testament Vol IV,* ed. Kittel, Gerhard (Grand Rapids: Eerdmans, 2006), 75.

when she is not beautiful.[23] You must be concerned with her soul above her external beauty. In all the descriptions of the excellent woman of Proverbs 31, it never mentions physical beauty. It is assumed that the husband is attracted to her, but that is not where her true value lies. You must also love your wife in her sin, but strive to love her out of her sin by pointing her to Christ.

Wives, remember where your beauty and value lie. This is true for every saint, male or female. Our value is defined not by our physical attractiveness, bank accounts, or any other standard the world throws at us. If I showed you a one-hundred-dollar bill and asked you what it was worth, there are actually two answers you could give me. You could also say that it was only worth a few cents in ink, paper, and design. The world will value us as next to nothing, what it can get out of us, as we saw with Hosea's wife. Yet you could also say that piece of paper is worth one hundred dollars, as you can exchange it for that valued amount of gasoline, or two buckets of popcorn at your local movie theatre. Why? Because the powers that be have said it is worth that much. Our value is imputed by God as the blood of Christ.

Believers, stop rolling in the mud. This is what we do when we make allowance for sin and the flesh. God describes our idolatry as adultery and our sin as defilement. We would be appalled to see a bride mud wrestling at her reception and chasing after lovers, yet this is what we do in our sin. Come again in repentance and seek the loving washing of your Savior.

Yet we each must ask ourselves the question, *Is this me?* Have I declared my allegiance to Christ the Bridegroom and knit my life to His? Are you reading this thinking that you must first make yourself acceptable before you come to Christ? You must be wed to be cleansed. You cannot pay your debt by your own works; you can only increase it. You must flee to Christ for both the blood and the water that flow from His side. To quote Toplady's hymn one last time, "Nothing in my hands I bring, Simply to Thy cross I cling; Naked, come to Thee for dress, Helpless, look to Thee for grace: Foul, I to the fountain fly, Wash me, Savior, or I die."

Nourish and Cherish—Ephesians 5:28–30

In Samuel Stone's hymn "The Church's One Foundation," we see much of what we are examining in these verses. As we examined above, Christ came and sought her to be His holy Bride, a new creation by water and the Word. Jesus feeds her by "holy food" and sustains her in spite of schisms, heresies, false sons, and those who outright hate her. "The church shall never perish! Her dear Lord, to defend, to guide, sustain, and cherish, is with her to the end."

---

[23] Pro tip: Never tell your wife that you love her even though she is not beautiful.

Paul returns to his threefold metaphor: head and body, husband and wife, Christ and church. Each informs the others, so considering and learning of one increases the understanding of the other two, but only one of these is perfect: Christ's love for the church. A man may abuse his body (Col. 2:20–23), and a husband may fail his wife, but Christ loves His Bride supremely, wisely, and perfectly. We also see a unique application of the second table of the law, summarized in Leviticus 19:18 ("love your neighbor as yourself") and cited multiple times in the New Testament. Isaiah 58:7 even describes one's fellow man as "your own flesh." If this is true for all peoples, and especially the church, how much more ought a man to love his wife as such? As we progress through these concepts, we want to remember again the breadth of the application. Men are to see here what is required for a husband to love his wife, and women are to see what they are to expect and respect in a husband. Believers are to see the love of Christ toward them, and unbelievers should see what they lack.

Let us just take a moment to examine the head and body in isolation. This assumes what we saw before in terms of the head governing the body. These two share more than formal and legal relationships; they are interdependent with a living, vital union. They are invested in one another. You do not spontaneously stop using your legs or make plans for what to do if you lose them. The head makes choices according to what is best for the body as a whole. One instance of where this fails is in gluttony (Prov. 23:20–21; Phil. 3:19). The head suffers with the body and for the good of the body in cases of self-discipline (1 Cor. 9:25–27). A head can suffer without the body suffering, but the body cannot suffer without the head suffering. Likewise, when the body feels pleasure and joy, so does the head.

What we see Paul lay out here in terms of love is not the emotional infatuation of narcissism, but love in action. This is not a man standing in front of the mirror adoring his own frame; that would be infatuation. A man loves his body in the sense that he tends to its needs. He nourishes his body, feeding it good things. He does not poison himself. He cherishes it or, more accurately, he nurtures and clothes it so that it will be warm and healthy. Paul uses the same word in the description of the nursing mother in 1 Thessalonians 2:7.

How does this apply to Christ and the Church? Christ, by the incarnation, provided for and created that mystical, vital union with His church. He is her prophet, declaring truth to her. He is her king, protecting and leading her. He is her priest, wherein He sympathizes with her and mediates on her behalf. He feels her joy as well as her pain. As we observed before, a head can suffer without the body suffering, but the body cannot suffer without the head. Christ suffered alone on behalf of the church, but when she suffers, Jesus suffers with her. The church gains everything she needs by this vital union with her Savior. He is the source of her life, wealth, righteousness, and joy in abundance.

While Christ does feel emotional affection for His church, Jesus's love is shown in action. It is common to reference the "love languages," and we find all five in our Savior. There is loving contact by the indwelling of His Holy Spirit. There are words of affection and affirmation in the promises of Scripture. We see love in gifts of the graces we need. We have all the quality time we could ask for in prayer and studying the Word. Christ most supremely loves in service by the incarnation, which is also what is most necessary.

Christ nourishes the church. We see in Ruth how she was both fed directly by Boaz as well as by his servants from the abundance of his crops. But Christ has fed our souls by His very being, which we receive by faith and see displayed in the Lord's Supper. He feeds the church by His Word, which gives her all she needs for growth, strength, and maturity. It is true that the church is often malnourished and weak in parts, but this is not due to any defect in the Word. This can happen in two different ways: when Christ's servant ministers have not faithfully distributed the Word to her members, and also when the members of the body have not made use of the spiritual nutrition provided.

Christ warms and nurtures His church by His providences. He gives her good gifts and works all things together for her sake (Rom. 8:28). He clothes her in His righteousness. We are accustomed to the bride's parents or even the bride herself paying exorbitant prices for the wedding dress. Entire TV shows revolve around this strange ritual. Yet in Esther, we see her clothed in royal garments at the King's expense. With Christ we see what all that symbolized. He has woven the cloth and sown every stitch of the bridal gown of the church. As Spurgeon once said of Psalm 138:8,

> The Psalmist was wise, he rested upon nothing short of the Lord's work. It is the Lord who has begun the good work within us; it is he who has carried it on; and if he does not finish it, it never will be complete. If there be one stitch in the celestial garment of our righteousness which we are to insert ourselves, then we are lost; but this is our confidence, the Lord who began will perfect. He has done it all, must do it all, and will do it all.[24]

Now we come to the earthly husband and wife. Husbands, we must be connected to our wives in joy and in sorrow. Be invested in her life in such a way that you rejoice when she rejoices and weep when she weeps. Her loss is yours, but so is her gain.

---

24 Charles Spurgeon, *Morning and Evening* (New Kensington: Whitaker House, 2002), May 23.

Provide for your wife in finances and what is needed for her emotional, physical, and spiritual well-being. Here we also see the limitations of the husband. You cannot be the entirety of her need for spiritual health and growth. You cannot be the fullness of Christian fellowship, *koinonia*. Yet you can provide for this by encouraging your wife to be in church and facilitating her presence among the saints and under the means of grace.

Earlier we examined how a godly marriage should give a wife a spirit not of bondage and fear, but of boldness in love. She should have that stable ground of the home in order to face a world that incessantly tells her she is not worthy. Have you created an environment where your wife is encouraged to succeed, or does she feel she fails your standards in everything? Even though Christ is perfect in His righteousness and standards, He takes joy in the sincerity of our striving. Nourish and cherish her in terms of physical need, by loving contact and words, time invested, gifts, and service. A godly woman's value is above jewels, but you are responsible for nurturing that. Pray with your wife, and pray for your wife. A large portion of your job as a husband is to be a billboard that displays Christ and points the way to Him.

To love your wife is to love yourself, and to wound your wife is to wound yourself. Every husband has felt the empathetic joy of his wife's delight. Unfortunately, most husbands have also sought satisfaction in a disagreement by wounding their wife with unnecessary words. And what do they gain except sorrow themselves? We are slow to learn this, and astoundingly forgetful. Meditate on Christ as your example. He works all providence together for His Bride, always seeking what is best for her. Jesus is firm with the church when He must be, but never in anger and never more than is necessary for her good. He corrects her and, at times, allows her to undergo part of the consequences of her actions. But He does not seek justice or satisfaction in her sorrow, and when justice was required for her sins, Jesus took the suffering on Himself so that she would not suffer.

Wives, your husband is imperfect, but God has given him to you for a purpose in His perfect wisdom. Praise God where your spouse is faithful to supply your needs. Praise God for wherever your husband reflects Christ to you. Wherever he falls short, look to Christ for the rest.

We see the beauty of God's design for marriage and the safety within the covenant in all of these things. We live in a broken world, and the relationships between men and women display this most sorrowfully. We have been designed for love, intimacy, and vulnerability, and the covenantal relationship of marriage provides the environment for this. Abortion exists primarily because of the absence of selfless marriages that reflect Christ and His church. If men acted like Christ, if they lived Christ, there would be no single mothers seeking a way out. Praise God for the Bridegroom of the church who is faithful to us, her children.

Two Become One—Ephesians 5:31–33

I will admit that the kind of emphasis I have placed on the extraordinary nature of marriage in Scripture is a bit unique in terms of commentators, but there is a reason for that. As I said in the introduction, we have a hard time not overreacting to Roman Catholicism. The Reformers and Puritans had some emotional baggage, which is understandable given the whole burning-at-the-stake thing. We need to be cautious, and examine Scripture "as it is" with as few of our presuppositions as possible.[25]

Rome used this passage to say that marriage is a sacrament, which translated into something for which people depended on clergy as an "automatic" means of grace.[26] This was based on Jerome's Vulgate translating "mystery" as "sacrament." So the Reformers and their children recategorized marriage, but went a bit far. Calvin shows this when he writes,

> But the present question is, Has marriage been appointed as a sacred symbol of the grace of God, to declare and represent to us something spiritual, such as Baptism or the Lord's Supper? They have no ground for such an assertion, unless it be that they have been deceived by the doubtful signification of a Latin word, or rather by their ignorance of the Greek language. If the simple fact had been observed, that the word used by Paul is Mystery, no mistake would ever have occurred.[27]

As we will see, Paul is saying that marriage is a unique symbol. It does "declare and represent to us something spiritual." Yet, it is not a "sacrament" in the full sense of the term because those are reserved for Christ's church. Unbelievers can marry one another and still unwittingly mirror the mystery of Christ and His church. All that being said, let us return to the text.

Paul points us back to when God created the first marriage in the garden. There are many ordinances and institutions of God through history, but marriage is unique in that it predates the fall. Hebrews 13:4 calls us to keep the marriage bed undefiled because it begins as undefiled and has a peculiar place in redemptive history.

God specifically created man in a way that required a complement for companionship, productivity, and bearing children. A cursory reading of Genesis 2 may sound like God was surprised that Adam needed help, but make no mistake, this was God's design in His perfect wisdom. We see from nature

---

25 I say as few presuppositions as possible because we cannot entirely eliminate them.
26 In Roman theology, by performing the ritual, grace is imparted.
27 Calvin, *Commentaries XXI*, 325.

that God could have made man an asexual, independent creature, but he was designed as a puzzle piece for interdependence.

God formed Eve from the side, or rib, of Adam. By God's design, women owe their origin to God and man, and every subsequent generation of men owe their origin to God and women. Neither man nor woman can create life without the other.

As we saw before from Daniel Rogers, Eve was not taken from the head that she might lead, or from his foot to be trampled. She was taken from his side to be a companion and under his arm to be protected. We might add to this that she was made from his body to be subject, nourished, and cherished. Adam was meant to see himself in Eve, and Eve was to see herself in Adam.

Paul specifically quotes Genesis 2:24, where Moses describes how this creation of Eve created and catalyzed the pattern for marriage. Boys and girls are born into subjection to their parents, which constitutes their primary responsibility for their childhood. When they are all grown up and God brings them to a spouse by providence, a huge shift takes place. The woman leaves her parents' authority to cleave to her husband and his leadership. The man leaves his parents' home, where he submits to his parents but also has relative comfort and safety. He now becomes the head of his own household. Both of them shift their *primary* allegiance to their spouse. Every other human relationship is to take a backseat to the marriage. They do not cease to honor their fathers and mothers, but that becomes secondary to the marriage. It is important that parents keep this in mind, as fathers teach by words and example what a head of a household ought to be, and mothers do the same in regards to the helpmate.

In marriage, the two become one flesh. This refers first to their physical intimacy within the marriage covenant, where they are set free to be vulnerable to one another (1 Cor. 6:15–20). Marriage should be the true "safe space," as we see in Proverbs 27:8. This vital union is more than just physical, however. It is financial, emotional, and psychological. They surrender autonomy in order to become something greater than they were alone.[28]

In our last verse, Paul applies this alongside everything laid out so far. The husband is commanded to love his wife as himself or his body. This means he is to love her selflessly and sacrificially. He is to love her in such a way that she is bold, powerful, and self-controlled. Colossians 3:19 calls husbands to love without harshness to this end. He is to be the supplement of her weaknesses, nourishing and cherishing her physically, emotionally, and spiritually. His love should point her to Christ.

---

[28] It is like Voltron, where the individual robot cars join together to make a giant robot samurai warrior.

Paul says that each man is to love his wife this way in order that she might respect or revere her husband. While that word can be translated as fear, it is clearly a concept of reverence. As we saw before, the husband is to love without harshness. 1 John 4:18 tells us that love casts out fear, and 1 Peter 3:5–6 shows that wives are to submit to their husbands and fear nothing as daughters of Sarah. The only fear here is that of disappointing or offending their loved one.

Notice that Paul says the husband must fulfill his role in order that the wife might revere and defer. While this is not excusing wives from subjection to an imperfect husband, it does mean that the wife is equipped to defer to him insofar as the husband loves his wife in a Christlike fashion. When the husband is selfish, he makes it difficult for his wife to respect and defer to him. Especially when there are children, a husband who considers himself first makes it complicated and, in extreme cases, impossible for the wife to honor and obey him. Husbands, love your wives sacrificially if you want her to follow you.

Now we return to verse 32, where Paul inverts the metaphor. He has primarily used Christ's example to teach husbands and wives their roles until this point. But now he comes to the great mystery. We have seen this concept already in Ephesians 1:9, 3:3–4, and 8–9. This is the plot twist where the servant is revealed to be the master. Here we see what was once in shadow brought to light. Steve Baugh writes,

> In the instance of Gen 2:24 cited in 5:31, Paul has cited it in such a way that it follows this same pattern but in a more "profound" way. Paul declares in v.32 that the original created institution of union of husband and wife was itself modeled on Christ's union with the church as his "body" as its archetype. On the historical plane, marital union then becomes a type of the historical antitype of fulfillment in Christ.[29]

This is to say that the whole institution of marriage was created by God to teach the most important truth, the gospel. God did not give us the gospel to help us have better marriages; He gave us marriages to teach us about the gospel. That is the primary reason marriage was created and now exists.

God created Adam as incomplete in order to show Christ's incarnational purpose we saw in Ephesians 1:22–23. The Son, the Word in eternity as the second person of the Trinity, was complete and self-sustained, but in the incarnation, Christ was "incomplete" in order to take the church as His Bride. Jesus will count Himself incomplete until the last of the elect is saved and brought safely to glory. What a great mystery this is!

---

29 Baugh, *Evangelical Exegetical Commentary: Ephesians*, 494.

Of course, the greatest joy and mystery of this all is the union we now have with Christ (John 17:21–23). Colossians 3:4 declares Christ to be our very life. And 2 Peter 1:4 says we become partakers of His divine nature. In Revelation 3:12, it is said that Christ places His name upon us. These are the greatest purposes of marriage.

It is true that we are commanded to follow these principles for marriage for the sake of obedience to God. It is true that in doing so, we follow God's ordained pattern for married life. It is true that when these things are followed, both husband and wife will flourish and the children will be raised in a healthy and protective environment. Yet the greatest reason for these things is to convey Christ and His church. When spouses follow these commands, they proclaim the gospel to the degree they are successful. They teach the most important truths to each other, their children, and the world.

Unmarried saints, do not feel as though you are excluded in these things, for you have that to which marriage points. You are created in the image of God and born again into the body of Christ. We best reflect Christ in love, and the ways that love works its way through all our behavior. The Ten Commandments become something beautiful when we examine them in terms of loving God and one another. While the worldly person looks around and asks, "What can these people do for me?" the Christian is to look around and ask, "Who needs to be loved and how can I best love them?"

Children Obey in the Lord—Ephesians 6:1–3

It is helpful for us to remember the nature of an epistle. These were not chapters in a book, but letters written on specific occasions. The elders of the church would receive the letter and then read it aloud, maybe with some exposition, in the Sunday service. At this point in Paul's letter to Ephesus, he is exploring what it means to be filled with the Holy Spirit in various contexts. After he tells the husband and wife how to be Spirit-filled and love one another, he talks to the kids.

Paul's direct address to the children of the church teaches us two things. First, it assumes that children were present and sitting under the preaching of the gospel, especially believing children. Paul includes a similar address in Colossians 3:20, calling children to obedience because it is pleasing to the Lord. The second is that children are worth talking to from the pulpit. Mark 10:13–16 shows us Christ's exhortation to not prohibit the children from coming to Him. While parents should try to keep their children from being a distraction in the service, we should be happy that children are present.

As adults, so long as our parents are alive, this command has bearing on us, though we need more wisdom than we did as kids to pull it off. This is part of being Spirit-filled Christians and loving others above ourselves in relational contexts.

First, we have to see a hierarchy of responsibility. Your primary responsibility is toward God, and anything contrary to this must be ignored. This is what Christ spoke of in Matthew 10:34–39. It is interesting that Chrysostom goes so far as to say, "If the father be a gentile or a heretic, we ought no longer to obey, because the command is not then, 'in the Lord.'"[30] Yet this cannot be absolute because we still have to honor government leaders when they are unbelievers.

Your secondary responsibility is toward your spouse and children. If you are married and if you have children, they take precedent. If your parents make demands of you that are detrimental to them, you have to say no.

The third is that you have a responsibility to be an adult bearing the image of God. You are not meant to be in constant dependence on your parents, even in guidance. You need to make your own decisions as an adult, even if you seek your parents' wisdom, and take responsibility for those decisions.

Beyond these things, we ought to honor and even obey our parents wherever possible. If you have been blessed with parents who are believers, then the words of Proverbs 1:8–9 still apply to you. Heed their instruction.

But we are to love our parents and live the gospel to them, especially if they are unbelievers, as a testimony to the grace God has shown us. In Romans 1:28–32 and 2 Timothy 3:1–2, we see a list of heinous sins that mark the unbelievers, and included in this list is disobedience to parents. Our lives are a public declaration of the gospel that we adorn by our works.

Honoring parents looks different in different circumstances. Yielding to the financial requests of a parent squandering money on an addiction is not loving. When caring for a parent with dementia, fulfilling a demand might be detrimental to their very livelihood. Yet even in these things, we should strive to love and honor.

Christ speaks indirectly of our responsibility to care for our parents in Mark 7:9–13, and He honored Mary while on the cross. Matthew Henry writes, "'Honor thy father and mother,' which honor implies reverence, obedience, and relief and maintenance, if these be needed."[31] In 1 Timothy 5:8, Paul says that abandoning and failing to provide for your family makes you worse than an unbeliever. While parents may not be financially dependent on their children to survive, as it was in Paul's and Christ's time, the absolute neglect of one's parents is still a serious thing.

---

30 Chrysostom, *Homilies on Galatians, Ephesians, Philippians, Colossians, Thessalonians, Timothy, Titus, and Philemon.*
31 Henry, *Commentaries*, 577.

The broadest application of this passage comes from examining who our spiritual parents are as believers. Martyn Lloyd-Jones writes, "So in a very wonderful way the relationship between the parent and the child is a replica and a picture, a portrayal, a preaching of this whole relationship that subsists especially between those who are Christian and God himself."[32] When we are obedient to our spiritual parents, Christ and the church, by the Holy Spirit's work within us, we "obey . . . in the Lord."

As we have seen already, there are corresponding components. You are born again through Christ and His church, and then, by virtue of Christ and His Sonship, you are adopted by the Father. Ephesians 3:14–15 declares God to be the origin of fatherhood itself.

So you are commanded by Scripture to honor your father and mother, that it might go well for you in the land which the Lord gives you. Our mother in this is not yet perfected. The church on earth sometimes makes grievous errors to the detriment of her children. Therefore, it takes wisdom as to how, but we are to honor her. We are to obey her and her ministers insofar as she is subject to her husband. Proverbs 31:28 should be true of the church, where her children rise up and call her blessed and her husband honors her also.

The greater portion of honor is due to Christ and the Father who provide, protect, and guide in perfect wisdom. We honor God in loving obedience to His Word. We honor Christ by mirroring Christ. We honor the Lord by honoring His Bride, the church. And we honor Him by loving His children, which brings us into the next segment.

Admonishing Parents—Ephesians 6:4

Having examined Spirit-filled marriage and childhood, now we come to Spirit-filled parenting in wisdom. This is in contrast to the wine-soaked foolishness of Ephesians 5:18. While these truths are most useful for parents of little ones, the principles Paul addresses still have bearing for those with adult children. If you do not have children, I urge you to hear the breadth of Paul's exhortation as a reflection of God perfectly loving His imperfect children.

Paul is literally addressing the fathers, but it applies to both parents. This is important because it assumes the father is present and has an important role in the home. It also assumes that he is actively involved in raising the children. Paul places the responsibility of the children on him, even if he delegates some of it.

Paul tells dads to not provoke their children to anger. He uses similar language in Colossians 3:21, where we see the addition "lest they become discouraged." This is about unnecessary provocation and discouragement. Just

---

[32] Lloyd-Jones, *Life in the Spirit in Marriage, Home, and Work*, 245.

because a child is momentarily angry or unhappy does not meant the parent has failed this, though a child being habitually or perpetually angry may indicate a deeper problem.

Paul was addressing parents in a context of unmitigated authority over their children. William Barclay observes, "A Roman father had absolute power over his family. He could sell them as slaves, he could make them work in his fields even in chains, he could take the law into his own hands, for the law was in his own hands, and punish as he liked, he could even inflict the death penalty on his child."[33] I bring this up because that is the context for God, for Christ as our Father. There is univocal and absolute authority, which makes the tender love of Christ for us as His children all the more beautiful. We see certain types of parents who characteristically and habitually provoke and fail their children in any era. For the sake of simplicity, we will stereotype these, but I urge parents to be honest about identifying where they match up.

The dictator: The parent who leads his household predominantly or exclusively by force, fear, and punishment. Parents need to periodically examine whether their punishment of bad behavior significantly outweighs praise of good behavior. The dictator parent is often applauded while the children are young, but shamed when the offspring rebel as adults. God permits us to make mistakes for our good, and our kids need an environment where they can make their own mistakes without merciless judgment.

The absent parent: The angriest and most frustrated of children are often those who have received no parenting. The broken home is the most common, but a parent can be physically present yet emotionally absent and fail to lead. Eli (1 Samuel 2–3) had his children in the house of God but never actively taught or disciplined. In David and Absalom (2 Samuel 13–15), we find the father who ignores the problems and hopes they will just go away. It fails to reflect our Heavenly Father, who is never absent from us or neglectful.

The pre-fabricator: It is natural for parents to have hopes and dreams for their children; that is part of deciding to have a child. There are certain things that we ought to discourage our children from (e.g., playing in traffic, wearing socks with sandals) or encourage toward (saving for the future) for their basic well-being. Yet there is a line that is easily crossed wherein we presume ourselves sovereign over their future and then provoke our children when they stray from the script. Saul and Jonathan in 1 Samuel 20:30–34 is an excellent example of this. God has decreed our future as His children, but, even in that, no violence is done to the will of the creature (us).

The capricious parent: Children need consistency, but we are inconsistent people. This stereotype is the parent whose structure of discipline and reward

---

[33] Cited by John Stott, *Ephesians*.

are constantly shifting. They are ruled by their emotions. Such a parent is more akin to the drunkard than the Spirit-filled saint. As Lloyd-Jones said, "What right have you to say to your child that he needs discipline when you obviously need it yourself?"[34] Our children need us to be the same parents today that we will be tomorrow, just as Christ has set the example being the same yesterday, and today, and forever (Heb. 13:8).[35]

One thing that is strikingly absent in each of these is the understanding of stewardship. Parents are entrusted with an eternal soul. Each child has his own developing personality and destiny that owe their authorship to God, not the parents. This is as humbling as it is informative.

Now we switch from what Paul tells us not to do to the positive responsibility of the parent. In other words, this is the answer to the question, "How should I love my child?" We need to think of instruction, discipline, and provision in terms of acts of love.

First is this concept of *nourish*, which Paul already used in 5:29 for the wife and the body. In the ESV, this is reflected in "bring them up." Immediately, the connection to the body shows us that this is about providing what is best. Nourishing is not gluttony for the body or spoiling the child, and it is not starving the body or neglecting the child.

It indicates the responsibility to provide. The parents are to provide for the child's emotional, psychological, physical, and spiritual needs. Anselm, while talking about raising children without affection, said, "If you were to plant a tree in your garden and were to enclose it on all sides, so that it could not extend its branches, what would you find when, at the end of several years, you set it free from its bounds? A tree whose branches were bent and scraggy, and would it not be your fault for having so unreasonably confined it?"[36] These provisions are made with an eye toward the goal of adulthood. You are not trying to raise boys and girls, but godly men and women.

To love them without coddling, to protect without sheltering, requires a lot of wisdom. It takes a lot of grace. So pray for both and seek them where God says they are to be found. Again, each child is different and has different needs. This is especially true as we come to our next exhortation.

The parent is to give instruction and discipline in the Lord, which is one word in the original text, *paideia*. This word has quite a range: 1 Corinthians 11:32 refers to God's discipline by illness or death, 2 Corinthians 6:9 refers to

---

[34] Lloyd-Jones, *Life in the Spirit in Marriage, Home, and Work*, 237–302.
[35] There is one important qualification to this. Our relationship to our kids will grow and the rules adjust to where they are in life. Some have said this is the nature of the OT to the NT.
[36] Quoted in Phillip Schaff, *History of the Christian Church Vol 2* (Grand Rapids: Eerdmans, 1970), 543.

punishment, 2 Timothy 2:25 describes gentle correction of an intellectual opponent, 2 Timothy 3:16 describes the Scriptures' instruction in righteousness, and Titus 2:12 refers to the training of grace. Paul indicates the whole range of parental instruction and discipline by placing this alongside nourishing.

This does touch on the general instruction and education of the child. Some parents will decide to homeschool, and others will send theirs to public school.[37] Now, this responsibility may be delegated to varying degrees, and sometimes it has to be, but parents need to be involved in their children's education.

Next is education in God's law. The parent has an obligation to teach the child right from wrong with its anchoring point in the moral law. Morality is not determined by majority opinion but by God's character. Of course, a large portion of this is in practical terms of discipline and correction—Proverbs 13:24, 22:15, 23:13–14, 29:15, 17.

Yet discipline is never to be done in anger or excess. Calvin says, "It is not the will of God that parents, in the exercise of kindness, shall spare and corrupt their children. Let their conduct towards their children be at once mild and considerate, so as to guide them in the fear of the Lord, and correct them also when they go astray"[38] Lloyd-Jones tells us, "A Christian, balanced discipline is never mechanical; it is always living, it is always personal, it is always understanding, and above all it is always highly intelligent. It knows what it is doing, and it is never guilty of excess."[39]

The greatest instruction, the most crucial, and the privilege of the parent is in terms of the gospel. The intellectual side of this is in terms of teaching your children in home devotions and gospel-centered conversations (Deut. 6:5–7; 20–25). Part of that is bringing your child into God's house, for which Chrysostom uses Hannah as an example. But you must also live the gospel to your child. In discipline situations, walk them through what repentance and forgiveness look like. Do you show real forgiveness that reflects God to your child? Every parent should be well-practiced in sharing the gospel with sinners.

We all need an example to follow in our roles in life. The wife has the church as her standard, the husband has Christ, and the parent has God the Father. This is the greater weight of "nourishing and discipline of the Lord," which is to say, we nourish and discipline our children after the pattern of the Lord. He protects us without coddling us to prepare us for heaven (Rom. 8:28–30, 35–39). He chastises us in perfect wisdom, love, and measure. As Spurgeon observes, there is not a drop of God's wrath in his chastisement of

---

37 Finances, availability, parental ability, the parents' education, and wisdom will all play part in this decision-making process.
38 Calvin, *Commentaries*, 329.
39 Lloyd-Jones, *Life in the Spirit in Marriage, Home, and Work*, 237–302.

us because Christ drank the dregs of the cup in the cross.[40] He instructs us in the law and the gospel (Heb. 1:1–3). As we saw before, God has provided prophets, apostles, evangelists, pastors, and teachers for our growth and education in that which matters most.

He accomplishes grace for us. He is eager to forgive on grounds of repentance (1 John 1:9). He is constant in His love for us, and we never have reason to doubt His love. He is eager to give good gifts according to our needs, especially in the Holy Spirit (Luke 11:9–13). The Christian who seeks his supply from the Father has all that is best for their growth and maturity. How this transforms our concept of covetousness! Flee to your Heavenly Father, if He is yours, and find rest in His arms. If He is not your Father, run first to the cross in repentance and faith, that you might know Him as Father rather than Judge.

Warrior Bride—Ephesians 6:10–20

When we talk about Ephesians, people with a theological bent first think about the passages on predestination, total depravity, and salvation by grace through faith. Others, like myself, go immediately to the description of marriage and its counterpart in the church with Christ. Yet most rush to the armor of God, as many preachers and practical Christians are prone to do. It seems empowering to use a modern buzzword to think of ourselves as noble soldiers, fighters on the battlefield, but a closer examination is quite humbling. Every piece of the armor marks us as God's, is gifted by God, is an aspect of Christ's work, and properly belongs to Christ.

Many exhaustive treatises exist on this segment of Ephesians, but we do well to pass it through that lens of the Bride. The bridal train has a long-standing tradition of tripping distracted guests, but Christ's Bride is girded with the belt of truth because she is under attack and must be agile. A traditional bridal gown is designed only for beauty, but the Bride of Christ is clothed in something more akin to Frodo's Mithril chain mail. She wears a breastplate of Christ's righteousness that cannot be pierced and protects the heart and emotions from Satan's wiles. Yet this armor is beautiful and befitting a bride adorned for her husband. While most brides wear insensible shoes, Christ's Bride is shod with the readiness of the gospel of peace, a warrior's studded sandal that gives traction on unstable ground, allowing her to run swiftly and dodge attack. The earthly bride carries a bouquet of flowers, but the church carries the heavy *thuros* shield, which quenches the darts of the evil one and reflects the collective working of the faith of the saints united.[41] Her veil is

---

40 Charles H. Spurgeon, "It Is Finished," *The Treasury of the Bible Vol. 3* (Grand Rapids: Zondervan, 1968), 672.

41 The thuros was a giant shield used by Roman soldiers in formation. It was unwieldy for

replaced by a helmet of salvation which preserves her from the most lethal blows of powers of darkness. She carries a sword of God's truth revealed in Scripture, double-edged and lethal to the enemy. Though she speaks of gratitude and the wedding feast, her lips are constant in prayer of confession and petition, as the day is fraught with peril.

She is beautiful in all her adornments, but these are not purchased by her or her parents; they are the gifts of the groom. She is both lovely and fierce, as she must be.

Benediction—Ephesians 6:23-24

We cannot possibly leave any treatment on Paul's epistles without dealing with benediction, the proclamation of good. To examine benedictions through the bridal lens gives us a new appreciation for their beauty. We will look at who is being blessed, who is actually blessing, and what is contained in the blessing.

When Paul declares the benediction in Ephesians, the audience is not the same as that of the letter. It is both broader and narrower than the Ephesian church.

It is broader because it applies to the whole of Christ's church, including us today. Paul draws attention to this with the third person, "peace be to the brothers," in keeping with the content of the letter. Chapter 4 showed how God is growing the entire body into union and peace, of which Ephesus is only a tiny portion.

Yet it is narrower because it only applies only to the elect, pointing us back to predestination in chapter 1. Here, he describes it as *those who love Christ*. The broader context of Scripture teaches us how the love for Christ, for God, and for God's people are interwoven. In John 13:35, Christ tells us, "By this all people will know that you are my disciples, if you have love for one another." And 1 Corinthians 16:22 states, "If anyone has no love for the Lord, let him be accursed. Our Lord, come!" So also in 1 John 2:9–11 and in 4:19 we are told that we only love because God first loved us. We will come back to this shortly.

What is the source of blessing? The blessings of the benediction find their origin in the triune God. First is God the Father because He is the one who loved us enough to send His only begotten Son to die for us. He holds all the blessings in heaven meant for us. Second is the Lord Jesus Christ, who gave Himself for us, who purchased blessings on our behalf in His righteousness. This is where that phrase "in incorruption" properly goes.[42] Christ in glory

---

one-on-one combat, but in a phalynx formation, the shields formed a kind of proto-tank that made the squad invulnerable to arrows from above and swords in the front.

42 Baugh, *Evangelical Exegetical Commentary: Ephesians*, 576.

dwells in incorruptibility. He will never again die, nor can He be tainted by sin. There, in incorruption, He intercedes on our behalf. In 2 Timothy 1:10, Paul writes of that "which now has been manifested through the appearing of our Savior Christ Jesus, who abolished death and brought life and immortality (incorruption) to light through the gospel." Finally, the Holy Spirit is not directly mentioned, but He is the authority in Paul's benediction and the agent applying the blessings sought and proclaimed therein.

Now we come to the benediction itself. A benediction, whether in Scripture, a worship service, or even a wedding, should be more than a marker that things have come to an end. It was common to close a letter with "wishes," but the benediction is older and mightier than that in Paul's day. Steve Baugh tells us, "The benediction in our service is not a pious wish of the minister. What makes it so special is what God is doing. He puts his name on us and blesses us with his smile and with his peace."[43] The benediction is the prayer of the pastor as well as God's promise to His people. God promises these things in varying degrees and forms to all of His saints through history and in perfection in glory.

The first promise is for peace. This is reconciliation with God and the unification of the universal church in all its diversity. Second Thessalonians 3:16 tells us, "Now may the Lord of peace himself give you peace at all times in every way. The Lord be with you all." So, too, 2 Corinthians 13:11 gives both charge and promise, "Finally, brothers, rejoice. Aim for restoration, comfort one another, agree with one another, live in peace; and the God of love and peace will be with you."

Love with faith is next. It is important that we see the indivisibility of these two. Wherever there is saving faith, it will work in love. Paul says in Galatians 5:6, "For in Christ Jesus neither circumcision nor uncircumcision counts for anything, but only faith working through love." And true love only exists where there is trust (1 John 4:7–10).

Finally, there is grace: the overarching provision of God from eternity in election, through history in redemption accomplished, through our lives of redemption applied, and into eternity. These are the promises of God for His people.

We are called to live our lives with an eye toward heaven, with Christ "in incorruption" as our great hope, because He is the first fruits of the resurrection. As the bride hears the benediction in the wedding service, she looks lovingly and longingly at her new husband. As 1 Corinthians 15:20 says, "But in fact Christ has been raised from the dead, the firstfruits of those who have fallen asleep." Romans 2:7 adds, "To those who by patience in well-doing seek

---

43 Baugh, *Evangelical Exegetical Commentary: Ephesians*, 577.

for glory and honor and immortality, he will give eternal life." This means we are to hold all things in this world with open hands before God because we know that something far greater awaits us.

Knowing that the benediction here is more than a wish, but a promise from the sovereign God, we must ask what we do with a promise. The Westminster Confession speaks of the Christian embracing the promises of Scripture "for this life and that which is to come."[44] This means that we are to pray for those four things: grace, peace, love, and faith. We should rejoice in the degree they are already granted, trust that more will be given as they are needed, and that they will be full in glory. It also means that we are to expect these things from God and not the world. Paul lacked freedom and many comforts of the world when he was in chains in Rome, but he had more of these four things than Caesar himself.

Would you have these things? Do you desire grace for the day, peace beyond understanding, faith which grounds you, love for others, and to be loved beyond measure? Has God shown you yet how the world promises these things but never delivers? You cannot find the real form of them in a way that lasts outside of Christ. Flee to the cross in prayer. Confess your sins, your failures and faults, and plead for Christ. Cast your hope on Him alone.

These benedictions of Paul and others are conveyances of love from the husband to the wife. They were whispers of the husband's wedding vows in the Old Testament, and they are reminders to saints today. A husband might remind his wife in a rough season of life, "I promised to be with you in sickness and in health, richer or poorer, until death do us part." The Bridegroom of our souls has a greater promise. "I will be with you, and give you grace, mercy, love, peace, faith, and so much more. I will be with you until the end of the age" (see Matt. 28:20).

---

44 WCF XIV.2, 2nd LBC XIV.2

XI
Paul Outside Ephesians

The Contented Spouse

Before leaving the Pauline corpus, we need to address a couple of topics that are not explicitly covered in Ephesians, the first of which is our contentment in Christ. We have briefly addressed this theme in its connection to temptation to idolatry, delighting in Christ, the challenge of submission, and others.[1] But this is a subject we need to hear again and again. As the Bride, we have an obligation to find our contentment in the marriage of our souls to the Messiah. As with every aspect of our relationship to God, the obligation is also benefit. We all yearn for greater joy, peace, love, and contentment, though we rarely think past the pursuit of the stuff we think will bring contentment. If we did, we would quickly see how futile many of those efforts are.

A quick example of this is adultery. The man or woman who commits adultery, generally speaking, does so because they think another sexual partner will give them love, joy, satisfaction, and contentment, which they do not currently have. They rarely think it through that far, but that is the subconscious drive. If they were to pause and think about it long enough, they would realize that adulterers do not have lives marked by love, joy, satisfaction, or contentment. Were you to ask them, "Would you still have an affair if you could find all those things you want in your current marriage?" their response would probably be, "No, I wouldn't, but I can't find what I'm looking for with my spouse, at least as much as I want." Often, the truth behind this is that they do not want to do the work to find those things in their marriage. It is hard work to build contentment in a marriage. So they think they can find satisfaction more easily in the arms of another.

But how could we ever say that of our Savior? How could we ever think that idolatrous spiritual adultery can give us something our Savior could not? The problem is that our actions betray a belief that the idols of our hearts can give what God cannot. Again, the reality behind it is that we do not want to put in the work to find our satisfaction in Christ. We think that the things we desire are more easily found in the arms of another.

---

[1] Much of what will follow is derived from Jeremiah Burroughs' book, *The Rare Jewel of Christian Contentment*, which I have referenced before and highly recommend.

In Philippians 4:11, we find that Paul put in that work, and how God did it in him: "For I have learned in what I am, content to be." The phrase "what I am" has been translated a variety of ways, normally along the lines of "whatever state I am in" because Paul goes on to address his contentment amidst both trial and blessing. When Paul is hungry, sick, poor, and tired, he is content. When he is fed, healthy, rich, and rested, he is content. Yet we should not lose sight of the literal reading. Paul is content in what he is; he is comfortable in his own skin.

So what is it that Paul is, which gives him such otherworldly contentment? We could sum it all up in "Paul is a sinner saved by grace," but that has many layers. He was lost and now found, dead made alive, alienated now reconciled. He has experienced the profound love of Christ, the Bridegroom of his soul, and, to the degree he understands it, has found contentment. Indeed, he has understood it better than most of God's children through history. He did not earn this love; it was grace. He was unlovable as a sinner, but God loved him anyway, even sending His son to bear Paul's sins to the cross and suffer the punishment thereof.

But Paul had to learn it. God taught him, to be sure, but Paul also had to seek it. As Burroughs puts it, "Contentment in every condition is a great art, a spiritual mystery. It is to be learned, and to be learned as a mystery."[2] It requires an eternal perspective. We have to learn who we are without Christ, who Christ and God are, and what we are in Christ. Returning to our metaphor, it requires learning about the marriage and its riches.

In Proverbs 15:6, we are taught, "(In) the house of the righteous one is great wealth, and the harvest of the wicked is to be troubled." To be the Bride of the Righteous One is to be part of His household and to be one of God's children. In that relationship, we are heirs to great treasure, a portion of which we taste even now. It is like Jean Valjean's peasant cloak, which had untold wealth sown into secret pockets.[3] To again quote Burroughs:

> The righteous man can never be made so poor, to have his house so rifled and spoiled, but there will remain much treasure within. . . . There is the presence of God and the blessing of God upon him, and therein is much treasure. . . . There is more treasure in the poorest body's house, if he is godly, than in the house of the greatest man in the world.[4]

Oh what contentment may be ours if only we learn it! How envy may be slain!

---
2 Burroughs, *The Rare Jewel of Christian Contentment*, 17.
3 In *Les Miserables*, the main character has this heavy coat with money sewn into it that he periodically removes to support his adopted daughter and himself while he is on the lam.
4 Burroughs, *The Rare Jewel of Christian Contentment*, 35.

It is the nature of my calling that I often work late, long after my family has gone to bed. In turning in, stepping carefully over toys, and cringing at squeaking floorboards, I climb under the covers and see my wife. I have often thought, "I am a rich man." But even if God were to send me through Job's gauntlet, though I might stutter in saying the words, I could still rightly say as a sinner saved by grace, "I am a rich man."

In Psalm 16:5, David said, "Yahweh is my portion and my lot." For us as the biblical Bride, Christ is our portion. Yahweh in flesh is our lot. He is sating and satisfactory. When we seek our portion elsewhere, we find discontentment. How much more peace would we find if we prayed for Christ instead of past Christ for other things? As Augustine once put it, "It is one thing to seek any thing from the Lord, another to seek the Lord Himself."[5]

One of my favorite things about getting to know a married couple is hearing stories of their early life together, especially when they met young. They talk about life in small apartments or mobile homes, eating copious amounts of spaghetti, ramen noodles, and peanut butter and jelly sandwiches. Traditional wedding vows often articulate "for richer or for poorer," but the sequence is normally the other way around. People often recall those simple, poorer days with such joy and sweetness, when they were young lovers too happy to realize they were poor.

This concept is found sprinkled throughout the Scriptures in Christ's Bride. It is found in both Old and New Testaments, particularly in Paul's writings. Such love is embedded in Job's words, "Though he slay me, I will hope in him" (13:15).

One of my favorites is found in Hebrews 10:32–34, where the author recounts how those saints suffered in the earliest days of their faith. We can almost hear the wedding vows, "richer or poorer, in sickness and in health." So they vowed in faith, and so they lived. He says, "you received these things with joy." Having been enlightened by God, you rejoiced in suffering. What a contrast this is to the "gospel" of health, wealth, and prosperity! Scripture actually exalts and portrays the joys and benefits of suffering (Acts 14:21–23; Rom. 5:3–5; 8:16–17; 1 Thess. 3:3; 2 Tim. 3:12; 1 Peter 4:14).

Those sufferings sanctified saints by drawing their eyes heavenward, purifying them, and preparing them for glory (Prov. 25:4–5; Mic. 2:10; 2 Cor. 4:17–18). They knew their real treasure, better and abiding, was in heaven (Matt. 6:19–21; Phil. 1:23). The Bride finds joy amidst the sufferings which identified her with her Husband. Yet she ends her journey in eternal and complete joy with her Husband in glory.

---

5 Augustine, *Expositions on the Book of Psalms*, "Psalm 16."

Reader, are you enduring trial and suffering? If not, then store these things away in your heart for harder days. If you are suffering, either personally or vicariously, rejoice in your suffering. How? Return to your first love. Revelation 2:4 says, "But I have this against you, that you have abandoned the love you had at first." Look heavenward at your inheritance and cling to God's sovereignty. Joyfully strive in suffering without resentful plowing or fatalism and resignation. Rejoice in what God is doing in you. Rejoice in what he is doing through you. Pray for your enemies and live Christ in all circumstances. In suffering with joy, we adorn the gospel we proclaim.

Divorce

John Owen writes, "It is confessed by all that adultery is a just and sufficient cause of a divorce betwixt married persons."[6]

Throughout this book, I have tried to explore both the marriage above and the marriage below, primarily in terms of their correlation. Unfortunately, this raises the question of divorce. In Hosea, we saw God's divorce from national Israel under the Mosaic covenant[7] while upholding the unbreakable marriage in the covenant of grace with true, spiritual Israel. But is divorce valid in the context of the full revelation of the gospel? The other question we will be addressing along the way is whether or not remarriage is valid, which groups like the Novatians and Tertullianists denied.[8]

First, we have to see divorce in the world of Moses. Leviticus 21 shows us that a priest is forbidden from marrying a woman who has been divorced or a widow. Deuteronomy 24 gives us some case law regarding divorce and remarriage. In rabbinical tradition, a man could divorce a woman over slight offenses. Perhaps the only strong exhortation against divorce in the whole of the Old Testament is found in Malachi 2:16, where divorce is compared to a garment of violence.[9] All this is important when we come to examine what Christ says in the gospels.

Matthew 5:31–32 is perhaps the most famous and frequently quoted passage on divorce. After making reference to Mosaic law, Jesus tells us that divorce for any reason other than adultery causes adultery.[10] Basically, if the

---

[6] This is the opening of a magnificent treatment of divorce, "Of Marrying After Divorce in Case of Adultery," *The Works of John Owen Vol XVI* (London: Banner of Truth, 1968), 254–257.
[7] We find a similar reference in Isaiah 50:1.
[8] David Dickson, *Truth's Victory Over Error* (Carlisle: Banner of Truth, 2007), 185.
[9] Admittedly, this is a difficult passage to work through, but likely is speaking of cloaking their sins of adultery by divorcing their wives, which is "violence."
[10] Likewise, we ought not to fall into the foolishness of viewing divorces as a *mensa et thoro*, or a kind of separation wherein remarriage is forbidden. As John Owen said, "This ... is no true divorce, but a mere fiction of a divorce, of no use in this case, nor lawful to be made use of, neither by the law of nature nor the law of God."

divorce is for invalid grounds (not adultery), the man encourages the woman to commit adultery by remarrying because the first marriage was still valid. This passage has led many pastors and theologians to claim that any divorce under any circumstances other than adultery is invalid. Yet there is one important thing to note before we examine some other passages. Christ is speaking to what we might call the covenant community, those claiming faith in the God of Israel and claiming to be His people. So, immediately, this changes the qualification from "no divorce without adultery" to "no divorce *between believers* without adultery."

Matthew 19:3–9 gives us a similar account. Christ again condemns divorce among believers except for adultery cases, but he further explains that the easy-divorce climate of the Mosaic economy was on the grounds of the sinfulness of the people, the hardness of their hearts. Remember, this was a system where birth made you part of the covenant people, not a profession of faith paired with evidences. It was also in that "scale model" system explained in our chapter on Cycles of History. The standards for the New Testament church are heightened because of the fullness of revelation. There are parallel accounts in Mark 10 and Luke 16. Part of the reason, if not the primary reason, for Christ's language in this case is pointing to the divorce of national Israel that we examined back in Hosea. Divorce was permitted under Sinai because of the hardness of men's hearts; it exposed that cardiac callousness and their inability to earn righteousness before God. "But from the beginning it was not so," meaning that the covenant of grace that preceded Sinai was never able to be broken because it relied on Christ's righteousness, not that of the elect.

Returning to earthly marriage, the next two sections come out of 1 Corinthians 7. Verses 10–11 almost appear more severe than what Christ prescribes, but are really an abbreviated examination of the same situation. A husband and wife should not separate (meaning divorce), and if they do, they are not to remarry. Bringing everything together so far, if a divorce occurs between two believers for any reason other than adultery, they are not permitted to remarry, or they commit adultery. If you have divorced for illegitimate reasons, and are now remarried, that does not mean you have to get a second divorce. It just means that you should not have divorced in the first place, and you need to seek forgiveness if you have not already done so. Remain faithful in the second marriage and seek to honor God in it.

Verses 12–16 are crucial for us to understand divorce and remarriage in a fallen world. Paul tells us if you are married to an unbeliever, try and make it work. You are a living testimony to that unbeliever, and they are "made holy" by you, meaning they are set apart from the rest of the world. God may use your living testimony, words, and conduct to bring them to salvation, and they certainly benefit from being married to someone who is imitating Christ. This sustains marriage's purpose in reflecting how Christ saves His Bride.

If your spouse leaves, if they abandon the marriage, then you are not "enslaved." This means you are not bound to the former marriage. You are free to remarry. So let us say a woman is married to an unbeliever or, as was likely a common case in Corinth, she was saved after they were married. That woman is only bound to the marriage so long as the unbelieving spouse is faithful to the marriage. This is broader than just serving divorce papers and skipping town. If a husband is physically abusive, the wife is not obligated to remain in the marriage until he sleeps with another woman or leaves her. He has abandoned the marriage and wants a victim, not a helpmate. He may even profess to be a Christian, yet he proves himself unrepentant and an unbeliever by his abusive actions, and the woman is just in divorcing him. An abusive marriage does not reflect Christ and His church or glorify God.

We have to be cautious in approaching divorce; it is never something to be taken lightly. Our marriages are meant to reflect Christ's relationship to His church. Even when a spouse has been unfaithful, they should seek repentance and reconciliation. In marriages between true believers, divorce should be nonexistent because Christ has forgiven us more than we will ever forgive our spouse.

Yet we live in a fallen world. When one spouse is an unbeliever, divorce may occur on valid grounds. In these cases, the believing spouse is not "enslaved" but is free to remarry a believer. As the early church father Chrysostom said, "But what will they say, who are knit together in second marriages? I speak not at all in condemnation of them, God forbid; for the Apostle himself permits them, though indeed by way of condescension."[11] Many have said that there should never be divorce, and marriage after divorce is always wrong, even using the bridal metaphor as the reason. Yet we know that we were once bound to the world, even to Satan in our flesh, but we are divorced from it and now wed to Christ.[12]

---

11 Chrysostom, *Homilies on Galatians, Ephesians, Philippians, Colossians, Thessalonians, Timothy, Titus, and Philemon*, on Eph. 5:33.

12 One of my church members, Jan Wills, has asked that I include a footnote that she disagrees with me on this section. So here you go, Jan.

XII
REVELATION OF THE BRIDE

WE HAVE TOUCHED ON John's book of Revelation here and there as we have progressed, but it deserves its own treatise. As the saying goes, "Finis Coronat Opus" or "the end crowns the work." Many use John's last book as an eschatological bingo game, watching the news and stamping the antichrist, false prophet, earthquakes, and plagues, while anxiously waiting to shout "Armageddon!" Debates abound over amillennial, post-millennial, pre-millennial, pro-millennial,[1] and pan-millennial[2] views, but I hope this chapter will benefit you regardless of which interpretation you have adopted. It is easy to become consumed with all the imagery of prophecy, but several elements of that sacred text are glossed over even though they are abundantly clear. My hope here is to draw out the bridal imagery and recapture a bit of the beauty with which God comforted the church through John.

The First Love

In Revelation 2:7, Christ charges the church at Ephesus with abandoning their first love. This charge is so grave that they are near to losing their status as a true church and having their "lampstand" removed. As time has passed, the church collectively waned in its love for the Bridegroom and the gospel which betrothed them to Him. As such, their labors in love for Christ had diminished. It is unfortunately common for a spouse to wax cold in their marriage, to pull away, and diminish their service toward their spouse. Modern culture calls it "falling out of love," as if this were some accidental and unpreventable thing, like tripping on a sidewalk. Yet Christ's response is to call them to repentance and return to their labors.

There will be seasons in our relationship with God wherein our emotions grow cold in a "winter of the heart," but the remedy is repentance, service, and prayer. Like David in the Psalms, we must plead before heaven until relief

---
1 This is the "I do not know what will happen, but I am for the reign of Christ." I classify myself as Pro-Millennial Anti-Trib (I'm against the tribulation of the saints).
2 "It will all pan out in the end."

comes, even drenching our couch with tears. So, too, as earthly spouses, we must pour ourselves out in repentance and service when emotions grow cold.

Heavenly Currency

In Revelation 2:9, Christ tells the church at Smyrna that He sees their tribulation and poverty, but clarifies that they are still rich. How strange this sounds to our earthbound ears! Yet this is far from an isolated concept. In 2 Corinthians 6:10, Paul describes himself and other servants of God as being poor and yet making others rich, having nothing and yet possessing everything. In Matthew 6:19–21, Christ tells us to lay up our treasures in heaven, not on earth, because where our treasure is our heart will also be.

Being wed to Christ, we are immeasurably rich with an inheritance we strain to imagine. Yet we find ourselves like royalty sojourning in a foreign land with unexchangeable currency. We have to make do with a small allowance in the local Naira, dispensed according to our heavenly father's wisdom.[3] Even when we are impoverished in this world, we know it cannot diminish the wealth which awaits us on entering our homeland.

Taking His Name

It is a well-known practice for the bride to take the name of the bridegroom, for a man to place his name upon his beloved. She shares the surname, symbolizing the sharing of life and estate. In Revelation 3:12, Christ promises that His people who conquer in His name will get three names. They will receive the name of God, the name of heavenly Jerusalem (which is the bride adorned at the end of this book), and the name of Christ himself. This feeds into Revelation 3:21–22, where the believer is promised a seat on the throne, as the queen is given a throne with her husband.

The Bridal Gown—Scarlet & White

In 2015, the goofiness that we call the internet was embroiled in controversy over a dress. Some people thought it was white and gold, while others were adamant it was blue and black. When John sees the robes of the righteous, he says that they are white, when logic would dictate they are red. As we have only briefly touched on the subject of the bridal gown up to this point, let us pause to examine what clothes the Bride of Christ in glory.

In Revelation 7:14, one of the elders tells John that the men he sees have endured the tribulation, washed their robes in the blood of the lamb that is Jesus, and made them white. As Meredith Kline observes, "Strange detergent,

---

[3] Naira is the currency of Nigeria.

staining blood."[4] Earlier, in Revelation 6:11, the martyrs were given white robes. In Revelation 4:4, the elders were described as wearing white garments. The white represents purity; the saints are unstained because they have been washed and made clean. This is the same concept as the dressing of Joshua, the high priest in Zechariah 3:1–5, where his filthy garments are taken away and replaced with clean garments.

Yet we should not be so quick to dismiss the red. One of my favorite gems of all the weird Mosaic ritual material is the scarlet thread. This scarlet yarn is a repeated key element in cleansing rituals and covenant ratification.[5] Not only is it scarlet, but it is also wool. Wool is naturally white, and obviously taken from a lamb, but it was then dyed in crushed berries.[6] It is the "bloody" thread necessary to make us clean and acceptable before God. We are clothed in the righteousness of Christ, a garment derived from Him.[7] It is white in its purity, and it is red in its costliness.

The Multi-Ethnic Bride

In Mary Shelley's *Frankenstein*, the monster presses the troubled doctor to make a bride for him. The doctor sets to work, piecing together corpses in an attempt to create something beautiful and provide a suitable companion for the one raised from the dead. Upon nearing completion, Frankenstein examines his work and is horrified. He tears the lifeless body apart and enrages the monster by dooming him to isolation for his seemingly endless life.[8]

One of the elements brought to life in Revelation is the diversity of the Bride, drawn together from every tribe, tongue, and nation, expressed in Revelation 7:9. This was one of Paul's greatest focuses: Christ's church is not only Jewish, but also Roman, Corinthian, Galatian, Ephesian, Colossian, Philippian, Greek, Barbarian, Scythian, and otherwise Gentile. She is a Bride of many origins and nationalities, and we can see today an even broader spectrum from continents around the world. Christ Himself bore an earthly lineage that included the Moabitess Ruth and the Canaanite Rahab.

This is a transformative truth for the Christian in a world that lists toward ethnic divisions. Countries are often unified by ethnic identity, but it can never be to the exclusion or despising of other people-groups for the Christian. Born again into God's family, adopted by grace through Christ, my "race" is first and foremost Christian. This supersedes my identity as an American or

---

4 Meredith Kline, *Glory in Our Midst* (Eugene: Wipf and Stock, 2001), 111.
5 Lev. 14:4–6, 49–52; Num. 19:6; Heb. 9:19.
6 Reminiscent of the "blood" of the crushed grapes, conveying Christ crushed for our sins.
7 The scarlet thread was also used in the tabernacle, which is an image of Christ, and the priestly garments.
8 Mary Shelley, *Frankenstein* (New York: Dover, 1994), 121.

my ancestry of Irish, German, and who knows what else. So every person that I meet may currently be my brother or sister, or destined by God to become such. I cannot assume what truly matters about an individual on the basis of their skin or language. I do not bear much physical resemblance to my dear Nigerian brothers, but I am far closer in heart to them than people with whom I share a bloodline.

The same is true for interracial marriage. Rather than this being an abomination before God, as some have claimed in the past, it is a more accurate reflection of Christ and His Bride. Though it may be a bit anachronistic, I have often mused on the statement on marriage in the WCF, "It is lawful for all sorts of people to marry, who are able with judgment to give their consent; yet it is the duty of Christians to marry in the Lord."[9] Ethnicity does not enter into the equation, only faith.

Thankfully, Christ is far more artful and skillful in drawing together His Bride than Frankenstein was, but it is a once-lifeless Bride infused with the "spark of life" for an immortal Husband.

The Mother and the Dragon

Revelation is full of fantastic and bizarre imagery, and chapter 12 is no exception. The first thing we have to understand about this passage is that it is not chronologically sequenced, meaning it is not a set of events taking place after the seventh trumpet. Like the Old Testament prophets, much of Revelation is cyclical, jumping back and forth in time. Even the chapter on its own is not entirely sequential, but thematic.

We see a woman who is clothed in the sun (as the sun is an image of Christ, this is her clothed in His righteousness), the moon at her feet, and stars in her crown showing her final destiny as the queen of heaven. This is the Bride, the church, particularly as it existed in national Israel at the time of Christ. It is also Mary, but only insofar as she birthed the Messiah and represents that Bride who is clothed in the righteousness of Christ. She is a queen, enthroned insofar as she is partially in glory, and yet on earth for the sake of the incarnation. She is approached by Satan, who would destroy the Messiah to be born.

The child is born, who will rule the nations with a rod of iron, referencing the inauguration in Psalm 2. Here, Christ's earthly ministry appears for only a moment before He ascends into glory, as Luke records in Acts 1. The works of Christ's life, death, and resurrection are not explored here because they are not the focus.

---

9 WCF XXIV.3, 2nd LBC XXV.3a.

She then departs to the wilderness, where God feeds her. What a beautiful presentation of the book of Acts and the diaspora! God prepared the way for Paul, Barnabas, and others to go out into the world, the wilderness, carrying the good news of Jesus Christ. God fed them and those who were saved by the Holy Spirit in extraordinary ways, even raising up prophets and performing miracles through them. This was how God nourished and sustained the Bride until the New Testament was written down in its entirety and distributed. Even today, God feeds His church while sending out men to preach the gospel.

The scene changes to heaven, where Satan and other reprobate angels are thrown down by Michael and others. This is difficult to place in the timeline of redemptive history. Isaiah 14:12–17 and Ezekiel 28:11–19 seem to treat the downfall of Satan as a past event, and most consider that all happened before Satan entered the garden. Christ says in Luke 10:18 that He saw Satan fall from heaven like lightning. To further complicate it, Job 15:15 speaks of heaven as being impure in some sense,[10] and Hebrews 9:23 indicates a kind of purification of heaven through Christ's blood. It could be that heaven is outside of time, and we cannot chart it on our timeline. Yet the simplest way to understand is this: We are seeing a second battle, as futile as the first, as Satan's power is fully crushed in Christ's accomplishment of redemption in the cross. John 12:31, 14:30, and 16:11 all support this concept.

Returning to earth, we see two efforts of Satan, which again are not likely singular or strictly chronological. Satan tries to destroy the Bride as a whole with rivers pouring out of his mouth. These are the lies of Satan in heresies and persecution, but God prevents them from destroying her. Satan also pursues her children individually, striving to consume them. It continues to this day, but God will not abandon His true children. This is the story of God's people between the first and second coming of Christ.

The Harlot of Babylon—Revelation 17–18

There is another kind of bride, a queen of this world, that we see depicted as the drunken whore riding on the beast. She is the bride of Satan with the reprobate as her offspring. She embodies humanity's rebellion against God. Depicted with fine clothing and jewelry, her rewards are in this life (Ps. 17:14). She revels in the persecution and death of God's faithful as we see in Revelation 17:1–6.

John repeats his focus on her delight in sexual immorality, which parallels the New Testament's emphasis on sexual sin. The Scriptures as a whole convey God's concern with the sanctity and beauty of marriage because it is

---

[10] Admittedly, this is Eliphaz speaking, so we treat it like that weird uncle where you have to fact check anything he says.

peculiarly designed to reveal the gospel. Sexual immorality in its forms of adultery, fornication, and homosexuality are mockeries of God's revelation of redemption. That is why God puts such a focus on them in Scripture.

Her boast in Revelation 18:7 that she is a queen, not a widow, who will never mourn, is particularly audacious and ignorant. It may even be a stab at Christ's Bride that mourned His death until the resurrection. The world continues to mock the church today, claiming that Christ is dead and will not return. She is like the fool often seen in the Psalms who says in her heart that there is no God. Her prosperity and power have deluded her into thinking there is no judgment to come, but Revelation tells us otherwise. Her time will come, and God's people must be sanctified, set apart from her.

The Marriage Supper of the Lamb —Revelation 19:6–10

At the very end of earth's history, the last of God's elect are saved by grace through faith in Christ. The final cells that form the complete beauty of the Bride are united to her, and the multitudes of heaven rejoice that the marriage has come. The wedding vows of the last saints are declared in faith.

Then we are told that she is clothed, not only in Christ's righteousness, but even in the works which God has accomplished through her by the Holy Spirit ("It was granted to her to clothe herself"). Her works are imperfect on their own, but they are filtered through Christ's intercessory work. What a day that will be! The Bride complete and we a part! We will stand before God with our meager works, our earthly labors for His glory, and God will delight in them. Christ will delight in them.

Then the angel tells John to write, "Blessed are those invited to the marriage supper of the Lamb!" The day will come, brothers and sisters in grace, that we will sit in the presence of the Bridegroom of our souls. We will feast in glory and be satisfied. How many times we have received a taste of that meal in the Lord's Supper? Yet it is nothing compared to the joy we will have on that day. We will be blessed and count ourselves as blessed, and nothing could be added to make that joy greater.

When John glimpses this, he falls down in worship. His impulse is right, but his direction is wrong. The angel refuses his worship, as if to say, "I have not made this meal. I have not paid the price for you to be here. The triune God has loved you and prepared this for you and the rest of His people. He alone deserves your praise."

One of my favorite expositions of this wedding feast is actually found all the way back in Psalm 22:22–31. David prophesies of a votive/thanksgiving sacrifice and celebration on the heels of a prophecy regarding Christ's crucifixion. In those verses, we see Christ resurrected and ascending, fulfilling His vows and proclaiming a feast of heaven. In feasting, Christ declares that He has fulfilled His vows to the Father from eternity to take on flesh and provide salvation for sinners, what we call the covenant of redemption. As Jesus feasts, He fulfills His vow to us, to send the Holy Spirit to apply salvation and preserve the elect unto glory. We see this in John 16:13–15: "When the Spirit of truth comes, He will guide you into all the truth, because He will not speak on His own authority, but whatever He hears He will speak, and He will declare to you the things that are to come. He will glorify me, because He will take what is mine and declare it to you. All that the Father has is mine; therefore I said that He will take what is mine and declare it to you."

This feast takes place in heaven and will continue into the new heavens and new earth. It is the feast of the prodigal son, seen in Luke 15:17–24. It is the feast prophesied in Isaiah 25:6–10. Yet even here and now we are given a taste of that feast in our worship and the Lord's Supper. As Calvin puts it, "Now, if the fathers under the law had their spiritual life renewed and invigorated by their holy feasts, this virtue will show itself much more abundantly at this day in the holy supper of Christ, provided those who come to partake of it seek the Lord truly, and with their whole heart."

Who is it that is invited to the wedding supper of the Lamb? For David, there is the distinction of Jew and Gentile, but these are taken away in Christ. "All who seek after God shall praise Him." So it was prophesied in Malachi 1:11, "For from the rising of the sun to its setting my name will be great among the nations, and in every place incense will be offered to my name, and a pure offering. For my name will be great among the nations, says the LORD of hosts." All who are saved by grace through faith are called Christ's seed, as in Isaiah 53:10: "Yet it was the will of the LORD to crush him; he has put him to grief; when his soul makes an offering for guilt, he shall see his *offspring*; he shall prolong his days; the will of the LORD shall prosper in his hand." John 11:51–52 says, "[Caiaphas] did not say this of his own accord, but being High Priest that year, he prophesied that Jesus would die for the nation, and not for the nation only, but also to gather into one the children of God who are scattered abroad." It was seen in Pentecost as the gospel was clarified and offered to the nations in Acts 2:7–11. Paul makes this clear in his letter to the Romans and in Galatians 3:7: "Know then that it is those of faith who are the sons of Abraham." And in Galatians 6:15–16, "For neither circumcision counts for anything, nor uncircumcision, but a new creation. And as for all who walk by this rule, peace and mercy be upon them, and upon the Israel of God." So also in Ephesians 1:9–10, "Making known to us the mystery of his will, according to his purpose, which he set forth in Christ as a plan for the fullness of time, to unite all things in him, things in heaven and things on earth." Finally, we see its fulfillment in Revelation 7:9–10: "After this I looked, and behold, a great multitude that no one could number, from every nation, from all tribes and peoples and languages, standing before the throne and before the Lamb, clothed in white robes, with palm branches in their hands, and crying out with a loud voice, 'Salvation belongs to our God who sits on the throne, and to the Lamb!'"

The poor and afflicted who seek after God will praise Him in that heavenly feast. As Christ said in Matthew 5:3–6, "Blessed are the poor in spirit, for theirs is the kingdom of heaven. . . . Blessed are those who hunger and thirst for righteousness, for they shall be satisfied." So also in Matthew 11:28–30, "Come to me, all who labor and are heavy laden, and I will give you rest. Take my yoke upon you, and learn from me, for I am gentle and lowly in heart, and you will find rest for your souls. For my yoke is easy, and my burden is light."

Though the prosperous are invited, they must come in humility. As we see in James 1:9–10, "Let the lowly brother boast in his exaltation, and the rich in his humiliation, because like a flower of the grass he will pass away." Going back to Psalm 22, the second half of verse 29 applies to all of the above. It literally says, "They who have bowed all the way down to the dust and his soul has not lived." While inviting the dead to a feast makes little sense in David's context, it is true of Christ's wedding supper. Those who were dead are made alive in Him, as Paul says in Ephesians 2:4–7.

This feast is for sinners called from every age, from Abel of Genesis to the last sinner saved. Like Paul, even those who persecuted Christ are offered the gospel of salvation for sinners. Peter preached in Acts 2:23, "This Jesus, delivered up according to the definite plan and foreknowledge of God, you crucified and killed by the hands of lawless men." All that is required for sinners to come to the feast is to repent and believe in the Lord Jesus Christ. So Paul describes it in Romans 1:16–17, "For I am not ashamed of the gospel, for it is the power of God for salvation to everyone who believes, to the Jew first and also to the Greek. For in it the righteousness of God is revealed from faith for faith, as it is written, 'The righteous shall live by faith.'" Isaiah 28:16 says, "Therefore thus says the Lord GOD, 'Behold, I am the one who has laid as a foundation in Zion, a stone, a tested stone, a precious cornerstone, of a sure foundation: "Whoever believes will not be put to shame."'" Finally, we hear it from Christ himself in John 6:37: "All that the Father gives me will come to me, and whoever comes to me I will never cast out."[11]

---

[11] "At the same time, on the other hand, there is some evidence that white stones were used to gain admission to public festivals. If one were to combine this evidence, then the 'hidden manna' they are to receive at the Eschaton, vis-à-vis their refusal to participate in the local pagan festivals, represents their form of admission to the final festive meal that believers are to experience at the 'marriage supper of the Lamb.'" Gordon Fee, Revelation: A New Commentary (Eugene: Cascade, 2011), re:2:18

The Bride Descends

Let us close this humble examination of God's greatest metaphor by meditating on the revelation of heaven. We turn to the new heavens and new earth, "for no subject will quicken the heart more than to lay open the riches of God's mercy, and the riches themselves, glory, and the unsearchable riches of Christ."[12] So I urge you, as Paul did to the Colossians, to set your mind on things above rather than those here below (3:2). The New Testament repeatedly describes God's people as those eagerly waiting (Rom. 8:19, 23, 25; 1 Cor. 1:7; Gal. 5:5; Phil. 3:20).

We have spoken often of the glory of God, and rightly so. All things are working together for God's glory, but yet we see they are also working together for the good of those who love Him (Christ's Bride collectively and the children of God individually). Here we see how God glorifies His people, and how doing that *is* His glory. Paul declares that those whom God foreknew—whom He fore-loved—He called, justified, and glorified (Rom. 8:28–30).

Paul told the Ephesians, "I do not cease to give thanks on behalf of your works remembered at my prayers, in order that the God of our Lord Jesus Christ, the Father of glory might give you a spirit of wisdom and revelation in knowledge of Him, the eyes of your heart enlightened to know what is the hope of His call to you, what the riches of the glory of His inheritance in the saints are" (1:16–18, author's translation). To abbreviate that further, Paul's prayer for them, and my prayer for you, is that God might reveal the riches of His glorious inheritance in the saints by the Holy Spirit.

As Thomas Goodwin states, "You know God is said to be rich in mercy, and rich in grace, and rich in love, and rich in power; all his attributes are called riches in Scripture. Now mark, wouldst thou know what heaven is? Thou shalt have all God's riches; not in bullion, for that cannot be, they are incommunicable, thou canst not have them in species; but thou shalt have them in comfort; thou shalt have all God's riches turned into comfort . . . all the riches in God shall be to make thee happy."[13]

You see, the glorious inheritance of God is in His saints. In other words, heaven is God with His people, the ultimate realization of Immanuel, where we are His and He is ours. What is our inheritance in Christ? It is true that we will each have a mansion in glory, a residence in a land without sickness or sorrow, streets paved with gold, securely guarded by angels, fed by the tree of life, never knowing need or hunger. All this is part of our inheritance, to be sure, but it is not the *heart* of our inheritance. The joy of glory is uninterrupted, uninhibited, unadulterated union with Christ, the Father, and the Holy Spirit.

---

12 Goodwin, *Ephesians*, 322
13 Goodwin, *Ephesians*, 314.

As the psalmist said, "The Lord is my chosen portion and my cup; you hold my lot" (16:5). In glory, we will be fully embraced by our God. Right now, we groan for the fullness of our adoption as sons and the redemption of our bodies (Rom. 8:23). Without this, heaven would not be heaven, and glory would not be glory. Taking full possession of our inheritance will be God taking full possession of us, "...that glory that shall arise to God, which he shall for ever live upon, as upon his inheritance, shall arise out of theirs; it is not said to be their inheritance, but his inheritance in them."[14] When I was younger, I wanted the mansion and the gold, sometimes as a parent and a pastor, I want the rest, but more and more, my heart is set on being with Christ, with God's people, and being unable to sin. The rest is details.

> There are two things to be considered in heaven. There is either the happiness that the saints themselves shall enjoy, which is "in the saints" saith the text, their happiness and their blessedness. And there is, secondly, communion with God, which is the cause of this happiness. Now of the two, communion with God is the greater. There is beatitutdo objectiva, the thing possessed, which is God himself; and there is beatitutdo formalis, which is the fruition of him; the happiness by enjoying God, and by knowing God. Now of the two, the knowing of God, communion with God, is more than our happiness; and therefore, if you mark it, the Apostle putteth that first, "That you may have a Spirit of Wisdom," saith he, "and of revelation in the communion and knowledge of him"; and then cometh, "That you may know what happiness you shall have, what are the riches of the glory of his inheritance in you," in the saints: there is the beatitutdo formalis, your fruition of it. Of the two, my brethren, it is the greater, therefore it is put first here, and therefore is not meant as a means only of knowing the other, but as a distinct thing from the other.[15]

When we behold the heavenly Jerusalem descending from heaven, we are carried back to the Messianic prophecy of Psalm 9:13–14. David was confident God would draw him back from the brink of death to again give praise in the gates of earthly Jerusalem. But this foreshadowed when God would draw Christ back from the gates of death to more glorious gates than Jerusalem. He was taken to the wedding arch of Zion's daughter, the heavenly Jerusalem, His church and Bride. It is a glimpse of the fulfillment of Malachi 3:17, "They shall be mine, says the Lord of hosts, in the day when I make up my treasured possession ..."

In these closing chapters of John's book, we behold our mother in completion. As Calvin describes her, "The heavenly Jerusalem, which derives its

---

14 Goodwin, *Ephesians*, 320.
15 Goodwin, *Ephesians*, 297.

origin from heaven, and dwells above by faith, is the mother of believers. To the Church, under God, we owe it that we are 'born again, not of corruptible seed, but of incorruptible,' (1 Peter 1:23), and from her, we obtain the milk and the food by which we are afterwards nourished. Such are the reasons why the Church is called the mother of believers."[16] But one day soon, she will be complete with all the elect within her doors to adore the Bridegroom forever. As W. M. Thomson said, "The temporal Zion is now in the dust, but the true Zion is rising and shaking herself from it, and putting on her beautiful garments to welcome her King when he comes to reign over the whole earth."[17]

There is surprisingly little for us to examine as to the application of the metaphor in these chapters, beyond what has been said above. The Bride descends, but we are given the vision in terms of a city. John walks us around her walls to count her towers and consider her palaces in fulfillment of Psalm 48. It is the eternal honeymoon suite, where the joy of God, of Christ with His people, is complete and consummated. We long to have described the bliss of that relationship, which is ultimately beyond words and our current comprehension. Instead, God inspired John to spend the bulk of the description on what it is for heaven and earth to meet without sin to divide them.

At the end, all we are left with is a longing for these things. We trace the words of 22:7 like a spouse with a letter from their beloved overseas, "Behold, I am coming soon..." Then we do the same with verse 12, then in 21. And we cry the words of the rest of that verse as our own. "'Amen. Come, Lord Jesus.' This is as true for me as it was for John. Come, Lord Jesus."

Closing

As I write this final segment, I am on sabbatical in Toronto, looking back on a decade in the pastorate during which I have written this book. It has been an incredible journey with a lot of laughter and a lot of tears (ministry is just that way). I have taught or preached nearly every section of this book to my congregation at Miller Valley Baptist Church, and that alone was worth the time invested. But I pray these words pass well beyond the borders of Arizona and the boundaries of my own lifetime. I look forward to the day when you and I meet in glory as perfectly united in our Bridegroom.

May God bless and keep you until that day. May His Word guide, sustain, and comfort you. May the Holy Spirit testify to that glorious adoption of grace in your heart. May we soon stand together at the throne of grace, for what God has joined together in the covenant of grace, no man can tear asunder.

---

16 John, *Commentaries Vol XXI*, 140.
17 Cited in Spurgeon, *The Treasury of David: Psalms 27–57 Vol. 2*, 364.

Bibliography

(Or How I Learned to Stop Worrying and Love Footnoting)

1 Clement, The Apostolic Fathers: Greek Texts and English Translations 3rd edition,

Ed. and trans. Michael W. Holmes. Grand Rapids, MI: Baker Academic, 2007.

A Pilgrim's Theology blog article "Calvin and 'Prophetic Idiom'" June 17, 2010.

Alford, Nicolas *Doxology: How Worship Works* (Free Grace: Conway, 2017).

Alighieri, Dante. *The Purgatorio*

Augustine *Concerning the City of God Against the Pagans* trans. Henry Bettenson (Penguin Books: London, 2003).

Augustine, *Expositions on the Book of Psalms*

Augustine, *Marriage and Virginity*, Trans. Ray Kearney (New City Press: Hyde Park, 1999).

Barcellos, Richard *The Lord's Supper as a Means of Grace…* (Bell and Bain: Glasgow, 2013).

Baugh, S.M. *Evangelical Exegetical Commentary: Ephesians* (Lexham: Bellingham, 2016).

Bavinck, Herman *Reformed Dogmatics: Holy Spirit, Church, and New Creation. IV* Trans. John Vriend (Grand Rapids: Baker Academics, 2008).

Belgic Confession

Bercot, David "Divorce" in *A Dictionary of Early Christian Beliefs* (Peabody, MA: Hendrickson, 2003).

Berkhoff, Louis. *Principles of Biblical Interpretation* (Baker Book House: Grand Rapids, 1950).

Bible Illustrations…Vol.1. James Lee (Alfred Gadsby: London).

Block, Daniel. *The Book of Ezekiel NICOT* (Eerdmans: Grand Rapids, 1997).

Bonhoeffer, Dietrich *Letters and Papers from Prison* (Fontana Books, Glasgow. 1962).

Bromiley, Geoffrey, *God and Marriage* (Eerdmans: Grand Rapids, 1980).

Brown, John *The Epistle of Paul the Apostle: The Galatians* (Sovereign Grace: Marshallton, 1970).

Bruce, FF *The Epistles to the Colossians… The New International Commentary on the New Testament* (Eerdmans: Grand Rapids, 1984).

Bunyan, John *Pilgrim's Progress* (Barbour: Uhrichsville, 1988).

Burroughs, Jeremiah *The Rare Jewel of Christian Contentment* (Banner of Truth: Carlisle, 1964)

Calvin, John *Commentaries* Trans. John King (Baker Books: Grand Rapids, 2005)

Calvin, John, *Institutes of the Christian Religion* (Westminster John Knox: Louisville, 1960).

Carson, D.A. editor *New Bible Commentary: 21st Century Edition* (Leicester: Inter-Varsity, 1994).

Cassel, P. *Joshua, Judges and Ruth Vol. IV of A Commentary on the Holy Scriptures* ed. J. P. Lange (T. & T. Clark: Edinburgh, 1872).

Catholic Church, *Catechism of the Catholic Church* (Doubleday: New York, 1995)

Chavasse, Claude *The Bride of Christ: An Enquiry into the Nuptial Element in Early Christianity* (Faber and Faber: London, 1911).

Chrysostom, John. *Homilies on Galatians, Ephesians, Philippians, Colossians, Thessalonians, Timothy, Titus, and Philemon* (B&R Samizdat Express. iBooks).

Civilizations of the Ancient Near East Vol 1. Ed. Jack M. Sasson (Hendrickson: Peabody, 1995).

Clowney, Edmund *Called To The Ministry* (Presbyterian and Reformed: Phillipsburg, 1964).

Covenant Legacy's article "Adam and Eve and The Problem of Polygamy" parts 1 and 2

Davis, Dale Ralph. *Slogging Along In The Paths of Righteousness: Psalms 13-24* (Christian Focus: Geanies House, 2016)

Dickson, David *Truth's Victory Over Error* (Banner of Truth: Carlisle, 2007).

Ellis, Peter *Celtic Myths and Legends* (Running Press: Philadelphia, 2002).

Fairbairn, Patrick *An Exposition of Ezkiel* (National Foundation for Christian Education: 1969).

Fee, Gordon D. *Revelation: A New Commentary* (Cascade: Eugene, 2011).

Feinberg, John S. and Paul D. *Ethics for a Brave New World* (Crossway Books: Wheaton, 2010), Kindle Edition Location 5460.

Ferguson, Sinclair B. *The Holy Spirit* (Downers Grove: Intervarsity Press, 1996).

Foxe, John. *Foxe's Christian Martyrs of the World* (Barbour: Uhrichsville 1989).

Freeman, James M. *Manners and Customs of the Bible* (Logos: Plainfield, 1972).

Goodwin, Thomas. *An Exposition of the Epistle to the Ephesians.* (Sovereign Grace Book Club, 1958).

Hamilton, Victor P. *The New International Commentary on the Old Testament: The Book of Genesis Chapters 1-17* Ed. R.K. Harrison and Robert L. Hubbard, Jr. (Eerdmans: Grand Rapids, 1990).

Hendriksen, William *Galatians, Ephesians, Philippians, Colossians, and Philemon* (Baker: Grand Rapids, 2002).

Henry, Matthew *Matthew Henry's Commentary On the Whole Bible* (Hendrickson: US, 1991).

Horton, Michael *The Christian Faith* (Zondervan: Grand Rapids, 2011).

Horton, Michael *God of Promise* (Baker: Grand Rapids, 2010).

Hutto, Jessalyn, *Inheritance of Tears: Trusting the Lord of Life When Death Visits the Womb* (CruciformPress: Minneapolis, 2015).

Jones, Peter *The God of Sex: How Spirituality Defines Your Sexuality* (Victor: Colorado Springs, 2006).

Kalas, E. "Martin Luther as Expositor of the Song of Songs," *Lutheran Quarterly 2* (1998).

Keach, Benjamin *Preaching from the Types and Metaphors of the Bible* (Kregel, Grand Rapids, 1972).

Keel, Othmar *The Song of Songs* (Fortress Press: Minneapolis, 1994).

Kline, Meredith *Glory In Our Midst* (Wipf and Stock: Eugene, 2001).

Lloyd-Jones, D Martyn *Christian Unity: An Exposition of Ephesians 4:1-16* (Baker: Grand Rapids, 2003).

Lloyd-Jones, D. Martyn *God's Ultimate Purpose: An Exposition of Ephesians 1* (Baker: Grand Rapids, 1978).

Lloyd-Jones, D. Martyn *God's Way of Reconciliation: An Exposition of Ephesians 2* (Baker: Grand Rapids, 2003).

Lloyd-Jones, *Life in the Spirit in Marriage, Home, and Work* (Baker: Grand Rapids, 1973).

Lloyd-Jones, D. Martyn *The Unsearchable Riches of Christ: Ephesians 3* (Baker Books: Grand Rapids, 1979).

Longman III, Tremper and Garland *Expositor's Bible Commentary*,

Longman III, Tremper *Introduction to the Old Testament* (1961).

Longman III, Tremper *New International Commentary on the Old Testament: Song of Songs* (Eerdmans: Grand Rapids, 2001).

Luther, Martin *Galatians* Ed. Alister McGrath and J.I. Packer (Crossway: Wheaton, 1998).

Martyr, Justin *Dialogue*

Milton, John. *Paradise Lost*

Muller, Richard A. *Dictionary of Latin and Greek Theological Terms Drawn Principally from Protestant Scholastic Theology* (Baker: Grand Rapids, 2004).

Neufeld, Ephraim *Ancient Hebrew Marriage Laws* (Longmans, 1944).

Ortlund Jr, Raymond C. *God's Unfaithful Wife: A biblical theology of spiritual adultery* (Intervarsity Press: Downers Grove, 1996).

Owen, John *Communion With God* (Banner of Truth: Carlisle, 2013).

Owen, John *The Works of John Owen Vol XVI* (Banner of Truth: London, 1968).

Owen, John *An Exposition of Hebrews* (Sovereign Grace Publishers: Evansville, 1960).

Pearse, Edward *The Best Match or The Soul's Espousals to Christ* (Soli Deo Gloria Publications: Morgan, 1994).

Pink, Arthur W. *Attributes of God: A Solemn and Blessed Contemplation of Some of the Wondrous and Lovely Perfections of the Divine Character* (Bible Truth Depot: Swengel, 1961).

Pink, Arthur W. *An Exposition of Hebrews* (Baker: Grand Rapids, 2006).

Pink, A.W., *Gospel of John* (Baker: Grand Rapids, 2006).

Piper, John, *This Momentary Marriage: A Parable of Permanence* (Crossway: Wheaton, 2009).

Pope, Alexander *An Essay on Criticism* (W. Lewis: London, 1709).

Pope, Marvin H. *Anchor Yale Bible Commentaries: Song of Songs* (Doubleday: New York, 1977).

Robertson, Robert. #400. *Trinity Hymnal: Baptist Ed.* (Great Commission: Suwannee, 1995).

Rogers, Daniel *Matrimonial Honor* (Edification Press: Warrenton, 2010).

Schaff, Phillip *History of the Christian Church Vol 2* (Eerdmans: Grand Rapids, 1970).

Sibbes, Richard *The Complete works of Richard Sibbes* Vol IV by AB Grosart (London: James Nisbet and Co., 1863).

Silverstein, Shel *Where the Sidewalk Ends* (HarperCollins: New York, 2004).

Shelley, Mary *Frankenstein* (New York: Dover, 1994).

Smith, W. Robertson *Kinship and Marriage in Early Arabia* (Black, 1903)

Spurgeon, Charles "Adoption – the Spirit and the Cry" Gal 4:6 published as a tract. (Inheritance: Grand Rapids).

Spurgeon, Charles. *Flowers from a Puritan's Garden*

Spurgeon, Charles "God's Thoughts of Peace, and Our Expected End," sermon May 29, 1887

Spurgeon, Charles *Morning and Evening* (Whitaker House: New Kensington, 2002).

Spurgeon, Charles *Treasury of David* (Kregel: Grand Rapids, 1968).

Spurgeon, C. H. (n.d.). *The Treasury of David: Psalms 27-57* (Vol. 2, p. 364). London; Edinburgh; New York: Marshall Brothers.

Spurgeon, C H *The Treasury of The Old Testament Vol 1&3* (Zondervan: Grand Rapids, 1968)

Sproul, RC ed. Reformation ESV Study Bible Notes (Ligonier: Lake Mary, 2005). God wrote the Bible, but Sproul gave some good footnotes

Sproul, RC Twitter, @rcsproul, 3:15pm – 25 Mar 2015

Stott, John, *Ephesians* (Intervarsity Press: Downers Grove, 1979).

Theological Dictionary of the New Testament Vol IV Ed. Kittel, Gerhard (Eerdmans: Grand Rapids, 2006).

Thomas, Gary *A Lifelong Love: How to Have Lasting Intimacy, Friendship, and Purpose in Your Marriage* (David Cook: Colorado Springs, 2014)

Toplady, Augustus *Rock of Ages*

VanDrunen, David *Living in God's Two Kingdoms: A Biblical Vision for Christianity and Culutre* (Crossway: Wheaton, 2010).

Watts, Isaac "We're Marching to Zion"

Waltke, Bruce *The Book of Proverbs Chapters 15-31* NICOT (Eerdmans: Grand Rapids, 2005).

Watson, Thomas "The Mystery of the Lord's Supper" in *The Puritans on the Lord's Supper* ed. Don Kistler (Soli Deo Gloria: Morgan, 1997).

Westerman, Rob *The Millennium Mystery and Revelation Code Examined* (self-published, 2009)

Appendix

The Nature of Subjective Beauty[1]

It has become a repeated theme among Christians, particularly those bent toward philosophical constructs, that beauty is not subjective, but objective. The reasoning behind this is that God is the supreme object of beauty, as He is also the supremacy of being, love, grace, justice, righteousness, and all other virtues. So, if God is the ultimate origin and manifestation of beauty then levels of beauty can be defined by their adherence to or parallel to God Himself. Makes sense, right?

This provides a very useful argument against the unrelenting march of post-modern thought into realms of art. A piece of obscene "art" can be denied as beautiful because it runs contrary to God and His design in creation. A stark example would be the work of Andres Serrano: He once photographed a crucifix submerged in urine. This cannot be defined as "beautiful" because it is defying the God who is the definition of beauty.

To be clear, there are certainly objective elements to beauty like symmetry. The ability to accurately represent God's creation in an art form is truly the science behind the art. Yet if we only define the beauty of an artwork in terms of symmetry, order, proportions, and harmony, then it could be posited that Piet Mondrian's paintings (the ones with black lines and squares of white and primary colors) exceed the beauty of Michelangelo's *David*. No one in their right mind would actually claim that, though.

The whole discussion of beauty in art was much simpler before technology. A painter or sculptor was largely valued by their ability to recreate what occurred in nature. Picasso's work would have stood no chance in the 1600's amid portrait painters (though Picasso actually had the skill to paint realistically). Yet photography changed the landscape of art, and now with the advances of science, a precise recreation can be made which no artist can mimic with paintbrush or chisel. Art shifted from imitating an objective reality to capturing subjective emotion and experience, impressions upon the heart and

---

[1] This material was first published through the blog of Reformation 21

mind. And before you dismiss that notion, would you rather see a photograph of a lily pad or Monet's paintings?

This conceptualization of purely objective beauty does not really function in a world that has real subjectivity. When we use this word in our everyday lives, and not in a philosophical vacuum, it is connotative and subjective. The beauty of a thing is enhanced or diminished by both knowledge and experience. Durer's painting of the praying hands becomes more beautiful to the viewer when the history behind it is known. I may find certain songs more beautiful than you do because of the memories I have attached to them. I can even say that my wife is more beautiful to me than to others because of what I have learned about her in 14 years together and the experiences we have shared. While God and truth are objective matters, we are still subjective creatures in a largely subjective world. Because a major component of "beauty" is the emotional experience of something, it will always have an inherent subjectivity. It is true that the full-blown post-modern, hyper-subjective view of the world is destructive and wrong, but that does not mean that the subjective baby should be thrown out with the Derrida bathwater. There is a reason we commonly distinguish between the "art" and the "science" of a thing.

I am not raising this issue simply because of personal preference or pet peeve. It has repercussions for our understanding of God's decree of history and our relationship to Him. Had God decreed a history without free will in the Garden of Eden, where no fall occurred and sin never entered the world, God would still have been glorious and worthy of endless praise. That is the science. But what makes God—specifically Christ—beautiful to us is enhanced by the revelation of mercy and grace in our lives. That is the art. God's glory is an objective thing, neither increased nor diminished by the creation, and yet we speak of glorifying God to describe the unveiling and contextualizing of God's glory.

Is God's perfection changed by His decree of my salvation? Absolutely not. Is God's beauty in my eyes increased by the love He has shown me when I was unlovable? Absolutely.

After all, what do we say when we see or hear a piece of art that speaks to our soul? "I love it!" It was not until God drew me out of death and into life to experience His grace and love that I was able to say, "I love Him!"

Scripture Index

Old Testament

Genesis	
1:1	7
1:26–28	180
2:17	185
2:20–25	12
2:22–25	12
2:24	25, 81, 218, 219
3:15	21
3:16	73, 203
3:17	26
3:20	15
4:8	29
4:19	29
8:22	136
16:3	30
16:11–12	30
18:12	34, 72, 81
18:14	146
19:36–38	30
23:4	62
24:10	36
24:12–4	36
24:22	36
24:26–27	36
24:30	36
24:33	36
24:34–36	36
24:52	36
24:53	36
24:54–56	36
24:57–58	36
24:61	36
24:63–67	36
29:3	94
37:9–10	182N26
38:12–15	93
49:10	80
50:19–21	29

Exodus	
3:14	109
4:22	39
4:25	65
19:10–14	160
20:12	40
21:2–6	41
21:3	128
22:16	73 N4
24:3	120
24:6–8	212
28:11–12	101
28:21	101
28:30	135
28:42	88
29:4	160
30:17–21	160
30:23–24	84
30:32	84
32:10	121
34:7	84
34:11-16	41

Leviticus	
14:1–8	212
14:4–6	239N5
14:49–52	239N5
17:7	41
18:18	31
18:21	48 N14
19:18	214
20:4–6	41
21:7	105N7

Numbers	
5:11–31	43
18:20	73
19:6	239N5
19:7–10	160
27:21	135
31:23	160

Deuteronomy			1 Kings		
1:36		68	1:1–4		30
4:25–26		120N29	3:10–14		80
6:3		64	4:26		80
11:22		16 N26	10:8		80
11:24		68	10:11		81
13:4		16 N26	11:1–8		30, 81
21:18–21		109	12:25–33		104
21:22		143	15:14		104N4
22:15		67	16:11		66
23:3		61	2 Kings		
24:1–4		110	14:23–26		116N25
24:19–21		62	1 Chronicles		
25:5–10		68	2:12–15		70
25:7		67	29:14		72
30:20		16 N26	Esther		
31:16–18		108	1:2		138
31:20		42, 116	Job		
Joshua			1:21		20 N36
1:3		68	3:5		66
7:24–26		122	4:18–20		10 N9
8:29		143	15:15		241
10:26		143	22:24		81
14:9		68	24:5–10		20 N36
Ruth			28:16		81
1:13–21		60	42:2		138N7
1:16–17		61	Psalms		
2:2		62	1:4		65
2:9		63	1:5		44
2:12		63	2:7–12		180
2:14		63	8:6		180
2:15		63	9:13–14		246
1 Samuel			16:2–3		74
7:12		32 N61	16:4		74
8:7–9		131	16:5		233
16:7		140	16:5–6		74
16:12		80	16:7–9		75
20:30–34		223	16:10–11		75
22:3–4		61	17:14		241
2 Samuel			19:4–6		77
6:5		123	19:6		78
7:1–17		98	19:13		149
7:10–17		80	22:22–31		242
12:11		30	23:1		160
16:22		30	34:10		73
20:3		30			

35:5	65	31:10	87
37:11	113N20	31:12	87
40:6	41	31:13	87
45:4	83	31:14	87
45:9	80	31:16	87
45:10–11	188	31:17	87
45:11	85	31:18	87
49:2	124N37	31:19	87
49:15	74	31:20	87
50:21	104	31:21	87
51:5	186	31:22	88
60:8	68	31:23	87
63:8	16	31:24	88
68:5	62	31:25	87
73:23–28	73	31:26	88
83:13	65	31:28	88, 222
84:11	73	31:29	88
104:15	152	31:30	88
119:96	4	31:31	88
119:105	73	3115	87
138:8	215		
139:23–24	104	Ecclesiastes	
		2:18–23	93
Proverbs		5:15	20 N36
1:7	201		
1:8–9	221	Song of Solomon	
3:11–12	24	1:3	80
5:18	28	2:7	95
5:18–20	30, 116	2:15	97
8:31	9	3:5	95
13:24	225	3:6–11	80, 98
14:28	85	4:1	93N44
14:32	74	5:1	92
15:6	232	5:7	66
16:33	135	5:8–16	99
17:15	80	5:10	101
20:28	83	5:13	80
22:15	225	7:10	101
22:22	68	7:12	91
23:13–14	225	8:2	157
23:20–21	214	8:4	95
25:4–5	233	8:6–7	101
25:24	86	8:8–10	94
26:15–16	96	8:10	101
27:8	218	Isaiah	
29:15, 17	225	1:2	45
31:3	30	3:23	93N44

8:18	175	18:16	20N36
9:6–7	175	23:19–21	46
11:6–9	124	28:11–19	241
13:12	81	Daniel	
14:12–17	241	4:35N7	138
14:27	138N7	Hosea	
17:13	65	1:1–5	105
20:4	20 N36	1:6–11	106
25:6–10	243	2:1	112
28:16	244	2:2	112
32:3	41	2:5–8	116
41:15–16	65	2:9–13	118
42:8	138	2:14–18	121
42:10	123	2:19–20	125
47:3	20 N36	2:21–23	126
50:1	110	4:6	129
50:1	234N7	4:15	130, 173
53:2	122	4:19	130
53:2	82N20	5:7	132
53:10	85, 199, 243	5:8	132
53:10–11	75	8:5–6	104
58:7	214	12:12	131
61:1–2	67	13:11	131
61:10	21	13:13	131
62:5	208	14:1–4	131
Jeremiah		14:5–6	132
2:20	46	14:9	103
3:1	110	Amos	
3:1–2	46	3:15	84
5:7	46	5:10–15	68
7:34	46	Micah	
16:9	46	1:7	52
25:10	46	1:11 N36	20
25:15	156N14	2:10	233
31:32	123	Nahum	
33:11	46	3:5 N36	20
33:17	16 N27	Zechariah	
Lamentations		3:1–5	239
1:8	119	11:12	128
Ezekiel		Malachi	
16:8	66	1:11	243
16:8–14	211	2:14–16	30
16:21	48	2:16	234
16:37–39	20 N36	3:17	246
16:59–63	49, 51		

New Testament

Matthew	
1:2–5	70
3:11	69
3:12	65
3:17	173
5:3–6	244
5:5N20	113
5:31–32	234
5:45	78
6:19–21	233, 238
6:34	98
10:34–39	221
11:28	120
11:28–30	244
11:29	83
15:21–28	61
16:4	74, 149
17:5	173
19:3–9	235
21:33–41	153
22:1–13	152
23:37	66
23:37–39	51
25:1–15	153
26:26–29	155
26:26–29	158N23
27:28–29	28
27:51	165
28:20	229

Mark	
1:7	69
3:27	82
3:31–35	149
7:9–13	221
8:38	149
9:24	35
10:2–9	31
10:13–16	220
10:43–45	203
10:49	158
14:22–24	158N23

Luke	
1:34	146
1:46	123N34
1:78–79	77
7:47	202
9:53	142, 164
10:18	241
11:9–13	226
12:35–40	154
14:8–11	154
14:15–24	153
15:17–24	243
18:18–30	60
22:44	28
22:61	202
23:46	74

John	
1:10–11	147
1:12	173
1:12–13	149
1:14	69
1:17	82
3:3	35, 174
3:28–30	147
4:19	198
4:34	74, 203
6:26	159
6:37	244
6:38	203
8:39–59	107
8:42	10
8:44	186
10:28	83
11:51–52	243
12:23–24	127
12:31	241
13:1–10	161N35
13:34–35	187
13:35	227
14:30	241
16:11	241
16:13–15	243
16:21	25
16:28	15

17:1–6, 19	74	8:29	173
17:5	15	8:31	108
17:10	17	8:35–39	225
17:17	212	8:37–39	83
17:21–23	220	9:4	39
19:25–27	25	9:5	82
19:34	212	9:24–26	112
19:39	84	10:17	17
20:10	25	10:17–18	77
		11:16–24	112

Acts
2:7–11	243	11:35	72
2:22–32	74	12:19	203
2:23	9, 244	13:1–7	203
2:24–36	178		

1 Corinthians
5:40–42	190	1:7	245
7:35	10	1:10	40
8:4	111	1:13	147
8:18–24	154	1:21	17
13:35–38	74	1:23	149
14:21–23	233	1:24	139
16:25–34	190	2:15	186
17:28	207	4:7	198
20:24	190	4:14–15	40
22:16	160	6:15–20	218
26:13	77	6:19–20	206
		7:6–8	31

Romans
1:16–17	244	9:25–27	214
1:17	4 N11	10:16	159
1:28–32	221	10:20	52
2:7	228	11:3	184, 203
5:3–5	201, 233	11:7	12
6:2–5	160	11:23–26	158N23
6:2–10	186	11:25	155
8:5–8	208	11:27–32	155
8:9–11	192	11:32	224
8:11	76, 178	12:14–31	184
8:14–17	208	15:10	179
8:16–17	233	15:20	77, 228
8:18	190	15:24–28	180
8:18–23	24	15:25	24
8:19, 23, 25	245	15:45–49	175
8:23	246	15:54–55	131
8:26	25	16:22	227
8:28	189, 201, 215		

2 Corinthians
8:28–30	7, 225, 245	2:14–16	199

3:12–15,	165	1:22–23	153N9
4:17–18	233	2:1–5	185
5:8	76	2:4–7	244
6:9	224	2:6	159, 191
6:10	238	2:11–12	186
10:1	83	3:1	189
13:11	228	3:3–4	219
Galatians		3:8–9	219
1:11	40	3:12	141
2:20	192	3:14–15	222
3:7	243	3:14–19	192
3:10–14	110	3:17–21	192
3:13	209	3:20	98
3:25–29	175N7	4:1	189
3:28	203	4:1-16	5 N14
4:1-5	6N13	4:3–7	183
4:4	69	4:5	161
4:4–5	27, 208	4:10	180
4:6	174N6	4:11–12	197
4:19	40	4:11–14	208
4:22–26	34	4:15–16	184, 206
5:5	245	4:16	183N31
5:6	228	5:1–2	198
5:22	140, 188	5:18	222
5:22–23	199	5:20–21	199
5:24	211	5:22–24	202
6:1	150	5:22–33	12
6:10	75	5:23	184
6:15–16	243	5:25	206
		5:25–27	31
Ephesians		5:26	161
1:3–6	172	5:26–27	210
1:3, 17	175	5:28–30	213
1:4–5	208	5:31–33	217
1:4–6	174N5	5:32	167
1:9	219	5:33	236N11
1:9–10	243	6:1–3	220
1:11–14	176	6:4	222
1:13	101	6:6	41
1:13–14	177	6:10–20	226
1:16–18	245	6:12	23, 97
1:19–20	178	6:23–24	227
1:20–23	203	Philippians	
1:20b–22	180	1:23	77, 233
1:21–23	180	2:3	187, 203
1:22–23	182, 219	2:5–8	208

2:9–11	180
3:8	76
3:19	214
3:20	188, 245
4:4	76
4:6	98
4:10–13	104
4:11	232
4:13	191

Colossians

1:17	207
1:18	184
1:19	194
2:9	194
2:9–10	184
2:15	180
2:19	185
2:20–23	214
3:1	180
3:4	220
3:5	133
3:18	205
3:19	218
3:20	220
3:21	222

1 Thessalonians

2:7	214
3:3	233
3:16	228
4:5	29
4:14	178

1 Timothy

2:13–14	19
3:2–12	31
3:2	31 N57
3:12	94N45
5:8	221

2 Timothy

1:7	208
1:8	189
1:10	228
2:25	225
3:1–2	221
3:12	233
3:16	46, 225

Titus

1:5–9	197N2
1:6	31 N57
2:3–4	205
2:12	225
2:14	15 N24
3:5	160, 211

Philemon

1	189
9	189

Hebrews

1:1–3	194, 226
1:8–9	83
2:8	180
2:10–18	149
2:13	175
2:17–18	173
4:8–11	120
4:13	20
4:15	200, 209
4:16	141, 189
8:9	123
9:19–22	212
9:19	239N5
9:23	241
10:5	41
10:19–22	189
10:22	211
10:32–34	233
11:11	34
11:13–16	62, 122
12:1	96
12:2	75, 84, 128, 164, 206
12:5–11	24, 150
13:4	217
13:8	139, 224
13:15	132

James

1:2–4	201
1:5	89
1:9–10	244
1:17	76

1 Peter

1:3	174
1:23	247

3:1–6	205
3:4	84
3:5–6	219
3:6	72, 81
3:7	26
3:15	100
4:8	187
4:14	233
5:8	23

2 Peter
1:4	220

1 John
1:9	226
2:9–11	227
4:7–10	228
4:18	219
4:19	227
5:6–8	212

Revelation
1:16	77
2:4	234
2:7	237
2:9	238
3:12	220, 238
3:17	21
3:17–18	85
3:17	20 N35
3:18	21
3:20	192
3:21	21
3:21–22	238
4:4	239
6:10–11	99
6:11	239
7:9	239
7:9–10	243
7:14	238
13:8	83
14:14–20	99
17:1–6	241
18:7	242
19:6–10	242
19:11–16	82
19:11–21	99
19:15	201
20:13	127
21:24–26	85
22:5	78

Other Titles from Founders Press

For the Vindication of the Truth: Baptist Symbolics Volume 1
By James Renihan

> I have longed to see a critical exposition of the First London Confession of Faith in print, one that provides a detailed examination of the provenance, structure, theology, editions, and impact of this notable text. This is that!
>
> – Michael A. G. Haykin, Chair & Professor,
> The Southern Baptist Theological Seminary

BY WHAT STANDARD? God's World ... God's Rules.
Edited by Jared Longshore

> I'm grateful for the courage of these men and the clarity of their voices. This is a vitally important volume, sounding all the right notes of passion, warning, instruction, and hope.
>
> —Phil Johnson, Executive Director,
> Grace To You

Truth & Grace Memory Books
Edited by Thomas K. Ascol

> Memorizing a good, age-appropriate catechism is as valuable for learning the Bible as memorizing multiplication tables is for learning mathematics.
>
> —Dr. Don Whitney, Professor,
> The Southern Baptist Theological Seminary

Dear Timothy: Letters on Pastoral Ministry
Edited by Thomas K. Ascol

> Get this book. So many experienced pastors have written in this book it is a gold mine of wisdom for young pastors in how to preach and carry out their ministerial life.
>
> —Joel Beeke, President,
> Puritan Reformed Theological Seminary

The Mystery of Christ, His Covenant & His Kingdom
By Samuel Renihan

> This book serves for an excellent and rich primer on covenant theology and demonstrates how it leads from the Covenant of Redemption to the final claiming and purifying of the people given by the Father to the Son.
>
> —Tom Nettles, Retired Professor of Historical Theology, The Southern Baptist Theological Seminary

Strong And Courageous: Following Jesus Amid the Rise of America's New Religion
By Tom Ascol and Jared Longshore

> We have had quite enough of "Be Nice and Inoffensive." We are overflowing with "Be Tolerant and Sensitive." It is high time that we were admonished to "Be Strong and Courageous."
>
> —Jim Scott Orrick, Author, Pastor of Bullitt Lick Baptist Church

Additional titles

A Primer for Conflict
By Josh Howard

Heirs of the Reformation: A Study in Baptist Origins
By James E. McGoldrick

Still Confessing: An Exposition of the Baptist Faith & Message 2000
By Daniel Scheiderer

By His Grace and for His Glory - By Tom Nettles

Getting the Garden Right - By Richard C. Barcellos

The Law and the Gospel - By Ernie Reisinger

Traditional Theology & the SBC - By Tom Ascol

Teaching Truth, Training Hearts - By Tom Nettles

Praise Is His Gracious Choice: Corporate Worship Expressing Biblical Truth - By Dr. Tom Nettles

Just Thinking: about the state - By Darrell Harrison and Virgil Walker

The Transcultural Gospel - By E.D. Burns

Ancient Gospel, Brave New World - By E.D. Burns

Galatians: He Did It All - By Baruch Maoz

Missions by the Book: How Theology and Missions Walk Together
By Chad Vegas and Alex Kocman

Order these titles and more at press.founders.org

WRATH AND GRACE

Wrath and Grace Publishing is committed to glorifying God through the publication of books in the Reformed tradition by classic and modern authors alike. With a focus on content that is biblically sound, doctrinally rich, and Christ-centered, we seek to publish works that will both engage the culture at large and teach Christians to enjoy Christ and His Kingdom in the world. Our books seek to engage both the head and the heart in conforming the lives of readers to Christ and His Word.

At Wrath and Grace Publishing, our gospel emphasis is in our name: Though we deserve Wrath because of our sin, we find Grace through the Lord Jesus Christ (Rom. 6:23). Our commitment to the Word of God keeps our content culturally engaging and eternally relevant.

So, whether you read a reprinted classic from an old, Reformed theologian, or a new work by a modern author, our pledge is to be faithful to God and His Word for the good of His Bride, the Church.

But that's not all. Wrath and Grace Ministries exists to create and produce not only biblically-sound, doctrinally rich, and Christ-centered books, but music, podcasts, teaching series, and much more. Our aim is to provide Reformed Christian resources for all ages around the world.

To view, listen, read, and use our content free of charge, please download the WG Universe App, available on all major app stores.

For more information, please visit our website at www.wrathandgrace.com

FOUNDERS
MINISTRIES

Founders Ministries exists for the recovery of the gospel and the reformation of churches.

We have been providing resources for churches since 1982 through conferences, books, The Sword & The Trowel Podcast, video documentaries, online articles found at www.founders.org, the quarterly Founders Journal, Bible studies, International church search, and the seminary level training program, the Institute of Public Theology. Founders believes that the biblical faith is inherently doctrinal, and we are therefore confessional in our convictions.

You can learn more about Founders Ministries and how to partner with us at www.founders.org.

- FoundersMin
- FoundersMin
- FoundersMinistries
- FoundersMinistries